Offshoring

Offshoring

John Urry

polity

Contents

Preface

This book develops debates and themes first initiated in various previous works, including *The End of Organized Capitalism* (1987, with Scott Lash), *Sociology beyond Societies* (2000), *Mobile Lives* (2010, with Anthony Elliott) and *Societies beyond Oil* (2013). These all documented the dizzying scale of movement of people, resources and institutions around the world. However, none explored in depth what is specifically examined here, namely that this movement now involves the systemic phenomenon of offshoring, which is 're-booting' contemporary societies in many significant ways.

It is shown below that there are pervasive offshore worlds which the social sciences need urgently to grasp. The emergence and sedimentation of these worlds is reshaping the contours of contemporary societies, reforming patterns of power, undermining notions of responsibility, threatening the conditions for democracy and transforming how societies are 'energised'. Offshoring is bringing into being shadowy sets of relations of work, finance, pleasure, waste, energy and security. These set huge challenges for researchers and more importantly for citizens. Offshore, out of sight, over the horizon are some of the troubling processes and related metaphors by which much life is being rendered opaque – full of secrets and some lies. This book documents and challenges the dark side to mobility and globalisation and considers whether and how offshoring can be reversed, whether it is possible to bring about reshoring.

I am very grateful for discussions with many colleagues on these various themes, including especially the late Heiko Schmid. Specific thanks for comments or recent discussions with Sarah Becklake, Thomas Birtchnell, Monika Büscher, Javier Caletrio, Rachel Cooper, Bülent Diken, Anthony Elliott, James Faulconbridge, Bianca Freire-Medeiros, James Freund, Tony Giddens, Michael Hulme, Glenn Lyons, Scott Lash, James Marriott, Katerina Psarikidou, Satya Savitsky, Mimi Sheller, Elizabeth Shove, David Sugarman, Bron Szerszynski, John Thompson, David Tyfield, Tom Urry, Sylvia Walby and Benno Werlen. I am especially grateful for collaboration with colleagues in the Centre for Mobilities Research at Lancaster and, in particular, Pennie Drinkall. Thanks also for comments from anonymous referees.

Some research reported in this book was supported by ESRC grant ES/J007455/1 entitled *Transport and Technology*, for which many thanks.

John Urry
Lancaster 2013

1

What Is Offshoring?

The problem

Warren Buffett, sometimes described as the twentieth century's most successful investor, recently maintained: 'There is class warfare, all right, but it's my class, the rich class, that's making war, and we're winning.'[1] This book describes in detail how this rich class did indeed wage class war and has so far won that war, partly through deploying the relatively new and striking strategy of offshoring. I document how this strategy came to be implemented as a key element in enabling the rise and rise of the rich class. The informal term 'rich class' refers to the putative global class made up of high net worth individuals and families, the owners/managers of major corporations and professional service companies, many thinktanks, and leading policy-makers.

To illustrate the significance of offshoring, consider ActionAid's major study published in May 2013. It reports that ninety-eight of the hundred largest publicly listed UK corporations (FTSE 100) own subsidiaries, associates, or joint ventures offshore in what

---

[1] Paul B. Farrell, 'Rich class fighting 99%, winning big-time', www.marketwatch.com/story/rich-class-beating-99-to-a-pulp-2011-11-01 (accessed 28.7.2013).

that charity defines as 'tax havens'.[2] Moreover, corporations typically hold many such accounts. ActionAid reported that advertising giant WPP held 618 offshore accounts, HSBC 496, Royal
Dutch Shell 473, Barclays 471, BP 457, RBS 393, Lloyds 259,
British Land 187 and Prudential 179. The banking sector is the
most prolific user of tax havens, with over half of the overseas
subsidiaries of major banks being located in 'treasure islands' of
low tax.[3]

Tax havens are also sometimes known as 'secrecy jurisdictions'.
Most corporations and wealthy people locate their income and
wealth offshore in such secret locations. Often it seems that 'only
the little people pay tax',[4] with the rich class able to direct their
wealth and much else 'offshore' and very often out of sight.

Moreover, these companies are built rather like Russian dolls,
with multiple layers of secrecy and concealment.[5] For example,
there is a company called Goldman Sachs Structured Products
(Asia) Limited based in the tax haven of Hong Kong. It is controlled by another company called Goldman Sachs (Asia) Finance,
which is registered in another tax haven, namely Mauritius. That
is administered by a further company in Hong Kong, which in
turn is directed by a company located in New York. This is controlled by another company in Delaware, a major tax haven, and
that company is administered by yet another company, also in
Delaware, GS Holdings (Delaware) L.L.C. II. This in turn is a
subsidiary of the only Goldman company that most people have
actually heard of, namely the Goldman Sachs Group which occu-
pies a glitzy tower completed in 2010 and located in Battery City
Park in New York City. This company generated in 2012 a worldwide turnover of around US$34 billion and employed nearly
30,000 staff.

This chain of ownership is one of hundreds of such chains
within the single company Goldman Sachs. Overall Goldman

---

[2] https://www.actionaid.org.uk/news-and-views/ftse100s-tax-haven
-habit-shows-need-to-tackle-a-hidden-obstacle-in-the-fight-against
(accessed 22.7.2013); www.guardian.co.uk/news/datablog/2013/may/12/
ftse-100-use-tax-havens-full-list (accessed 13.5.2013).
[3] Nicholas Shaxson, *Treasure Islands* (London: Bodley Head, 2011).
[4] http://en.wikipedia.org/wiki/Leona_Helmsley (accessed 30.4.2012).
[5] See http://opencorporates.com/viz/financial/ (accessed 22.7.2013).

Sachs consists of more than 4,000 separate corporate entities scattered across the world, many offshore. Some of these entities lie ten layers of control below the New York headquarters. Around one-third are registered in tax havens; and in the world of Goldman Sachs the Cayman Islands are larger than South America, and Mauritius is bigger than Africa!

This book explores how this world of offshoring came into being and some of its major consequences. Offshoring affects countries losing taxation, especially in the developing world, and the seventy or so tax havens. Moreover, this is an issue not just of money and taxation but of many other processes that are offshored and wholly or partly rendered secret, including manufacturing industry, pleasure, energy, waste, carbon dioxide emissions and security. All of these are to some degree offshored and situated in 'secret locations'. As they go offshore they are linked together in various chains of concealment. As Shaxson more generally argues: 'offshore is how the world of power now works.'[6] This world of offshored power is what this book seeks to reveal. In the next section the strategy of offshoring is placed within a brief historical context.

Beyond borders

All societies entail the movement of peoples and objects, but capitalist societies elevate its scale and impact. Much social thought has described capitalism's continuous and restless movement.[7] In 1848 Karl Marx and Friedrich Engels described how, over the previous century, the bourgeoisie had created more extensive productive forces than all preceding generations.[8] The need for a constant expanding market caused the bourgeoisie to chase over the surface of the globe, forcing fixed, fast-frozen relations to be swept away. All that is solid, Marx and Engels maintained, melted into air. The cheap prices of commodities produced by capitalist

---

[6] Shaxson, *Treasure Islands*, pp. 7–8.
[7] See the classic study Marshall Berman, *All that is Solid Melts into Air* (London: Verso, 1983).
[8] Karl Marx and Friedrich Engels, *The Manifesto of the Communist Party* (Moscow: Foreign Languages, [1848] 1952), pp. 54–5.

factories 'battered down all Chinese walls', undermined 'national one-sidedness' and created a world in its own bourgeois image. Marx and Engels pointed to the increasing 'cosmopolitan charac- ter' of production and consumption, describing how the exploita- tion of workers was regularly 'shifted elsewhere' as new cities and factories were developed, while older ones were destroyed.[9]

So capitalism is all about movement and especially the move- ment of capital and of workers. Capitalist societies involve a rest- less acceleration of economic, social and political life. This speeding up of movement is thought to have developed especially during the last quarter of the last century. Much academic and policy writing emphasised how the contemporary world was becoming 'borderless', with many frontiers increasingly irrelevant to how people's accelerating lives were lived and experienced.[10]

Writing in 1990, Ohmae famously described this borderless world: 'the free flow of ideas, individuals, investments and indus- tries . . . the emergence of the interlinked economy brings with it an erosion of national sovereignty as the power of information directly touches local communities; academic, professional, and social institutions; corporations; and individuals.'[11] Ohmae opti- mistically argued that this borderless world would engender boundless economic and social growth. Borderlessness would gen- erate new business opportunities, international friendship, family lives organised across distance, international understanding, greater openness of information and more wealth.

At least a hundred studies each year documented the nature and impact of many global processes. Overall it seemed that econo- mies, finance, media, migration, tourism, politics, family life, friendship, the environment, the internet, and so on, were becom- ing less structured within nation-states and increasingly organised across the globe.[12] Some analyses emphasised an increased density

---

[9] On capitalism and its changing geographies, David Harvey, *The Enigma of Capital and the Crises of Capitalism* (London: Profile, 2011).
[10] Hartmut Rosa and William E. Scheuerman (eds), *High-Speed Society* (University Park: Pennsylvania State University Press, 2009).
[11] Kenichi Ohmae, *The Borderless World* (London: Collins, 1990), p. 269.
[12] See material and books listed at www.polity.co.uk/global/whatis globalization.asp (accessed 10.2.2013).

of interactions across the globe, with the liberalising of world trade, the internationalising of production, the globalising of commodity consumption, the declining costs of transport and communications, and the internationalising of investment. Global corporations seemed able to operate on a worldwide basis, with reduced long-term commitment to specific places, labour forces or societies.

Other studies detailed the global infrastructures that linked together people and places around the world. Further analysts argued that the 'global' is to be viewed more as a set of effects brought about by powerful actors undermining national limitations upon the free flow of information, images, people and money. The 'global' here is something performed through the actions and writings of free-market consultants, such as Ohmae, as they contest the powers of 'old-fashioned' national states to make and uphold national laws and regulations.[13]

Overall it was thought to be good to move, as well as to receive these various flows of people and objects arriving from other places. Many analysts believed that mobilities would reinvigorate societies through new ideas, information and people, thus making societies, places and people more 'cosmopolitan'. Old-fashioned structures would dissolve.[14] Social theorist Bauman conceptualised these processes as constituting a 'liquid modernity', contrasting it with a more fixed and stable older modernity.[15]

In developing such a mobile global order, a cluster of system changes occurred around 1990 as Ohmae was analysing and advocating the notion of borderlessness. First, Soviet communism disappeared almost overnight, partly because of its failure to develop and embed new informational technologies. Especially following the demolition of the Berlin Wall in 1989, many significant barriers to the flow of information, people and capital dissolved across Europe, with some Soviet bloc countries joining the European

---

[13] See John Urry, *Global Complexity* (Cambridge: Polity, 2003), on various approaches to global analysis.
[14] Ulrich Beck, *Cosmopolitan Vision* (Cambridge: Polity, 2006); Bron Szerszynski and John Urry, 'Visuality, mobility and the cosmopolitan: inhabiting the world from afar', *British Journal of Sociology*, 57 (2006): 113–32.
[15] Zygmunt Bauman, *Liquid Modernity* (Cambridge: Polity, 2000).

Union – which has as its goal reducing many barriers to movement.

Second, new systems of global news reporting developed. The First Gulf War in 1991 was the first major event in which there was 24-hour real-time reporting around the world. This generated a 'global stage/screen' for many major events: wars, terrorist atrocities, sports events, concerts, celebrity scandals, and so on. These became more mediatised, visible and apparently shared. New social media transformed the character and temporality of information and rumour circulating around the world and arriving from 'elsewhere'.

Third, during the late 1980s, many major financial markets moved to online real-time trading that was accessible somewhere or other 24 hours a day. This increasingly global system of electronic financial trading resulted in the much greater speed and volatility of financial and other markets, often involving high-frequency computer-based trading.[16]

Finally, the World Wide Web was 'invented' by Tim Berners-Lee between 1989 and 1991. He defined HTML (hypertext markup language), HTTP (HyperText Transfer Protocol) and URLs (Universal Resource Locators). The web initially stemmed from the need for more extensive communications within scientific communities, but it soon led to the proliferation of countless virtual worlds which so transformed economic and social life. The internet is characterised by mostly seamless jumps from link to link, person to person, company to company, without regard to conventional national boundaries through which information was historically located, stored and curated.[17]

This cluster of changes came together in the 'West' to generate a 1990s 'global optimism' as to a progressive open future. The economist Stiglitz described the 'roaring [nineteen] nineties'.[18] Having 'won' the Cold War, the West set about making the rest of the world in its own global, consumerist and borderless image.

---

[16] Robert Holton, *Global Finance* (London: Routledge, 2012).

[17] Manuel Castells (ed.), *The Network Society* (Cheltenham: Edward Elgar, 2004), and *Communication Power* (Oxford: Oxford University Press, 2009).

[18] Joseph Stiglitz, *Making Globalization Work* (Harmondsworth: Penguin, 2007).

A vast array of food, products, places, services, friends, family and experiences became available to those with reasonable incomes. The world was indeed 'open' and full of choice for many living, working and consuming near the centre of this borderless global society.

Moreover, this open world was seen as lasting well into the new century through continued American global dominance. The Project for the New American Century (PNAC) developed during the 1990s, involving many figures who held high office in the Bush administration of 2000–8. This project sought to ensure continuing American pre-eminence by guaranteeing that the US and its allies could access sufficient oil and related resources, so preventing other powers from challenging the 'West's' capacity to spread 'freedom' worldwide.

But, significantly, this 1990s global decade did not turn out to be the harbinger of a long-term, optimistic and borderless future. The 1990s were more like a *fin de siècle*, of intense opulence and decadence for some, combined with the anticipation of a doom laden ending. And that ending came fast with the dramatic attack on the Twin Towers of the New York World Trade Center on 11 September 2001. This generated the most dramatic images viewed in real time upon the 24-hour global media.

The ending of the decadent 'roaring nineties' engendered various apocalyptic visions for this new century. A different academic and political agenda developed, focused upon the many dark sides of these liquid processes, including the possibility of an environmentally induced 'collapse' of societies. Just as previous major civilisations, such as the Roman, Mayan, or Soviet, collapsed, so various analysts now argued that this might happen to contemporary Western civilisation through its own unfolding contradictions.[19]

This dark agenda was described in some of Bauman's books published in the last decade documenting the 'collateral damage' resulting from a liquid modernity characterised by process and

---

[19]The first of these doom-laden texts published in Britain was written by Martin Rees, president of the Royal Society; see *Our Final Century* (London: Arrow, 2003). Jared Diamond's *Collapse* (London: Penguin, [2005] 2011) is an international bestseller establishing how and why societies do sometimes collapse and disappear.

flow.[20] His texts, as well as those of other scholars, reveal
that moving across borders are not just consumer goods, new
experiences and pleasurable services. Also there are many
'bads', of environmental risks, terrorists, trafficked women, drug
runners, international criminals, outsourced work, slave traders,
smuggled goods and workers, CO_2 emissions, oil spills, untaxed
income, asylum seekers, property speculators, financial risks,
hurricanes, and so on. There is a dark side to borderlessness and
movement.

From the turn of the century onwards it became clear that many
risks move across borders, these risks fuel the imagination of
further powerful and threatening risks, and these real and imagined risks engender and legitimate new systems of 'security' to
monitor and regulate such risks.[21] And it is difficult to know how
serious many of these risks actually are and therefore what is an
appropriate security response. For the 2012 Olympics, London
was transformed into a security fortress, with an air exclusion
zone protected by surface-to-air missiles primed for all eventuali-
ties. London was made 'secure' through a security operation
involving more British people than were at the time fighting in
Afghanistan.

Offshoring

So it has become clearer that much of importance in economic,
social and political life involves movement, relocation and concealment. Rather than there being a general process of increased
open movement across borders, movement is often out of sight
and involves elaborate forms of secrecy. A borderless world develops new borders and new secrets. Borders are regularly created,
policed and surveilled. This book describes how a world of accelerated movement across borders is a world of secrets and sometimes lies.

---

[20] See for example, Zygmunt Bauman, *Liquid Love* (Cambridge: Polity,
2003); Zygmunt Bauman, *Collateral Damage: Social Inequalities in a
Global Age* (Cambridge: Polity, 2011); Zygmunt Bauman and David
Lyon, *Liquid Surveillance: A Conversation* (Cambridge: Polity, 2012).
[21] See the classic Ulrich Beck, *The Risk Society* (London: Sage, 1992).

There has come into being a general offshore world which is restructuring global power and domination. This book dissects these offshoring practices and examines the offshore world being assembled. An offshoring analysis examines the moving of resources, practices, peoples and monies from one national territory to another, and how they are wholly or partly hidden from the view of the public and/or public authorities. Such offshoring normally involves rule-breaking in one or more of three ways. There is the getting around of rules and regulations in ways that are simply illegal (tax evasion); there is going against the spirit of the law even if what is done is technically 'legal' (tax avoidance); and there is the use of laws in one jurisdiction to undermine laws that operate in another (much maritime practice). The point of offshoring is to operate outside sets of specific regulations, often going 'off-state', involving some combination of these different forms of rule-breaking.

Offshoring practices have been made possible by various 'post-national' systems of contemporary mobility, although this is not to suggest that there was once a 'golden age' when secrets were absent. These systems include container-based cargo shipping; extensive aeromobility; the countless virtual worlds; car and lorry traffic; electronic money transfer systems; taxation, legal and financial expertise enabling particular national systems of regulation to be evaded; and proliferating 'mobile lives' engendered through frequent legal and illegal movement across borders. Each such system entails a combination of mobilities and immobilities. Central to most systems are de-localised virtual environments enabling information, money, trades, images, connections and objects to move digitally as well as physically, often along routeways in the shadows. Virtual environments are part and parcel of contemporary offshoring and the de-localising of production, consumption and sociability that characterises the past few decades.

In particular, Gill writes how in this world the 'mobile investor becomes the sovereign political subject', with much governance around the world transformed to make secure the paramount interests of mobile investments.[22] Or, as Panen argues, offshore

---

[22] Stephen Gill, 'New constitutionalism, democratization and global political economy', *Pacific Review*, 10 (1998): 23–38, at p. 25.

worlds mean that 'foreigners are given an advantage over local residents'.[23] These offshoring worlds are pervasive and not accidental or incidental – part of a strategy of class warfare, according to Warren Buffett. Indeed, we might see offshoring as the means by which the rich class came to develop as a distinctly international 'class for itself' rather than a 'class in itself'.[24]

The processes of 'offshoring' range from those where there is a mere dependence upon overseas resources, to those which are onshore but which enjoy offshore status and may be concealed, to those which are literally out to sea, over the horizon, secret and often illegal. Offshoring has become a generic principle of contemporary societies, and it is thus impossible to draw a clear divide between what is onshore and what is offshore. Indeed, offshoring worlds have inflected much of contemporary life. They are dynamic, reorganising economic, social, political and material relations between and within societies, as populations and states find that resources, practices, peoples and monies can be made or kept secret and that vast advantages thereby accrue. Interests develop seeking to strengthen the institutional machinery that makes possible offshored worlds.

Some societies indeed developed as specialist and interconnected 'offshore societies' based around intersecting secrecy flows and jurisdictions, often parasitic upon powerful 'onshore' societies. This book examines the workings of those societies from which resources disappear and societies where people or resources arrive from elsewhere, often along secret channels. All societies in the contemporary world are transformed by powerful offshoring relations.

This new order is one of multiple concealments, of many secrets and some lies. Offshoring erodes 'democracy' and, more generally, notions of fairness within and between societies. It can generate a kind of regime-shopping as well as preclude the slowing down of the rate of growth of CO_2 emissions, which presupposes shared and open global agreements between responsible states, corporations and publics.

---

[23] Ronen Palan, *The Offshore World* (Ithaca, NY: Cornell University Press, 2006), p. xviii as well as pp. 158–9.
[24] This distinction is made by Marx in many of his historical works.

Moreover, some people now live partially offshored lives. Runciman suggests that, before the fall of Gaddafi's Libya, Saif Gaddafi was a typical offshored person. He lived in London but possessed offshored corporations, charities, houses, friends and contacts around the world. He bought property through secret tax-avoiding ownership arrangements involving the British Virgin Islands. Gaddafi was 'just an offshore guy, living in an offshore world', and hanging out with many other 'offshore guys'.[25]

Other very different offshored lives involve those poor individuals and households who are moved from one detention centre to another or from one unregistered ship to another in an endless round of never being properly located. Such offshored persons may not possess rights to stay and act as citizens of their preferred nation-state; indeed, some are made literally stateless.

The argument of *Offshoring*

This book establishes the current scale and significance of offshored processes and especially how this is a strategy of class warfare. The next chapter considers the nature of secrecy within societies, a topic not much explored in social science, although secrecy and power are significantly intertwined in most societies. I examine the contribution of Georg Simmel, who maintained that the growth of a 'money economy' generates new levels of 'consciously willed concealment', or secrets. I examine how contemporary societies entail novel kinds of visibility between citizens and the powerful, especially through the role of the media and scandal. These developments have in turn fostered the importance of 'exit' and 'secrecy' for the powerful in society. The chapter ends with an account of neo-liberalism as a set of discourses and practices which developed from around 1980 and which set the preconditions for the emergence of many offshored secret worlds.

Subsequent chapters explore different elements and forms of offshoring. Chapter 3 examines production and work, which is often how the world of offshore is confronted within public policy and the media. Especially significant has been the offshoring of

---

[25] David Runciman, 'Didn't they notice?', *London Review of Books*, 14 April 2011, pp. 20–3, at p. 20.

much manufacturing work, especially in 'free zones' away from most protection by state laws, regulations and trade unions. Goods are increasingly produced offshore and are then transported thousands of miles to where they get consumed, so undermining domestic production. This all involves highly complex divisions of labour that spread around the world, necessitating extensive transportation of goods in vast container ships. I briefly consider the potential effects of additive manufacturing, or '3D printing'.

The following chapter 4 turns to the second major public issue noted with regard to offshoring. This is the extensive scale and impact of the movement of finance and wealth through tax havens. Such offshoring presupposes the overlapping movement of legal and illegal money around the world at incredible electronic speeds and then being located offshore for periods. The financialisation of the world economy has been utterly intertwined with the development of places where tax 'dodging' is facilitated. Analysis is provided of the importance of a haven's 'façade', with Switzerland providing the most successful such façade during the last century. And yet it is also shown that there is a new politics of taxation which has placed the issue of financial offshoring onto many political agendas. The offshoring of income and wealth is in turn bound up with most other forms of offshoring discussed below.

Chapter 5 examines how much leisure and pleasure happens offshore, especially the 'pleasures' of 'sex, drugs and rock and roll'. Some of these are illegal (sex with minors) or normatively disapproved of 'back home' (gambling). These offshore sites are often also places of taxation avoidance. Many people are seduced by the allure of journeys to places of fun and freedom, so escaping disapproval of those living in their home neighbourhood. This reflects the shift in contemporary societies from people living neighbourhood lives to those experienced 'beyond neighbourhood'. The chapter also considers the offshoring of much sport and of its ownership.

Chapter 6 considers how energy has been increasingly offshored. There have been long-term shifts from local and decentralised forms of energy to forms which are offshored, literally, financially and metaphorically. This is often interconnected with other offshoring processes examined here. A shift towards energy resources that can be moved, such as oil, makes the energising of any society more likely to be offshored. Almost all current societies depend upon offshored energy. It is also shown how difficult it is to reverse energy mobility, extreme energy and financialisation. And many of the processes of offshoring in other spheres are themselves dependent upon mobile energy resources – especially resource-limited oil and its overwhelming significance for providing energy to transport people and objects offshore.

In chapter 7, attention is directed to the forms and practices of the global waste industry. It is shown how contemporary societies are sites of systemic wastefulness which is designed into products and places. As a result there is a vast scale of waste generated, and this is increasingly offshored. Especially hazardous waste gets exported to those societies which possess less strong regulatory regimes. Some such societies have developed what economists call a 'comparative advantage' in dealing with the world's waste, which includes dead ships and computers. Exporting manufacturing industry to various countries, and especially China, has the effect that CO_2 emissions are exported away from the places where many manufactured goods are bought, used and consumed. There is brief analysis of the complex politics of reassigning such emissions from societies of production to the societies of consumption.

The following chapter 8 examines the offshoring of security. Much contemporary security, including conducting wars, interrogating prisoners and extracting secrets, is conducted out of sight and away from oversight and legal regulation within a particular society. These activities have been conducted by secret services, especially seeking to determine who is friend and who is foe. As more people are on the move, so it is increasingly no simple matter to determine those who are and remain friends. And yet much contemporary politics rests upon the simple dichotomy of 'them and us', of foe or friend. I go on to analyse 'extraordinary rendition', which enables the offshoring of torture on a factory scale. Analysis is also provided of how new forms of miniaturised weaponry, especially drones, enable security to be offshored, with one's own side not being placed in the front line at all.

Chapter 9 examines the sea, seeking to recentre analysis of the earth's surface which is nearly three-quarters water. An offshoring world is particularly dependent upon various water worlds, upon power at sea and the power of the sea. Central to moving off-land are water worlds. At sea many rules and regulations are evaded; oceans are literally and metaphorically over the horizon. Much is invisible, out of sight of states, law enforcers and regulators. The outlaw sea comprises pirates, rubbish, sinkings, mysterious deaths, deregulation, and a race to the quality bottom. It is shown how the sea, and especially its slow-moving sea-borne traffic, provides a model of offshored neo-liberalism, with minimal states and regulations.

The final chapter documents the centrality of secrecy and exit for reconstituting the dominant global class and enabling 'democracy dodging'. Many 'offshore societies' are undemocratic. Much has been moved offshore – hidden from view, legally protected and not subject to potential democratic oversight, control and regulation. This offshore world is detrimental to democracy. Also offshoring prevents effective action on global climate change through precluding a powering down to a lower carbon future.

This chapter thus tries to establish a radical programme of onshoring or reshoring to re-establish democratic control. Democracy needs activities to be brought back 'home', and I examine a range of measures as to how this might be achieved. I further consider whether offshoring entails such high carbon costs that future oil shortages and more extreme weather events will bring offshoring worlds to a slowdown or even an abrupt end. Since these secret worlds are not fully stabilised, they will not necessarily last forever.

Alternatively it is possible, as various dystopian futures remind us, that we may not have seen anything yet and that the twenty-first century could be a century of 'extreme offshoring'. This would have dark consequences for both democracy and the possibility of moving to a viable post-carbon world.

The costs of this offshoring world described in the book are indeed high. Brittain-Catlin summarises how, in this secret realm, 'the negative, dark spirit . . . today pervades the offshore world and its network of secret paraphernalia and hidden practices that are so closely bound into the global economy.'[26] Offshoring provides a different theory of the workings of the contemporary world to that of 'globalisation'. It is an account that emphasises avoidance, rule-breaking, irresponsibility, and secrets as the 'rich class' remade the world in its interests.

---

[26]William Brittain-Catlin, *Offshore: The Dark Side of the Global Economy* (New York: Picador, 2005), p. 118.

2

Secrets

Simmel on secrets

The analysis of offshoring requires examination of this 'negative, dark spirit' and especially of the role of secrecy within social life. I examine this first through sociologist Georg Simmel. A century ago Simmel argued that all social relationships between people rest 'upon the precondition that they know something about each other'.[1] Social life is founded on exchanging information, about what people can expect from each other, and how to manage this information. Exchanging information is key to social life, and it is generally presumed that transparency is desirable.

Simmel maintained that there are relatively few secrets in small-scale societies because everyone is rather similar to everyone else and there is little development of a money economy. But 'modern civilised societies' depend upon more varied conceptions. Secrets are necessary because people are so different; there has to be some 'reciprocal concealment' between people.[2] People need knowledge to live among others, but such knowledge is so important and at times so dangerous that what is known about oneself has to be

---

[1] Georg Simmel, 'The sociology of secrecy and of secret societies', *American Journal of Sociology*, 11 (1906): 441–98, at p. 441.
[2] Ibid., p. 448.

'doctored'. Understanding the exchange of social information requires people to discriminate what is hidden, to conceal what should be kept hidden, and to dismiss much other information that gets proffered from others.

It is especially the money economy that Simmel says generates new levels of secrecy, or 'consciously willed concealment'.[3] Money permits many transactions to be made 'invisible', so people can hide purchases and sales, acquisitions and changes in the ownership of objects. Three secrecies are especially made possible through a money economy. First, someone can get rich through a tiny transaction surreptitiously slipped into their hand and barely noticed by anyone else at the time. Second, transfers can be covered up and 'guarded from publicity in a fashion impossible so long as values could be possessed only as extended, tangible objects'. And third, with the growth of distance, changes in value can happen in ways that are hidden 'utterly from the view of our nearest neighbours'. The money economy escalates the scale and impact of transactions that can be made and kept secret. Also the power of money makes it possible to buy the silence of others so as to keep secrets.

Simmel presciently emphasised that these concealments are more likely and significant in 'dealings with foreign money' and provisions to conceal the 'financial operations of corporations'. Secret transactions are central to a money economy especially in the case of dealings involving foreign money and corporations.

Simmel thus thought that modern societies both permit and require high degrees of secrecy. This is taken to the extreme with secret societies such as masonic lodges, where the society is held together through the need to maintain its secrets. Essential to a secret society is the reciprocal confidence of its members, partly engendered through initiation rites, as well as many ways of teaching silence. Secret transactions, Simmel says, make it easier for people to come to agree with each other.[4] In Simmel's time capitalism saw many examples of such secret societies. This current book examines other examples of 'secret societies', now often located across different countries and engaging in a wide array of monetary and policy transactions.

---

[3] Ibid., pp. 449, 467, for quotations in this paragraph.
[4] Ibid., p. 492.

So, for Simmel, secrecy combines concealment and revelation. It sets boundaries and offers temptation to break through those barriers with gossip or confessions. The development of the money economy escalates new forms of concealment and invisibility.

Secret powers

Historically secrecy has been a key feature of power relations in most societies.[5] The ruling household often lived in a secret world, a castle, palace or fortress, such as eighteenth-century France's Palace of Versailles or China's Forbidden City. The life of the emperor or monarch and their household was secret. The monarch/ emperor was visible to their court but offered more or less no visibility to the wider society. This secrecy reinforced the mysterious qualities of the ruler and of their household, even though much of their behaviour transgressed societal values.

In some societies, an occasional ritual procession or 'progress' of the monarch or emperor would be made around their kingdom. This turned subjects into a community as they caught a glimpse of the ruler's carriage as it passed swiftly by. Subsequently the European empires developed 'royal tours' so that colonial subjects could catch a passing sight of their imperial ruler before they returned to their palace or castle, away from the inquisitive eyes of their poor subjects. The glimpse of the swiftly passing monarch was a kind of royal tease.

Modern forms of citizenship came to rest upon greater mutual visibility both between citizens and the state and between citizens. From its emergence in the Greek city-state, citizenship involved interaction in which individuals could appear to each other, face to face, in a public theatre to perform and remember exemplary actions. This understanding and practice of citizenship grew especially in eighteenth-century Europe, where new social spaces emerged, such as the coffeehouse and the salon, in which the new (male) bourgeoisie assembled as equals to discuss political and social matters of the time.

---

[5] Bron Szerszynski and John Urry, 'Visuality, mobility and the cosmopolitan: inhabiting the world from afar', *British Journal of Sociology*, 57 (2006): 113–32.

Modern liberal democracies in particular presuppose more transparent forms of behaviour and visibility. Communications spread from the written and printed form, to audio, film, TV and the digital and social media. These transformations of communications importantly altered the scale and significance of secrecy. There are various changes here.

First, new technologies enable the novel surveillance and monitoring *of* citizens through what has been called *qualculation*. This involves the almost instantaneous collecting and ordering of abstract, numerical information about populations, especially as that population is on the move and engaged in social activities, such as shopping, holidaymaking, driving in certain areas, and so on. This making of private actions un-secret is often realised automatically through algorithms which sort, classify, map and monitor citizens, particularly when they are on the move.[6]

Second, modern citizenship involves seeing the powerful, not just the powerless. This seeing occurs in various ways. There is the mediatised seeing of the powerful through reading newspapers or viewing YouTube videos; there is seeing through being co-present in extraordinary, planned sports or political events or though extraordinary, unplanned events, such as disasters, rescues or deaths; and there is seeing 'rulers' who may show compassion and sympathy or scandalous behaviour and excess at moments of national or corporate crisis. So much is on show, although almost all these moments of disclosure have been historically resisted or at least stage-managed by rulers and their fearful advisers.

This fear of disclosure results partly from the third element here, that of scandal.[7] The position of those in leading roles in companies and states rests upon a trust that has to be earned. But, as those subject to scandal say, although they took years building up their good 'name', 'their world collapsed overnight' as the scandal 'swept' over them and their unfortunate friends and family. In a scandal the private transgressive act is exposed to the wider public. This almost always involves various media, which increasingly employ technologies of observation, surveillance and

---

[6] Nigel Thrift, *Non-Representational Theory* (London: Routledge, 2007).
[7] See especially John Thompson, *Political Scandal: Power and Visibility in the Media Age* (Cambridge: Polity, 2000); and John Urry, *Global Complexity* (Cambridge: Polity, 2003).

monitoring, often developed within the secret services of states (notably used recently by Murdoch's News Corporation). Exposure makes frontstage or 'public' what is supposedly backstage or 'private', and this can generate a media feeding frenzy that takes no prisoners.

Moreover, with the development of digital worlds, there are few images of private lives that can be 'locked away' forever. There are no true secrets, since actions leave 'digital traces'. Furthermore, the competitive nature of the mass media means that the tiny actions of the 'wrongdoer' can get replayed again and again and their shame made globally visible. Once the media have peered 'backstage' there is an escalating exposure and visualisation of the scandalous figure. Scandals often possess an all-consuming flow, where any attempt to stem the opprobrium becomes another element of the scandal, sometimes even the greater scandal.

'Financial' and 'abuse of power' scandals often occur at moments of global scrutiny that depend upon the world's media. Especially important are big public meetings when the brand of the company or country is put on display and its practices revealed to the world. Avoiding such moments of potential disclosure is energetically sought by those with plenty to hide, often using the power of money to buy or physical threats to enforce silence. Later I examine the characteristics of various taxation scandals.

Fourth, in order to avoid scandals at moments of global exposure, corporations increasingly erect new barriers of 'consciously willed concealment'. This book is about some of these new concealments, and especially those wholly or partly offshore from the main activities of the organisation. Simmel underlined how even the late nineteenth-century money economy enabled concealment. But changes occurring from around 1980 made it possible for power to escape into many new channels of secrecy.

Bauman emphasises how one element of contemporary stratification is the power to 'exit'. Power involves, he says, 'escape, slippage, elision and avoidance, the effective rejection of any territorial confinement' and the possibility of escape from potential regulation and scandal into 'sheer inaccessibility'.[8] There are many examples of such 'exitability' for elites through outsourcing or offshoring activities of corporations.

---

[8] Zygmunt Bauman, *Liquid Modernity* (Cambridge: Polity, 2000), p. 11.

Richardson, Kakabadse and Kakabadse demonstrate the attractions of offshored discussions and networking practices at the annual secret meetings of the shadowy Bilderberg Group. They document the overlapping links between economic and political elites possible in the secret off-the-record discussions characteristic of such meetings of the 'rich class'.[9] As elites escape and circulate spatially, so they leave 'residues' which develop further their connections. In chapter 5 we see the importance of other kinds of offshored meetings in places of leisure and pleasure which serve to cement strong and often secret connections between elites.

Overall, Brittain-Catlin argues that members of the contemporary bourgeoisie behave more and more like criminals, hiding undercover, obliterating traces and protecting their freedom to make money secretly and mostly out of sight. With contemporary offshoring: 'wealth is protected against its uncovering through mechanisms that remove the identity or trace of ownership.'[10] Indeed there is much overlap and linking between legal and illegal money and wider social practices. Brittain-Catlin talks of the progressively undifferentiated character of 'corporate, private and criminal wealth'.[11] The offshore system provides cover for the proceeds of organised crime and white-collar financial crime, money launderers, and corrupt presidents who have stripped their countries bare of assets. This parallels Graeber's more general claim as to the centrality of pillage and crime in the very formation of global income and wealth. Money derives, he says, from conquest and extortion.[12]

---

[9] Ian Richardson, Andrew Kakabadse and Nada Kakabadse, *Bilderberg People: Elite Power and Consensus in World Affairs* (London: Routledge, 2011); Charlie Skelton, 'Bilderberg 2012: bigger and badder and better than ever', www.guardian.co.uk/world/us-news-blog/2012/jun/01/bilderberg-2012-chantilly-occupy (accessed 15.5.2013). See Thomas Birtchnell and Javier Caletrio (eds), *Elite Mobilities* (London: Routledge, 2013).

[10] William Brittain-Catlin, *Offshore: The Dark Side of the Global Economy* (New York: Picador, 2005), p. 145; Nick Kochan, *The Washing Machine: Money, Crime and Terror in the Offshore System* (London: Gerald Duckworth, 2006).

[11] Brittain-Catlin, *Offshore*, p. 145.

[12] Daniel Graeber, *Debt* (New York: Melville House, 2011).

I turn now to so-called neo-liberalism, in which the multiple practices of offshoring became a central element of a broader class struggle.

Neo-liberalism

In 1947 in Switzerland, the country that was and in a way still is the world's premier tax haven, a senior bank official brought together various scholars to a secret meeting at Mont Pèlerin, near Geneva. This meeting was organised to revive liberalism under the direction of the Austrian liberal economist Friedrich Hayek, author of the bestselling *The Road to Serfdom*.[13] This meeting, and the general development of the Mont Pèlerin Society funded by Swiss banks, was central in commencing the global fightback against dominant Keynesian justification for state interventionism, including the American New Deal.[14] For some while this struggle to reverse Keynesianism was organised through many further secret meetings.

Their bête noire was John Maynard Keynes, whose ideas became exceedingly influential following the Great Crash of 1929 and the subsequent 1930s economic depression. These dire events led many to a belief in the virtues of tax-funded state expenditures, systems of national planning, and the idea of a collective national interest separate from the interests of specific individuals and companies. It was believed that economic systems would not themselves rectify unemployment and economic depression. As Keynes pointed out: 'Economists set themselves too easy, too useless a task if in tempestuous seasons they can only tell us that

---

[13] Friedrich Hayek, *The Road to Serfdom* (London: Routledge, 1944). Hayek, like Thatcher, was a strong supporter of General Pinochet, a leader notorious for inflicting his brand of serfdom upon the Chilean people during the 1970s.

[14] See David Stedman Jones, *Masters of the Universe* (Princeton, NJ: Princeton University Press, 2012), chap. 2; and George Monbiot, 'A rightwing insurrection is usurping our democracy', www.guardian.co.uk/commentisfree/2012/oct/01/rightwing-insurrection-usurps-democracy (accessed 27.12.2012) on the role of recent thinktanks.

when a storm is past the ocean is flat again.'[15] There were many tempestuous seasons during the 1930s, which meant that there was no flat ocean that would be returned to with ease. According to Keynes, economies are not self-regulating and automatically equilibrium-restoring.

One person present at that fateful 1947 Mont Pèlerin secret meeting was Milton Friedman, who with others subsequently went on to develop what is widely known as neo-liberalism. Since the 1970s, neo-liberalism has become the dominant global orthodoxy of economic and social policy and practice, developing ideas first broached in the Mont Pèlerin Society designed to organise the struggle against Keynesianism.[16] Neo-liberal doctrine and practice developed within, and then spread out from, the Friedman-dominated Economics Department at the University of Chicago. By 2000 Chicago School alumni included twenty-five government ministers and more than a dozen central bank presidents.

Keynesianism was significantly challenged by a pro-free-market transatlantic network of thinktanks, businessmen, economists, journalists and politicians. Carroll identifies various transnational organisations as being particularly significant in often secretly developing the economic, social and political conditions for the global spread of neo-liberalism: the Paris-based International Chamber of Commerce; the annual Bilderberg Conferences; the Trilateral Commission; the World Economic Forum held in Davos; and the World Business Council for Sustainable Development.[17] What Stedman Jones terms the 'masters of the universe' of neo-liberalism secretly conspired to take over and ensure the

---

[15] Cited in Bryan Lovell, *Challenged by Carbon* (Cambridge: Cambridge University Press, 2010), p. 63; see Keynes's seminal text *The General Theory of Employment, Interest and Money* (London: Macmillan, [1936] 1961).

[16] https://www.montpelerin.org/montpelerin/index.html (accessed 19.7. 2012). It should be noted that Keynes had already died, in 1946 aged sixty-three.

[17] See William K. Carroll, *The Making of a Transnational Capitalist Class: Corporate Power in the 21st Century* (London: Zed, 2010), p. 50, on the interlocking connections between these organisations.

transformation of economic, political and social life during the latter part of the twentieth century.[18]

Overall, this increasingly dominant neo-liberalism asserted the importance of private entrepreneurship, private property rights, free markets and the freeing of trade. It was thought that these objectives would be realised by deregulating private activities and companies, privatising previously 'state' or 'collective' services, lowering taxes, undermining collective powers of workers and professionals, and providing conditions for the private sector to find many new sources of profitable activity.

Neo-liberalism especially minimises the redistributive role of the state and the need for taxation, to redress the balance, as it argues, between 'bad' states and 'good' markets. Neo-liberals hold that states are inferior to markets in 'guessing' what should be done. States are seen as inherently inefficient and easily corrupted by private interest groups. Markets, by contrast, are presumed to move to equilibrium if unnatural forces or elements do not get in the way. Neo-liberalism elevates market exchanges over and above other sets of connections between people. The 'market' is the source of value and virtue. Deficiencies in markets are seen to be the result of market imperfections.

However, states are important within neo-liberal restructuring. First, they are often central in constructing the material infrastructures that make possible new kinds of profitable opportunity for private companies, such as new debt-based property developments that are undertaken once the roads, railways, ports, airports, sewage systems, or electricity grids are put in place by the state.[19]

---

[18] See Daniel Stedman Jones, *Masters of the Universe* (Princeton, NJ: Princeton University Press, 2012), for a detailed history of neo-liberalism, as well as Naomi Klein, *The Shock Doctrine* (London: Allen Lane, 2007), p. 166; David Harvey, *A Brief History of Neo-Liberalism* (Oxford: Oxford University Press, 2005); Sylvia Walby, *Globalization and Inequalities* (London: Sage, 2009); Colin Crouch, *The Strange Non-Death of Neo-Liberalism* (Cambridge: Polity, 2011); and Joseph Hacker and Paul Pierson, *Winner-Takes-All Politics* (New York: Simon & Schuster, 2011).

[19] See John Urry, *Societies beyond Oil* (London: Zed, 2013), chap. 2.

Second, states are crucial in eliminating 'unnatural' forces – the sets of rules, regulations and forms of life that are said to slow down economic growth through the constraints upon the private sector's freedom of operation. This 'freedom of the market' is often realised by states, through a 'shock treatment' which involves creating or responding to 'emergency'. The state wipes the slate clean and imposes sweeping free-market solutions.[20] Klein writes how 'only a great rupture – a flood, a war, a terrorist attack – can generate the kind of vast, clean canvases they crave. It is in these malleable moments . . . that these artists . . . begin their work of remaking the world.'[21] Hacker and Pierson document many ways in which American business and partially secret thinktanks conspired to 'reboot' the American state during the 1970s, so enabling the neo-liberal agenda of 'remaking the world' to be realised.[22]

Especially important were the ways in which neo-liberalism realised 'accumulation by dispossession', notably over various kinds of commons.[23] There are many examples of often secret dispossessions of the commons: peasants thrown off their land, collective property rights made private, indigenous rights stolen and turned into private opportunities, rents extracted from patents, general knowledge turned into intellectual 'property', states selling off or outsourcing their collective activities; trade unions' rights undermined; and new less regulated instruments and flows redistributing income and rights towards finance and away from more productive activities.

Through multiple dispossessions of the commons or the collective, neo-liberalism is 'incorporated into the common-sense way many of us interpret, live in, and understand the world'.[24] One consequence of multiple 'dispossessions' has been the growth of inequality within many societies and globally, and hence of

---

[20] Milton Friedman, *Capitalism and Freedom* (Chicago: University of Chicago Press, 2002).
[21] Klein, *The Shock Doctrine*, p. 21.
[22] Hacker and Pierson, *Winner-Takes-All Politics*, chap. 5 on 'organized combat'.
[23] Harvey, *A Brief History of Neo-Liberalism*, pp. 159–61.
[24] Ibid., p. 3.

powerful interests to protect and further extend the bases of such unequally distributed global income and wealth.[25] Offshoring is part and parcel of the realising of such unequal interests. And such inequalities matter a great deal. Access to significant 'services' depends upon each person's income and wealth, and so, the more unequal these are, the less chance there is that people will be regarded as in any way equal to one another. Moreover, the rampant marketisation of almost everything crowds out many other reasons why people may act, such as for reasons of service, duty and sociability. Neo-liberalism significantly challenges Sandel's argument that there should be 'moral limits of markets'.[26]

A number of processes have developed this corrupting influence of markets. Banks and financial institutions came to be regarded as a set of markets that should be less regulated. The distinction between commercial and investment banking was dissolved in many societies through lowering lending standards and developing business models to turn debts into products. Competitive individualism within banks was enhanced through a bonus culture that rewarded indebtedness and dangerous risk-taking. Hedge funds mushroomed. There has been the widespread removal of exchange controls. Apart from certain transitional economies, governments and international organisations such as the World Bank eliminated most exchange controls which limited the convertibility of domestic and foreign currencies. Significantly, eliminating exchange controls was one of the first actions in Britain in 1979 of the incoming Thatcher government, which then proceeded to limit many other forms of regulation.

Much of the offshore world analysed below developed because of the increasingly unregulated movement of finance across national borders, a scale of movement often dwarfing the budgets of national states. Neo-liberalism provided ways of extending the power and reach of ever larger conglomerations of private and corporate wealth that came to be increasingly located in secret jurisdictions. Offshoring is part and parcel of the exceptionally successful restructuring effected by neoliberalism over the past few decades.

---

[25] Hacker and Pierson, *Winner-Takes-All Politics*.
[26] Michael Sandel, *What Money Can't Buy: the Moral Limits of Markets* (London: Allen Lane, 2012).

Conclusion

In this chapter I have shown some ways in which secrecy and power have been and are intertwined. I considered Georg Simmel and especially how he argued that the growth of a 'money economy' generates new levels of 'consciously willed concealment', or secrets. I examined how contemporary societies entail new kinds of visibility between citizens and the powerful, especially through the media, scandals and deceptions. These in turn fostered the importance of 'exit' and 'secrecy' for the operations of power.

The chapter ended with an account of neo-liberalism, which developed from around 1980, although it had been partly planned in secret since the late 1940s. It was shown how the enhanced role of finance and indebtedness presupposes newly offshored secret worlds that neo-liberalism facilitated and sustained.

Much of this book documents the dynamic intersections of onshore and offshore. Indeed, although many secret offshore processes are examined, this distinction is not one that is finalised, fixed and secure. Secrets are rarely dealt with once and for all and kept forever out of sight. Secrets are waiting to be discovered, and they are increasingly revealed by 'whistleblowers', some of whom are themselves 'offshore' and operating through further secrets and lies.[27] Once something is a secret, then there are often reasons why others will seek to reveal that secret. So securing and revealing secrets form part of the complex processes in a neo-liberal world order, where reputations and profits can be made in both concealing and exposing those secrets. Offshore engenders yet more offshoring.

---

[27] In June 2013, Wikileaks founder Julian Assange, himself holed up in the Ecuadorian embassy in London, was providing advice and assistance to Edward Snowden, who was 'offshore' in Moscow's Sheremetyevo airport until granted a one-year entry visa by Russia. Snowden had blown the whistle on the National Security Agency's PRISM programme, which gave the US/UK government access to vast databanks from Google, Facebook, Microsoft, Skype and others. Also see the UK government website which supposedly encourages whistleblowing: https://www.gov.uk/whistleblowing/overview (accessed 27.6.2013). See chapter 10.

3

Work Offshored

Divisions of labour

The previous chapters established how a set of offshored econo-mies, peoples and places is being formed and sustained. Offshor-ing especially transforms often peripheral or marginal places. The rise of offshore is not contingent or opportunistic but central to the internationalising global economy and its neo-liberal restruc-turing. This chapter examines changes in the location and form of manufacturing industry in particular.

Until the eighteenth century, in Europe and North America most manufactured objects were produced by craft specialists working in a local area and using materials found nearby. Such craft workers included ironmongers (iron goods), blacksmiths (metalwork), coopers (barrels), cobblers (shoes), and so on. Neither raw materials nor final products travelled very far, and there was relatively little division of labour apart from between these predominantly male craft trades.

Beginning in England in the late eighteenth century, the momen-tous shift to industrial manufacturing meant that many of these crafts became less significant. Workers in very large numbers moved considerable distances to work in the emerging 'dark satanic mills' of workshops and factories powered by coal, and later in the twentieth century by electricity.

Here industrial fabrication was performed by new combinations of workers and machines involving routinised operations and processes of assembly. Much more complex work developed, first described in 1776 by political economist Adam Smith in analysing the division of labour in a pin-making factory.[1] He showed how the making of pins could be divided into about eighteen distinct operations, which in some factories were each performed by different people. The resulting division of labour generated large economies of scale in such factories, which made many products. The raw materials and final products were then moved often large distances by canal boat and later by the new steam railway.

In the twentieth century, raw materials and final products were transported appreciable distances on trucks along the increasingly complex road systems of North America, then Western Europe, and then in much of the rest of the world. Many factories exploited raw materials that had been appropriated from the empires that had extended especially during the nineteenth century. Their 'resources' were shipped in new oil-based steamers and then turned into manufactured products, and in some cases were sold back to the colonised populations.

By the 1960s, complex mechanics and computing introduced into factories led to automated mass-production manufacturing, allowing manufacturers to undermine and replace remaining skilled labour with standardised and mechanised assembly lines. During the golden age of Detroit, the car manufacturing capital and model of computerised factory automation, large-scale manufacturing controlled by computers and involving on-site production and assembly took place through increasingly large corporations. These large American corporations (and similar entities in Europe) organised production, employment, promotion, welfare and savings. They were staffed by 'corporation men', who would work for much of their career within vertically integrated organisations that provided significant welfare benefits for the mainly male employees and their families (through the so-called family wage).[2] Such large, relatively stable organisations

---

[1] Adam Smith, *An Inquiry into the Nature and Causes of the Wealth of Nations* (Oxford: Clarendon Press, [1776] 1979).
[2] See Anthony Jay, *Corporation Man* (Harmondsworth: Penguin, 1975).

producing low-cost manufactured goods were key elements within what Lash and Urry termed 'organised capitalism'.[3]

But with the 'disorganisation' of Western capitalism from the late 1970s, first in the US, the American industrial corporation became increasingly fragmented, ownership often being vested in financial institutions concerned with short-term 'shareholder value'. The large corporation became outdated, with the number halving over the past twenty years.[4] Corporate cultures providing reasonably generous benefits for corporation men were less common. Sennett and others lamented the resulting decline in people's long-term commitment and character that was ushered in by this new economy.[5]

Furthermore, manufacturing industry in the US increasingly moved from the rustbelt to the sunbelt states. New high-tech industries were located in the south and west states of North America. Many US industries and towns in the rustbelt experienced astonishing declines of income and employment. Similar shifts occurred in other developed economies, away from previous centres of manufacturing industry based upon large vertically integrated corporations. The rise and fall of Detroit, the world's original 'car city', especially symbolises such a dramatic shift. Its population fell from 2 million to now less than 750,000, and its government collapsed into bankruptcy in August 2013, somewhat similarly to what was presciently forecast in the 1987 movie *Robocop*.[6]

This stemmed partly from how much manufacturing work was offshored to countries offering cheap and non-unionised labour, as well as less regulation and lower tax rates often located within free or special economic zones. This was characterised as the 'new international division of labour'.[7] With technology becoming

---

[3]Scott Lash and John Urry, *The End of Organized Capitalism* (Cambridge: Polity, 1987).
[4]Gerald Davis, 'Re-imagining the corporation' (paper to American Sociological Association, Colorado, August 2012).
[5]Richard Sennett, *The Corrosion of Character* (New York: W. W. Norton, 1998).
[6]See 'Detroit legal battle over bankruptcy petition', www.bbc.co.uk/news/world-us-canada-23381456 (accessed 24.7.2013).
[7]F. Froebel, J. Heinrichs and O. Krey, *The New International Division of Labour* (Cambridge: Cambridge University Press, 1979).

more complex, cheaper labour in the global South meant that some elements of the manufacturing process could be moved offshore. As digital technology was introduced into manufacturing, greater levels of precision, efficiency and speed enabled some components of human labour to be pushed out to what had been the periphery of the world economy.

Much manufacturing work was relocated to various countries offering low wages for assembly-line work, using local energy, mostly coal, and where those countries bore the environmental costs. This offshoring of manufacturing was key in the growing economic power of the BRICS (Brazil, Russia, India, China, South Africa). At the same time company headquarters often remained in the global North, able to control these distributed and remote manufacturing processes through new communications technologies, digitised networks, air travel for intermittent visits, and sea travel for the movement of the resulting components and finished goods.

Blinder especially examined how such offshored production would be 'the next industrial revolution'.[8] This process is seen by him as being as important as previous shifts of entire economies, from agriculture to manufacturing or from manufacturing to service industries. He describes this offshoring shift as a seriously 'big deal'. Or as Walter and Dorothy Diamond presciently wrote back in 1998, the coming century will be the 'Century of Offshore Investment'.[9]

Blinder's work and much subsequent discussion examined offshoring from the viewpoint of the rich North of the world and what would happen to it through 'offshoring' especially manufacturing work. Particular concern has revolved around how jobs have been 'lost' from first-world manufacturing and increasingly now from service industries. This has been brought about through employing workforces in the developing world, sometimes within regulation-reduced zones where labour is much cheaper, less

---

[8] Alan Blinder, 'Offshoring: the next industrial revolution', *Foreign Affairs*, 85 (2006): 113–28; Jagdish Bhagwati and Alan Blinder, *Offshoring of American Jobs* (Cambridge, MA: MIT Press, 2009).
[9] See Ronen Palan, *The Offshore World* (Ithaca, NY: Cornell University Press, 2006), pp. 7–9.

unionised, deregulated, and more pliable than in the rich North. Some commentators describe this offshoring of much work as 'unfair', both upon the workers employed in exploitative and often dangerous conditions and upon the economies of the rich North, which suffer 'unfair competition' and consequential economic decline.

Other commentators view offshoring as demonstrating the theory of comparative advantage, that each economy should specialise in those activities in which they have 'comparative' economic advantage. This leads economies to develop areas of specialisation and concentration, and in the end all societies benefit through increased global income. This is linked to arguments that the free trade in goods and services will generate economic gains for all countries once appropriate adjustments take place. The workings of newly emerging divisions of labour will in the end benefit all, it is maintained.[10]

There is little doubt that offshoring has resulted in significant job losses within developed societies over the past couple of decades. These stemmed from three different components of offshoring often insufficiently distinguished. First, there is the specific export of jobs as a particular company outsources work elsewhere, normally because labour is for various reasons 'cheaper' in another country. This involves the 'direct substitution' of jobs, especially those in 'manufacturing', rather than those of management or research that may remain 'at home' in the developed world. A British example of this is Dyson, a world leader in innovative vacuum cleaners. In 2002 it began outsourcing its manufacturing to Malaysia, while maintaining research and management functions in Wiltshire in Britain.[11] Dyson still presents itself and is treated by the British government as a 'British' company.

Second, there is 'indirect substitution'. This occurs through the growth of factories or service centres elsewhere that are broadly

---

[10]See Bhagwati's contributions in Bhagwati and Blinder, *Offshoring of American Jobs*. Many books lament the outsourcing of US manufacturing jobs.
[11]'Dyson to move to Far East', http://news.bbc.co.uk/1/hi/business/1801909.stm (accessed 9.5.2012).

part of the same industry but which over time successfully compete against those more expensive factories or centres left in the developed world. The growth of automobile manufacturing in China is an example of this, so much so that the world's largest car market is now China.[12] Chinese auto manufacturers increasingly displace Western car manufacturers from existing markets, except the US, as the economic production of automobiles shifts 'east'. This in turn follows the earlier successful development of auto manufacturing in Japan and the rise of Toyota as the world's largest carmaker.[13]

The third kind of offshoring is in developing new products and services that, over a lengthy time, displace existing economies and workforces that had been located in the developed world. Much economic history is the history of new socio-technical systems that develop and replace in often complicated ways existing corporations, systems and workforces. I term this 'system substitution', an example being the worldwide growth of the new 'industry' of internet downloads since the early 1990s. This novel set of activities and capacities generated a long-term decline in music retailers on the high street, as well as of many postal services. One system of communications in effect replaced another, so changing the worldwide distribution of production and work within 'delivery'. Significant delivery-systems work was offshored, and this substituted for the direct postal delivery arriving in individual letter boxes. Most postal systems in the developed world are in deep crisis as a consequence of this and related system substitutions.

So there are three main components of the offshoring of work – through direct, indirect and system substitutions. In the next sections I consider two preconditions for this extensive offshoring of work: containerised shipping and the doctrine and practices of free trade.

---

[12] David Tyfield and John Urry, 'Greening China's cars. Will the last be first?', www.lancs.ac.uk/staff/tyfield/GreeningChinaCars _CeMoReWorkingPaper.pdf (accessed 28.11.2012).
[13] Chester Dawson, 'Toyota again world's largest auto maker', *Wall Street Journal*, 29 January 2013, http://online.wsj.com/article/SB10001424127 887323337520457826918106049375
0.html (accessed 11.5.2013).

Containerisation

The cargo container has made possible astonishingly cheap production and transportation of manufactured goods around the world. This small innovation, combined with the fragmentation of the large corporation, has led to huge increases in the miles travelled by goods and components. The world container-ship fleet consists of around 5,000 vessels.[14] Currently container ships can carry up to 16,000 containers, while the world's largest shipping company, Maersk, is planning a range of 'mega' triple-E container ships. These will each carry 18,000 containers, will be twenty storeys high and the width of an eight-lane motorway, will take four to five days to unload, and will be unable to enter most existing ports, which will need rebuilding.[15]

These container boxes, easy to load on and off ships, trains and trucks, almost eliminated the cost of transporting many goods, redrew the world's economic geography and ensured that most objects are available anywhere to consumers that can afford them. Over 90 per cent of the world's cargo travels by sea on these container ships, which are like slow-moving buildings. Almost all goods in the world are shipped within this intermodal system of containers, including most manufactured objects. Sekula summarises how the 'cargo container, an American innovation of the mid-1950s . . . is the very coffin of remote labour power, bearing the hidden evidence of exploitation in the far reaches of the world'.[16] During the period of very cheap oil the very low-tech container ruled the waves.

The Twenty-foot Equivalent Unit (TEU) cargo container is thus a key element of a wider socio-technical system. These coffins of

---

[14] www.worldshipping.org/about-the-industry/liner-ships/container-vessel-fleet (accessed 29.7.2013); Brian Cudahy, *Box Boats: How Container Ships Changed the World* (New York: Fordham University Press, 2006), pp. 236–41.

[15] www.worldslargestship.com/ (accessed 13.9.2013).

[16] Allan Sekula, 'Freeway to China', in Jean Comaroff and John Comaroff (eds), *Millennial Capitalism and the Culture of Neoliberalism* (Durham, NC: Duke University Press, 2001), p. 147; Allan Sekula and Noël Burch, 'The forgotten space', *New Left Review*, 69 (May–June 2011): 78–9 (accessed 14.5.2012).

labour shape and are shaped by global production, consumption, provision, investment, inequality, status and wealth. As a protective shell around the artefacts consumed mainly in the rich North but produced in the global South, container ships realised the greatest ever movement of material objects in human history. In a way everyone now lives in a containerised world.

This 'system' comprises the goods, the ships, the container ports and cheap oil.[17] It depends upon economies of scale, low energy costs and pollution standards, and flows of cheap and often unregulated labour originating chiefly from the developing world. Mass production by poorly paid and generally unskilled labourers in the global South is umbilically linked with mass consumerism in the global North. This linking is realised through the slow but steady movement across the oceans of these vast 'containers' of desire.

The containers are mostly laden with goods made in East Asia and destined for the rest of the world following the Walmart model. This is based upon the computerised management of extended supply chains relating to an exceptional array of components and products.[18] Container ships are constantly on the move along certain routes between a few vast ports that are themselves normally located a little away from city centres as well as from trade union organisation. The largest container ports – Shanghai, Singapore, Hong Kong and Shenzhen – are all in Asia.

In chapter 9 we see how shipping itself involves a major form of offshored work with unimaginably poor conditions of employment. I examine the role played by the offshoring of ship registration which first developed after the First World War but which grew especially in the post-Second World War period. These flags of convenience ships have no real nationality and are almost literally off all shores. Seafarers are an invisible workforce, while complex patterns of ship ownership avoid ownership obligations, scrutiny, decent conditions of work and taxation.

---

[17] See John Urry, *Societies beyond Oil* (London: Zed, 2013).
[18] Marc Levinson, *The Box* (Princeton, NJ: Princeton University Press, 2008). Every second container spends time in China during its journey: Paul French and Sam Chambers, *Oil on Water* (London: Zed, 2010), p. 43.

Free trade

Central also to offshoring has been the discourse and practices of free trade, involving the claim that there should be a general reduction in trade barriers between countries. This notion was key to neo-liberalism, part of the system of global governance that sought to stabilise Western dominance during the last century through imposing trade liberalisation around the world. The offshoring of work in part developed through reducing many barriers to trade.

Especially significant was the US, as the world's dominant economy significantly based upon the resource of oil. This provides over 95 per cent of transportation energy, making the world go round. Globalisation and indeed offshoring is inconceivable without the cheap and plentiful resource which lubricates increasingly free trade, which should be renamed 'high carbon' trade.[19]

Moreover, this doctrine of free trade is not 'freely' chosen; it has often been imposed by the US or the EU when suiting their interests. It is often an element of the so-called Washington Consensus by which the global order has been orchestrated over the past few decades.[20] If there are valuable resources in the world, then the US insists that they should be available to the highest bidder and also paid for in American dollars; thus there should be free trade. The rules of the World Bank, the International Monetary Fund and the World Trade Organisation all state that whoever has sufficient money, and especially dollars, to buy particular products then they must have the legal right to purchase them. The world is one's oyster if one is the world's richest economy and is able to print dollars to buy the oysters, we might say!

Furthermore, the US developed many client states especially through its global military reach, with hundreds of bases worldwide. On occasions this enabled the US and its allies to enforce free trade. There is not much democratic debate in free trade and much imposition. The US also engages in destabilising regimes

---

[19] See Urry, *Societies beyond Oil*; Richard Heinberg, *The Party's Over* (Forest Row, East Sussex: Clairview Books, 2005).
[20] See David Held, *Global Covenant: The Social Democratic Alternative to the Washington Consensus* (Cambridge: Polity, 2004).

which are not part of the Washington Consensus promoting and maintaining such 'free trade'.

In addition, the US wages trade wars when trying to impose particular products from US manufacturers upon other countries. An example of this is the current effort to make European consumers use genetically modified foodstuffs even against the opposition of the still powerful European Union.[21]

Casas-Zamora notes that trade is freest where developed economies have a large comparative advantage. Trade is much less free in the case of agriculture, where extensive subsidies are found within the developed world, so creating and maintaining particular crops and foodstuffs at the expense of the often smaller producers within the developing world. Nor can trade be allowed to be free where intellectual property is often legally protected in draconian fashion.[22] Hypocrisy is the name of the 'free trade game'.

Processes of offshoring work

Given these two processes, long-distance supply chains and free trade, how is the offshoring of work developing? In the economic literature it is common to distinguish between tradable and non-tradable products, a distinction partly mapping on to the distinction between manufacturing and service industries. But these distinctions are rapidly changing, with the consequence that more and more work is offshored.

This growing potential for offshoring work has various roots. First, in many developing countries there has been the growth of free trade or special economic zones, which provided incentives for significant parts of manufacturing and services (including health and education) to be located offshore. Developing these zones was endorsed as a strategy by the UN during the 1970s. Such zones were not normally considered part of the territory of

---

[21] Anthony Gucciardi, 'Leaked: US to start "trade wars" with nations opposed to Monsanto, GMO crops', www.activistpost.com/2012/01/leaked-us-to-start-trade-wars-with.html (accessed 9.5.2012).
[22] Kevin Casas-Zamora, 'Why the discomfort over free trade', *YaleGlobal*, 12 September 2008.

the home state; they are a kind of parastate.[23] Two-thirds of workers in special economic zones are in China, this following the initial Shenzhen zone dating from 1979. Some such zones are now termed 'cities' or 'knowledge villages', as with several Emirate states housing offshored American or British universities.

Second, the container-based system results in the rapidly falling costs of transporting many physical products – for example, the real costs of electronic goods. They enable entertainment services within the home, which then compete with those services available through travelling to and being co-present in live events within specific venues.

Third, many items in world trade are now digital and delivered through computer networks rather than through consumers travelling and receiving face-to-face delivery. Examples include SMS messages rather than letters, the use of internet banking services rather than local bank branches, or music that is downloaded rather than purchased in a record store.

Fourth, some services are in effect now generated through manufactured products such as e-readers, which enable books to be read digitally rather than in their physical manifestation bought at a bookshop, although bookshops are increasingly at a distance and not local. In such cases the product normally travels to the consumer virtually rather than the latter physically visiting the bookshop to make the purchase and acquire the 'book'.

Finally, in the neo-liberal period there is the widespread commodification of areas of life that were once thought to be 'naturally' public or which took the form of commons. These include water, security, health, children's play, education and leisure. These are often now delivered by international corporations rather than by neighbourhood groupings, with the consequence that elements of the delivery system are geographically very distant from customers.

Together these processes mean that many more products are now tradable and delivered partly or wholly offshore. As the range of tradable services expands, so service workers in the developed world compete with manufacturing and service workers in other

---

[23] Keller Easterling, 'Zone: the spatial softwares of extrastatecraft', http://places.designobserver.com/feature/zone-the-spatial-softwares-of-extrastatecraft/34528/ (accessed 11.10.2013).

societies. Blinder argues: 'the dividing line between the jobs that produce services that are suitable for electronic delivery (and are thus threatened by offshoring) and those that do not does not correspond to traditional distinctions between high-end and low-end work.' The only exception to the potential offshoring of work is where 'personal, face-to-face contact is either imperative or highly desirable'.[24] Examples of the latter include, says Blinder, child care, physiotherapy, political lobbying, waitering and taxi driving. Overall he argues that more education and training should be provided in the developed world for people undertaking personal service jobs, suggesting that, in the future, 'people skills may become more valuable than computer skills'.[25]

One important kind of offshoring work is where service jobs are outsourced to call centres, so that face-to-face advice is replaced by 'ear-to-ear' services. Over the past ten to fifteen years there has been an extensive development of call centres; they constitute a major source of new employment, especially within financial services, retailing and telecommunications.[26] Over 70 per cent of those employed in call centres are female, with workplaces being characterised by relatively flat hierarchies. Call centres in more coordinated economies have better conditions of work, although in general job discretion is low and workers typically remain within any one centre for less than a year.

'Ear-to-ear' services are often offshored. The proportion of call centres serving international customers was three-quarters in India, nearly two-fifths in Ireland, and over one-third in Canada (2007 figures). Indeed, while call centres are geographically mobile, their spread is shaped by language and culture, such as between France and Morocco, Spain and Latin America, and the UK/US and other English-speaking countries. Canada's proximity to the US and shared language, time zone and culture means that it is important in the offshoring of service work from the US. The geographic mobility of calls also makes it relatively easy to

---

[24] Blinder, 'Offshoring: the next industrial revolution', p. 119.
[25] Ibid., p. 125.
[26] David Holman, Rosemary Batt and Ursula Holtgrewe, *The Global Call Center Report: International Perspectives on Management and Employment* (Ithaca, NY: Cornell University Global Call Center Network, 2007).

outsource work to third-party companies rather than retaining this in-house. However, by 2007 most call centres were in-house, those in India being the main exception. Most employees work for subcontractors, with their workplaces being larger and taking advantage of economies of scale.[27]

In India, competence in the English language and effective tele-communications enable customer services to be provided to con-sumers often thousands of miles away. Most call-centre workers in India are graduates and work full-time, but they experience low levels of discretion and much monitoring of performance. Efforts are made to train workers to obscure or make secret that they are offshore and distant from customers within the developed world. Research reveals a managerial strategy of 'national identity man-agement', in which employees are expected to take on different national identities as part of their job and training. Through inter-views with eighty call-centre personnel, Poster analyses how acquiring another 'ethnicity and citizenship' is crucial to the labour process in these Indian call centres.[28] These workers have much to lose in terms of the costs to their bodies, family lives, psycho-logical states and sense of national identity, which are all in a way offshored through these processes.

Finally, it is important to note that, although it was once rea-sonable to talk of work being predominantly offshored 'east-wards' from the 'West', this is not still true. There are now many patterns of offshoring, the most striking being the movement of investment and employment from China to various other coun-tries.[29] Thus the first new computer manufacturing plant for some years is about to open in North Carolina and is being built by Lenovo, the Chinese group now the world's largest PC manufacturer.[30] The fragmentation or disorganisation of capitalist

---

[27] Ibid., pp. 4–6.

[28] Winifred Poster, 'Who's on the line? Indian call center agents pose as Americans for US-outsourced firms', *Industrial Relations Journal*, 46 (2007): 271–304. Some suggest that the Philippines are now an impor-tant location for call centres, since accents sound 'American'.

[29] See Dexin Yang, *China's Offshore Investments* (Cheltenham: Edward Elgar, 2005).

[30] Tamzin Booth, 'Here, there and everywhere', *The Economist*, 19 January 2013, p. 3.

corporations means that offshoring processes will flow in diverse directions and not just from the (once?) rich North.

3D printing

It is now argued that being both close and responsive to 'markets' is getting to be more important, and this will be increasingly relevant to future manufacturing location. Closeness to markets relates to how offshoring may not be the only game in town here. Various new machines now enable the 'printing' of three-dimensional shapes or objects, which can take place thousands of miles away from where designs were developed. Such designs are transmitted digitally and then turned into objects through remote 3D 'printing', and this can occur much closer to where the marketplace is located.

There are various technologies here, the main differences being in how the layers of the print are built up as they are laid one on top of the other while the material is extruded from a cartridge.[31] As they are laid down, so a 3D object is produced. Each layer is in effect a digital slice generated through a given computer-aided design. New layers are added until the object is fully printed or 'manufactured'. Normally a binding agent is added to the powder, which can be comprised of nylon, plastic, carbon, titanium or stainless steel. This process is technically known as 'additive' manufacturing, by contrast with most previous 'subtractive' manufacturing processes, which involved cutting, drilling or bashing wood or metal or other materials.

Such 3D printing was initially developed during the 1980s and 1990s to produce cheaper prototypes of objects before a workshop or factory was tooled up to manufacture thousands or more copies of the 'real' object through subtractive processes. Manufacturing individual prototypes is very expensive but much cheaper with 3D printing. But as 3D printing developed, so it was realised that a much wider range of shapes and materials

[31] This account draws on ESRC-funded research conducted by Thomas Birtchnell and myself; see Thomas Birtchnell and John Urry, 'Fabricated futures and the transportation of objects', *Mobilities*, 8/3 (2013): 388–405, http://dx.doi.org/10.1080/17450101.2012.745697.

could be produced, not just prototypes. Something like one-fifth of additive manufacturing is now of final products rather than prototypes, and this figure is rapidly increasing.[32] Objects that can now be 'printed' include medical implants, car parts, jewellery, football boots designed for individual feet, furniture, lampshades, batteries, parts for aircraft, stainless-steel gloves, dental crowns, cycle helmets, customised mobile phones and, soon, even artificial blood vessels.[33] Researchers are envisaging 'printing' the entire wings of an aircraft, an electric vehicle or even whole buildings.

This manufacturing system has many potential cost savings, such as customising objects for particular consumers, printing or manufacturing on demand, being able to make small modifications to products at almost zero cost, saving on raw materials (since little gets thrown away), and the local adaptation of design to suit particular environments. There are also significant possibilities of recycling both the unused powder and existing manufactured objects.[34]

But the biggest saving is that objects could be manufactured close to or even by consumers with their own 'printers'. What could proliferate are 3D printing shops on the high street or in shopping centres or even in the home. Overall there are many possibilities for the much greater localisation of manufacturing. For some products the capacity to scan the object and then make endless copies by or near consumers would produce large cost savings and reduce transport-related emissions and oil use – assuming that roughly the same number of products was being manufactured worldwide. This could be game-changing, involving a completely new 'system' which would transform the very notion of 'manufacturing'. Chris Anderson refers to it as a 'new industrial revolution'. A system may be forming here whereby 'manufacturing' is relocalised and undertaken on a smaller

---

[32] See 'The printed word', www.economist.com/node/18114221 (accessed 16.8.2011).

[33] Katia Moskovitch, 'Artificial blood vessels created on a 3D printer', www.bbc.co.uk/news/technology-14946808 (accessed 21.11.2011).

[34] Charlotte Ricca-Smith, 'Could 3D printing end our throwaway culture?', www.guardian.co.uk/technology/2011/nov/17/3d-printing-throwaway-culture (accessed 21.11.2011).

scale, involving potentially millions of 'makers', according to Anderson.[35]

The consequence of potentially vast savings in transportation costs could mean that, at some point, low-cost manufacturing centres, as in the Far East, would no longer possess the comparative advantage in manufacturing objects that, as discussed above, are 'containerised' over thousands of miles to the eventual marketplace. Digital objects can travel almost for free, although oil is the basis of many powders used in such printing/manufacturing.

Geels describes how all major innovations in science and technology tend to be very wide-ranging and not confined to the merely 'technical'. System innovations, such as the possible transformation of manufacturing discussed here, involve changes not just in technical products but also in 'policy, user practices, infrastructure, industry structures and symbolic meaning etc.'.[36] Both *The Economist* and *Wired* have characterised 3D printing as a potentially new socio-technical system, a 'third industrial revolution' which would transform the scale and impact of manufacturing work on a major scale.[37]

Conclusion

This chapter documented the changing nature of production and work. Especially significant have been the ways in which work and industry have been outsourced and offshored. This has been made possible partly by the fragmenting of the Western manufacturing corporation, combined with the innovation of containers, computerised supply chain management and the doctrine of free trade. The Walmart model is based upon long supply chains, containerisation and offshored manufacturing. Indeed, the largest

---

[35] See Chris Anderson, *Makers* (New York: Random House, 2012).

[36] Frank Geels, 'Multi-level perspective on system innovation: relevance for industrial transformation', in Xander Olsthoorn and Anna Wieczorek (eds), *Understanding Industrial Transformation* (Dordrecht: Springer, 2006), p. 165.

[37] See 'The third industrial revolution', www.economist.com/node/21553017 (accessed 18.11.2012); Anderson, *Makers*.

corporations are now based in retailing but without the same highly complex division of labour typical of manufacturing.

The chapter concluded by considering whether 3D or additive manufacturing is a world-changing innovation that will generate a new long wave of onshored socio-technical development. As analysts of long waves note, the structure of goods and services, of the dominant technologies, firms and social activities, do change over a fifty-year period. Will 3D printing reshore some of the offshoring of work that characterised the past thirty years? Could the offshoring of work go into reverse if factories themselves begin to dissolve? Davis argues that 3D printing will generate 'highly dispersed production', with the potential to relocalise production systems within homes, community centres and local factories. I discuss in chapter 10 whether this will reverse offshored systems and how it would have many far-reaching implications for the location of economies and societies in future decades.[38]

---

[38] See Davis, 'Re-imagining the corporation'; 'Outsourcing and offshoring', *The Economist, Special Report*, 19 January 2013.

4

Taxing Offshored

Introducing 'tax dodging'

It is remarkable that taxation issues have shot up the political agenda over the past decade. Taxation is displacing work as the most visible offshoring process. There is almost always a 'tax' story running in the world's media, and especially the new media, often involving brands otherwise well regarded (recently Starbucks, Amazon, Apple, Google, Facebook, Twitter). Various campaigning groups such as UK Uncut have brought issues of tax right up the political and moral agenda through highlighting individual and corporate tax 'dodging'. The term 'dodging' glosses the distinction between actions which are formally legal (avoidance) and those clearly illegal (evasion), tarring them all with the same critical brush.

Even George Osborne, the Conservative Chancellor of the Exchequer in the UK, describes 'aggressive tax avoidance' as 'morally repugnant'. Rather surprisingly, he recently promised to drive forward a 'new agenda of transparency', forcing oil, mining and gas companies to publish financial data project by project.[1] He argued that, while it was important to force multinationals to

---

[1] Daniel Boffey, 'George Osborne in pledge to help world's poor fight tax abuse', www.guardian.co.uk/politics/2013/feb/16/george-osborne-pledge-tax-abuse (accessed 17.2.2013).

pay their tax within the developed world, it was the world's poorest who needed the most help to ensure that taxes got paid where economic activities actually took place. Osborne also announced a new G20 transfer pricing group which would examine how to stop firms unjustifiably shifting taxable profits from one country to another.

David Cameron, the current Conservative Prime Minister, also entered the tax debate in Britain by critiquing a large tax avoidance scheme based in Jersey. However, once the media peered behind the tax returns of one rich person, lots of other 'dirty washing' is revealed.[2] Tax campaigner Murphy notes that the PM's comments opened a Pandora's box leading to the door of many senior Tories: 'Mr Cameron now seems to have realised that by raising this there will be an awful lot of issues affecting people in the Conservative Party. People might even ask questions about his dad.'[3]

Cameron's father, Ian Cameron, indeed made his fortune through tax avoidance. He took advantage in the 1980s of the new climate of less-regulated investment after Margaret Thatcher abolished exchange controls in Britain in 1979. This enabled money to be moved in and out of the country without it being taxed or controlled by the UK government. Ian Cameron established and directed investment funds located within various tax havens. He became chairman of Close International Asset Management, a multimillion-pound investment fund based in Jersey; a senior director of Blairmore Holdings Inc., registered in Panama City and currently worth £25m; and a shareholder in Blairmore Asset Management, based in Geneva. Blairmore Holdings was established in 1982. The lengthy prospectus written in 2006, designed to attract high net worth investors with at least

---

[2] Rob Evans and Rajeev Syal, 'Lord Ashcroft "avoided £3.4m in tax" ahead of rule change', www.guardian.co.uk/politics/2010/sep/27/lord -ashcroft-tax-conservative (accessed 2.8.2012).
[3] Jason Groves, 'Cameron's tax tangle', www.dailymail.co.uk/news/ article-2162697/Jimmy-Carr-tax-evasion-After-attack-avoidance-David -Cameron-backs-down.html#ixzz1zAsUD2ts; on Ian Cameron's tax avoidance schemes, see Ed Howker and Shiv Malik, 'Cameron family fortune made in tax havens', www.guardian.co.uk/politics/2012/apr/20/ cameron-family-tax-havens (both accessed 29.6.2012).

US$100,000 to buy shares, was explicit as to how investments would avoid UK taxation. It stated: 'The fund is not liable to taxation on its income or capital gains as long as such income or capital gains are not derived from sources allocated within the territory of the Republic of Panama.' The fund was not subject to UK corporation tax or income, and under Panamanian law it did not pay tax derived from income generated in other parts of the world. Ian Cameron's wealth was estimated on his death in 2009 as £10m. These tax-dodging companies located in various tax havens thus helped to finance David Cameron's 'posh' education and hence his progress to becoming British PM.

Core then to neo-liberalism has been the large growth in the movement of finance and wealth into and through the world's sixty to seventy tax havens. These include Switzerland, Jersey, Manhattan, the Cayman Islands, the British Virgin Islands, Monaco, Panama, Dubai, Liechtenstein, Singapore, Hong Kong, Gibraltar, the City of London and Delaware. The growth of what are also known as 'secrecy jurisdictions', or in France as *'paradis fiscal'*, are central to the neo-liberalisation of the world economy since around 1980. To have one's money parked offshore is to be in paradise, by contrast with the high-tax life onerously experienced onshore. Tax havens are places of escape and freedom, a paradise of low taxes, wealth management, deregulation, secrecy and often nice beaches. This system works directly and aggressively against transparency, making private what most consider should be public, transparent and visible to tax-collecting authorities.[4] These treasure islands have made it possible for the rich class to get even richer.

Roughly a quarter of contemporary states are in one way or another 'tax havens' as defined below.[5] Many new havens have become major players over the past thirty years (the Cayman Islands), while older financial centres have partly become tax havens (London). The scale of money that is offshored in such

---

[4] See Javier Caletrio, 'Global elites, privilege and mobilities in post-organized capitalism', *Theory, Culture and Society*, 29 (2012): 135–49, at p. 139.

[5] See the listing of tax havens based upon the index of financial secrecy: http://en.wikipedia.org/wiki/Financial_Secrecy_Index (accessed 28.1.2012).

locations has grown from US$11 billion in 1968, to US$385 billion in 1978, US$1 trillion in 1991, US$6 trillion in 1998, and US$21 trillion in 2010.[6] Conservative estimates thus suggest that offshoring has increased almost two thousandfold since the revolutionary year of 1968, from US$11 billion to US$21 trillion (in money terms).

Almost all major companies possess offshore accounts/subsidiaries, more than half of world trade passes through these havens, almost all High Net Worth Individuals (HNWIs) possess offshore accounts enabling tax 'planning', ninety-nine of Europe's hundred largest companies use offshore subsidiaries, and much of the offshore world examined in this book is utterly intertwined with this core offshoring of money and taxation.[7]

Overall, one-quarter to one-third of all global wealth is held 'offshore'.[8] The scale of this offshored money makes the world much more unequal than previous researchers ever imagined. Fewer than 10 million people own the astonishing US$21 trillion offshore fortune. This is equivalent to the combined GDPs of the US and Japan, the world's first and third largest economies.[9]

In the next section I examine the key characteristics of the offshore façade and especially how Switzerland assembled the most

---

[6] See various estimates in Nicholas Shaxson, *Treasure Islands* (London: Bodley Head, 2011), pp. 7–10; Mark Hampton and John Christensen, 'A provocative dependence? The global financial system and small island tax havens', in Feargal Cochrane, Rosaleen Duffy and Jan Selby (eds), *Global Governance, Conflict and Resistance* (London: Palgrave, 2003); 'The price of offshore', www.taxjustice.net/cms/upload/pdf/Price_of _Offshore.pdf (accessed 17.7.2012); 'Revealed: global super-rich has at least $21 trillion hidden in secret tax havens', www.taxjustice.net/cms/ upload/pdf/The_Price_of_Offshore_Revisited_Presser_120722.pdf (accessed 23.7.2012).
[7] Ronen Palan, Richard Murphy and Christian Chavagneux, *Tax Havens: How Globalization Really Works* (Ithaca, NY: Cornell University Press, 2010), chap. 2 for relevant estimates.
[8] http://en.wikipedia.org/wiki/List_of_countries_by_GDP_(nominal) #List (accessed 23.7.2012).
[9] 'Revealed: global super-rich has at least $21 trillion hidden in secret tax havens'. See www.thewealthreport.net/ (accessed 3.1.2013) on the economic, social and political concerns of High Net Worth Individuals. Less than 1 per cent of the world population owns this US$21 trillion fortune.

effective façade. I then elaborate the consequences for the world economy of the shift from the real economy to finance capitalism, which involves the move from onshore to offshore, from money as public to money as private finance. I go on to show just why taxation has become so subject to public debate in at least some countries. It is increasingly thought 'scandalous' and a matter of legitimate protest that companies and individuals pay low or zero amounts of taxation. The chapter concludes with a discussion of how offshoring is key to the power of contemporary finance and examines Keynes's views as to the dysfunctional role that finance often plays within modern economies.

The 'façade'

Central to an effective tax haven is its physical, virtual and meta-phorical 'façade'.[10] A good façade combines safety and secrecy, probity and privacy. As most commentators note, Switzerland has been best able to assemble and sustain a stable and enduring façade. The most effective façades are long established and possess many physical and symbolic signifiers of safety and secrecy, probity and privacy.

The respectable Swiss society has set the gold standard, provid-ing what Shaxson terms a 'theatre of probity' initially developed during the nineteenth century. This Swiss theatre or façade involves a powerful assemblage of polite manners, trustworthy law firms, multiple languages of business, careful paperwork, utter discre-tion, long-established banks, financial institutions and account-ancy firms, stable government, good public services, especially transportation, and the asking of no impertinent questions and hence no need to tell lies. The better the secret, the fewer lies to be told, and thus there is less chance of being caught out not telling the truth.

---

[10]There are many practical guides as to which are the 'best' tax havens, such as Lee Hadnum, *The World's Best Tax Havens* (Kirkcaldy: Taxcafé, 2011), and www.taxhavens.biz/ (accessed 4.7.2012). Amazon, which itself avoids paying UK corporation tax through locating its headquarters in Luxembourg, reports that many customers purchase both Hadnum's book and that by Shaxson.

Especially significant is the highly decentralised canton system, which has engendered competition between them so as to reduce taxation rates and offer stricter forms of secrecy. In Switzerland, two-thirds of total taxes are levied by the cantons, and they also wield other powers enabling them to compete for business by promising heightened secrecy. In a national referendum in 2010, the Swiss electorate overwhelmingly rejected a proposal to establish a minimum 22 per cent tax rate on incomes over around $315,000.[11]

The small and apparently sleepy canton of Zug is a leading tax haven. Up to the 1960s this was a poor farming region, but it has now become the haven of choice within the wider tax haven of Switzerland. Zug contains the highest concentration of US dollar millionaires and the widest wealth disparity inside Switzerland. It hosts 30,000 corporations, including major household names such as Alliance Boots, Foster Wheeler, Glencore, Informa, Thomson Reuters, Tata, Transocean and Xstrata. Some of these corporations only possess post boxes in the town's post office. Zug's highest personal income tax rate is 22 per cent, with most paying an average of 15 per cent. Much of Zug is packed with commodity traders, private equity firms and divisions of big multinationals, occupying mostly low-rise, modern buildings pleasantly located near Lake Zug.[12]

Swiss 'neutrality' in warfare was important in the country becoming the safe and secret banker to peoples and organisations, often servicing both sides in military disputes. This became especially marked during the First World War, as taxes increased across Europe to pay for warfare and European elites sought to find safe and secure locations for their monies so as to avoid paying taxes for the armies fighting in a way 'their war'.

But Switzerland's role during the Second World War came close to compromising this position. Much Nazi money was hidden

---

[11]David Runciman, 'Didn't they notice?', *London Review of Books*, 14 April 2011, pp. 20–3; Shaxson, *Treasure Islands*, chap. 3. Robert Harris's novel *The Fear Factor* (London: Random House, 2011) captures the power and allure of the Swiss façade for those establishing hedge funds.
[12]Deborah Ball, 'Tax haven's tax haven pays a price for success', http://online.wsj.com/article/SB10001424053111904875404576528123989551738.html (accessed 19.7.2012).

away in Swiss bank accounts, the details of which were released only slowly and reluctantly after the end of the war.[13] But somehow its role in protecting Nazi 'blood money' did not undermine Switzerland's façade – indeed, it helped to reinforce its reputation for utter secrecy. By 2007 accounts of non-residents in Swiss banks were worth US$3.1 trillion, half this money coming from the rest of Europe. It is estimated that at least four-fifths of the income and wealth in these Swiss accounts is not declared to the 'home' tax authorities.[14]

The good façade involves a singular assemblage of stability *and* mobility. The stability ensures that this is a place for business, that everyone trusts that money is safe, that companies can be formed and re-formed with ease and security, that a person's word can be trusted, that there is a secured legal environment, and that banks do not go bust or get accused of fraud. The mobility ensures that money can move safely and securely in and out of the 'treasure island', and also that people can move in and out easily, safely and effectively. This necessitates both absolutely secure communications for monetary transactions and good transportation systems for intermittent visits by 'investors'. The good façade thus necessitates the appropriate combination of stability and mobility, as found for decades in Switzerland, although less so more recently.

Other havens do not provide so effective a façade. Many offshore financial centres have developed more recently, some encouraged by the UK, the US and related 'imperial' states. Many were essentially small and poor developing countries forced in a postcolonial era to forge a new economic position within the emerging global economy. In some cases this consisted of a development strategy centred upon 'low taxation' and 'up-market tourism', often directed to the same offshore class.

These offshore financial centres developed financial and legal expertise to attract flows of money, so avoiding or evading taxation rules and regulations. Palan, Murphy and Chavagneux emphasise that tax havens are deliberately created entities which are designed to 'smooth' the transactions of those not normally

---

[13] See Tom Bower, *Blood Money* (London: Pan, 1997).
[14] Vivienne Walt, 'Zug's secrets: Switzerland's corporate hideaway', www.time.com/time/magazine/article/0,9171,2040142,00.html (accessed 19.7.2012).

resident within a society's borders and whose transactions are cloaked in veils of secrecy. Such havens or secrecy jurisdictions presuppose the active work of accountants, bankers, lawyers and tax experts to establish governance that is designed as opaque and benefiting those not normally 'citizens' of that society.[15] Palan summarises how 'Lawyers, businessmen, and criminals drawn, as a general rule, from the capitalist core spread these offshore techniques . . . "taught" ruling groups of many apparently sovereign and independent Third World countries how to develop offshore facilities.'[16] This strategy for development made sense as various micro-states took advantage of historic links with a 'host' power and good transportation connections. Such states were simultaneously developing as significant tourist destinations. Corporations and HNWIs within the rich North came to depend upon these offshore financial centres often located in what were fairly poor developing societies. Worldwide there are in 2013 thought to be 12 million HNWIs, each holding at least US$1 million in investable assets. The combined wealth of this 'rich class' is US$46 trillion, equivalent to two-thirds of annual world GDP.[17]

Powerful actors in various micro-states deployed links to the former British Empire to establish or guarantee their façade. Some successful tax havens are colonial outposts combining the façade of the City of London with very limited tax gathering, lax regulation and unaccountable local politics. The City of London, which is itself governed in a peculiarly undemocratic fashion, where corporations are electors and outnumber people, provides the appropriate façade for many tax havens within developing societies. Overall it seems that 'depositors are happiest putting their money in locations that have the feel of a major jurisdiction like Britain without actually being subject to British rules and regulations (or British tax rates).'[18] British Crown Dependencies (Jersey)

---

[15]Palan, Murphy and Chavagneux, *Tax Havens: How Globalization Really Works*, p. 236.
[16]Ronen Palan, *The Offshore World* (Ithaca, NY: Cornell University Press, 2006), p. 185.
[17]See www.indianexpress.com/news/high-net-worth-individuals-india -second-to-only-hong-kong-in-growth/1131137/ (accessed 27.6.2013), especially on the regional variation in growth.
[18]Runciman, 'Didn't they notice?', pp. 20–1.

or British Overseas Territories (the Cayman Islands) together account for around one-third of the global market in offshore financial services.[19]

Many tax havens are islands (Cyprus), a string of islands (Turks and Caicos Islands) or a small enclave within a larger entity (Gibraltar). Such 'micro-states' enable finance, taxation, consumption, exclusion and security to be governed away from the gaze of much of the world's population. They are normally undemocratic, with a governance system able to exclude those whose faces do not fit. Few will speak out against the lax regulatory regime for fear of being ostracised within a small society where everyone appears to know everyone else. These societies are like 'goldfish bowls' where it may be emphasised that, if you do not like it here, you can leave.[20] Tax havens are able to maintain the façade of 'respectability' that is required by those moving large amounts of money offshore.

The story of the Caymans illustrates well such offshoring processes over the last forty or so years.[21] This poor, undeveloped set of islands was formally established as an offshore financial centre in 1967 (although it had never in fact levied any income tax). It was supported in its development as an offshore centre by the UK Treasury and the Bank of England but opposed by the tax-gathering Inland Revenue.

The most powerful person in the Caymans is the Governor, appointed by the queen. He presides over a cabinet of locally elected Caymanians and deals with important items of governance and makes all appointments of significant power-holders. This strange place, where the national anthem is 'God Save the Queen', has a population of only 53,000. Without the British façade, this offshore centre would not function, and malaria-bearing mosquitoes might once more swarm along its beaches.

---

[19] www.telegraph.co.uk/finance/personalfinance/offshorefinance/880598 8/Tax-haven-activity-rife-despite-G20-crackdown-promise-says-Tax -Justice-Network.html# (accessed 4.7.2012).
[20] Runciman, 'Didn't they notice?', pp. 20–3.
[21] See William Brittain-Catlin, *Offshore: The Dark Side of the Global Economy* (New York: Picador, 2005), chap. 1, on how its growth was linked to the development of Eurodollars.

But the Cayman Islands developed into the world's fifth largest financial centre, with nearly $2 trillion on deposit,[22] and with 80,000 company registrations. Its per capita standard of living is one of the highest in the world, and there is more or less no unemployment. There is also no consumer law, social welfare or employment law. The Caymans receive income from company registrations, with each company being constituted as a legal entity separate from both its founder and its shareholders. Companies registered in the Caymans are beholden to no one, and they can change shape and form, being mutable, adaptive and very flexible. Most companies pay no tax on their income, profit and capital gains so long as their principal business is conducted elsewhere.[23] According to evidence revealed in the HSBC scandal that erupted in July 2012, the Caymans played a central role in the secret extensive laundering of South American drugs monies.

Many of these micro-states depend upon their offshored financial activities. Offshore finance is dominant within the local economy and state. This can be seen in the case of the British Virgin Islands (BVI), which in 1984 established a new kind of international business company and has prospered ever since. There are now 1 million companies incorporated in BVI, whose population is a mere 23,000. Its government normally has no idea who owns the tax-free companies or what they do; almost all having nominee directors. The only significant information supplied to the official registry is the name of the company's agent – a local firm which arranges the incorporations and collects an annual fee. These agents will not release further facts.[24]

---

[22] See *Cayman Islands: Off-Shore Financial Center Assessment Update*, www.imf.org/external/pubs/ft/scr/2009/cr09323.pdf (accessed 13.5.2013).

[23] Brittain-Catlin, *Offshore*, pp. 21–2; Shaxson, *Treasure Islands*, chap. 6; Carrick Mollenkamp, 'Senators doubtful as HSBC touts money-laundering fixes', http://uk.reuters.com/article/2012/07/18/uk-hsbc-compliance-senate-idUKBRE86H03J20120718 (accessed 23.7.2012).

[24] See Bill Maurer, *Recharting the Caribbean* (Ann Arbor: University of Michigan Press, 2000), chap. 8; www.bviincorporation.com/2/Other.Advantages/ (accessed 23.7.2012). See the video www.icij.org/offshore/video-how-dodge-tax (accessed 4.4.2013); www.bvifacts.info/ (accessed 18.5.2013).

BVI appears central in the recent spiralling of property prices in central London, where it is thought that £7 billion has secretly poured into purchasing property with the real owner able to evade stamp duty, capital gains tax and inheritance tax. Those purchasing property hide their identities even on the UK's official Land Registry, since they use fictitious names. Nearly 100,000 offshore entities have been set up holding secret UK property. British banks are complicit in lending to these secret, tax-avoiding purchasers, who are pushing up property prices and reinforcing the 'super-prime' market, so further squeezing out the tax-paying 'little people' – which is most of the population – from the London housing market.[25]

In some cases, offshore financial activities can crowd out manufacturing, service and tourist industries from the local economy, as in Jersey. Injunctions by the OECD, the EU or the G20 to curtail the scale of tax dodging within micro-states must also consider how to assist these smaller economies to diversify away from offshore financial services upon which they are dependent. These states are locked into offshore, and it is hard for them to move into other areas, to reskill the population, to acquire new knowledge bases and to escape links with big banks that can be laundering money.[26] They need an alternative growth strategy, which is often hard to identify and implement once they have been 'corrupted' by their offshore financial status.

An extreme version of a micro-state is the recently launched residential cruise liner called *The World*. This is like 'a luxury private island, a kind of free-floating, certainly isolated, but territorial property. Islands play an important role in fantasies of escape and control for celebrities and the super-affluent.'[27] *The*

---

[25] On the BVI, see *Guardian* reports at www.guardian.co.uk/uk/series/offshore-secrets (accessed 27.11.2012); on the super-prime London housing market, see www.opendemocracy.net/rowland-atkinson/car-parks-for-global-wealth-super-rich-in-london (accessed 20.7.2013).
[26] On Jersey, see Mark Hampton and John Christensen, 'A provocative dependence? The global financial system and small island tax havens', in Feargal Cochrane, Rosaleen Duffy and Jan Selby (eds), *Global Governance* (London: Palgrave, 2003).
[27] Rowland Atkinson and Sarah Blandy, 'A picture of the floating world: grounding the secessionary affluence of the residential cruise liner', *Antipode*, 41 (2009): 92–110, at p. 105.

World roams the world's oceans on a semi-permanent basis, detached from national jurisdictions, tax regimes, moral commitment to nation, local people and most limits upon consuming. It is connected to modern informational networks, being designed for the permanent offshore living of HNWIs. Seven further 'ships' are planned – places to avoid the world while floating around on a kind of 'moving façade'.

In chapter 5 it is shown how 'temporary' tax havens are created in sporting 'camps' in which major events such as the Olympic Games or World Cup are held. This tax requirement is normally insisted upon by the organising international organisations, which are themselves offshore, normally within the tax haven of Switzerland. Forty-seven global sports organisations are located in Switzerland.[28]

In the case of 'British' territories, knights or lords of the realm are often key in the banks and their governance structures. These honours help to stabilise that territory's façade. A notorious example of this was the Texan Allen Stanford, appointed a Knight Commander of the Order of the Nation of Antigua and Barbuda in 2006. Developing a plausible façade through the British honours system meant that, from his base in Antigua, Stanford could generate one of the largest Ponzi schemes in history. Subsequently he was indicted for a US$7 billion fraud, imprisoned for 110 years, and stripped of his knighthood, an increasingly common occurrence!

Hong Kong is one of the world's 'top ten' tax havens, according to a recent Christian Aid Report.[29] It functions as an offshore territory for China in a role similar to the one it played in relationship to Britain before ownership was transferred in 1997. Chinese elites require their own offshore centre, governed at a distance and deploying a hybrid British and Chinese façade that conceals resulting tax avoidance/evasion. It appears that this tax dodging is on a vast scale and involves many leading corporate and political figures in China.

---

[28] www.swissinfo.ch/eng/specials/switzerland_for_the_record/world_records/How_Switzerland_champions_champions.html?cid=8149794 (accessed 15.7.2012).
[29] www.telegraph.co.uk/finance/personalfinance/offshorefinance/8805988/Tax-haven-activity-rife-despite-G20-crackdown-promise-says-Tax-Justice-Network.html# (accessed 4.7.2012).

Thus almost all major societies seem to 'house' one or more tax havens within their sphere of influence. China has the tax havens of Hong Kong and Macao, Portugal has Madeira, the Netherlands has the Netherlands Antilles, Britain has the Channel Islands, Italy has San Marino, the US has Nevada and Delaware, Spain has the Canary Islands, many European countries have Liechtenstein and Luxembourg, and so on. Offshore territories often operate through an 'extended statehood system' by which they are governed by, or are extensively linked to, a major state such as the US, Britain, France, the Netherlands and China.

This 'extended statehood system' in turn enables almost all national corporate and political elites to be provided with secure systems by which much of their personal fortunes can be moved offshore, so avoiding or evading tax. This would seem to be an almost universal pattern characteristic of both developed and developing countries. It is, for example, thought that the single largest depositors in foreign banks are based in India, which loses US$500 billion per annum to tax havens.[30] An astonishingly high proportion of elected Indian politicians have criminal convictions. There is here what could be called an 'indiscriminate criminality'.[31] The offshoring of corrupt funds from China also seems to figure in the strange case of the British man Neil Heywood. He was apparently killed by Gu Kailai, the wife of Bo Xilai, who was at the time the secretary of the Communist Party in Chongqing, the fastest-growing urban centre on earth.[32] It is alleged that the Bo family had managed to send assets offshore, especially to Hong Kong, that were worth around US$136 million.[33]

Incidentally, there is no single definition of what counts as a tax haven, a category now bitterly fought over.[34] Many secrecy

---

[30] 'India "loses $500bn to tax havens"', www.bbc.co.uk/news/world-asia -india-17013314 (accessed 2.8.2012).

[31] I am indebted here for David Tyfield's observations.

[32] On Chongqing, see Jonathan Watts, 'Invisible city', www.guardian. co.uk/world/2006/mar/15/china.china (accessed 18.5.2013).

[33] 'Bo's family assets in HK being probed', www.ytlcommunity.com/ commnews/shownews.asp?newsid=59940&category=featured (accessed 18.5.2013).

[34] See Palan, Murphy and Chavagneux, *Tax Havens: How Globalization Really Works*.

jurisdictions seek to maintain the illusion that they are simply a law-abiding offshore financial centre. But a brief visit to that jurisdiction's online marketing normally reveals text which sets out its minimal regulation, low tax and limited disclosure requirements. A successful offshore tax haven often includes the following: it should not tax income, profits or inheritance; its banks should offer various currencies and operate online and not require personal visits; new accounts in banks require minimal documentation; there is bank secrecy with no Tax Information Exchange Agreements with other countries (about forty havens have no such agreements); and bank accounts can be opened using an 'anonymous bearer share corporation', so that people's names do not appear in any public registry or database.[35] A tax haven seeks to deliver secrecy above all else.

Thus various major states engender and facilitate their own treasure islands, often with geographical ties or excellent transportation or symbolic links with their 'homeland'. Since the neo-liberalising of economics, this tendency for 'housing' offshore tax havens by major economies has speeded up. The colonial or post-colonial power is key to supporting or guaranteeing each façade. In a globalising world, offshore banking is now huge business, and there is much competition between these many treasure islands.

Most financial elites within historically dominant societies have strong interests in constructing and sustaining their own treasure islands. In these havens their money and that of core corporations can be conveniently parked and moved offshore without publicity and scandal. Until recently, such convenient arrangements remained mainly secret; there were many 'complicitous silences'.[36] It was how business was done in a world where finance was in command. And although there have been some modest attempts at tightening up offshore banks by the OECD, the US government, the EU and various European governments, there is no evidence as yet that this will significantly undermine

---

[35] OECD policies are to be found at the Global Forum on Transparency and Exchange of Information for Tax Purposes, www.oecd.org/site/0,34 07,en_21571361_43854757_1_1_1_1_1,00.html (accessed 17.7.2012).
[36] Pierre Bourdieu, *The Logic of Practice* (Cambridge: Polity, 1990), p. 133.

the scale of taxation avoided and evaded. These secrets are essential to the power of finance and the dictatorship of financial markets as now discussed.

Too much finance

In chapter 2 I briefly discussed the development of the Mont Pèlerin Society, organised by Swiss banks plotting against Keynes's intellectual justification for state expenditure and regulation to deal with the economic depression of the 1930s. Although this society did not have much impact until the late 1970s, key figures being novelist Ayn Rand and economist Alan Greenspan, some developments as far back as the 1950s laid the foundations for a much more privatised, offshored world, a world that is part and parcel of the growing inequality of income and wealth and the enhancement of the rich class that developed toward the end of the last century.

During the 1950s, and especially after the Suez debacle in 1956, the British Empire rapidly shrank. Less world trade was financed in sterling and more in US dollars. And a whole new market for finance came to be developed, often called the Eurodollar market. The nationalised Bank of England could have regulated this new market as it grew but it chose not to do so, since the Bank remained, even after nationalisation, the mouthpiece of private financial interests. There was thus a regulatory vacuum at the heart of this growing market, enabling a free 'offshore market' in finance to develop nominated in dollars rather than in sterling, but located in a sense offshore and not in the US. This was the first time a major market for finance developed where there was no actual exchange building and few rules and regulations. Neither American nor British authorities regulated this market, but it has been central to sustaining what Carroll analyses through a detailed social network study as 'the enduring influence of a North Atlantic ruling class'.[37]

The Eurodollar market rapidly became the largest source of capital in the world and established the potential offshoring of

---

[37] William K. Carroll, *The Making of a Transnational Capitalist Class: Corporate Power in the 21st Century* (London: Zed, 2010).

financial markets.[38] The City of London transformed itself into an 'offshore island' and fourteen island states became British Overseas Territories, half of them as offshore tax havens. From these beginnings the Eurodollar market exploded during the 1960s and helped to re-establish the power of the City and especially the Bank of England. Shaxson brings out the libertarian nature of the City, with the governor of the Bank of England proclaiming in 1963 that 'exchange control is an infringement of the rights of the citizen'.[39] Even during the 1960s the stampede into this offshore market was making it increasingly difficult for states to develop national monetary policy. Policy-makers in the US were more and more worried by the potential instability of this new unregulated market.

A further key development was of Eurobonds, first established in 1963. These are unregulated bearer bonds, with no records kept as to who actually owns them. The Eurobond market expanded greatly so that, even by 1970, it was thought to be larger in value than the world's entire foreign exchange holdings. Such bonds could avoid taxation, with some commentators describing their significance as being as great as that of the banknote.[40] While normal banks had to keep reserves against future withdrawals, banks operating in Eurobond markets faced no such requirements and were far more profitable. This development helped to engender the rise and rise of so-called investment banking. The US was central to this system, since it possessed the special advantage of repaying its debt in dollars through the trick of printing more dollars when needed, such as for fighting the Vietnam War in the 1960s or for its citizens buying extraordinary numbers of goods manufactured in China during the 2000s.

What thus developed was an offshore world that consolidated the combined financial power of London and New York. The City of London was central to this corporate power, with long-established procedures thought to increase confidence in its façade. Some key features were that it was self-governing, and

---

[38] See earlier analysis in Scott Lash and John Urry, *The End of Organized Capitalism* (Cambridge: Polity, 1987), pp. 202–9; and Shaxson, *Treasure Islands*, chap. 5.
[39] Shaxson, *Treasure Islands*, p. 90.
[40] Ibid., pp. 91–3.

even overseas corporations were able to vote in elections to its government; it possessed much expertise especially in financing overseas investment; it was less tied into a dominant national industry in comparison with the US or Germany; and it was weakly regulated.[41] It was in a way both offshore and yet utterly core to the British economy and society.

Evans wrote how the rise of Euromarkets 'meant the beginning of an important shift from international financial relations being conducted through the official channels of the Bretton Woods system towards the private markets of the Eurodollar system.'[42] Because of the Eurobond market, bankers were able to reconstruct financial power with much debt offshored. Shaxson describes how, from the 1960s, 'these island semi-colonies and other assorted satellites of London came into their own as offshore Euromarket booking centres: secretive and semi-fictional way stations on a path through accountants' workbooks, hidey-holes where the world's wealthiest individuals and corporations, especially banks, could park their money, tax free and in secrecy.'[43] Even during the 1980s the scale of the movement of money was in no way directly proportionate to the 'needs' of trade and investment. The movement of money was at least twenty times greater than what was 'required' for financing international trade and desirable new investment.[44]

This parallels the process by which banks can conjure money out of thin air. As J. K. Galbraith famously wrote: 'banks create money'.[45] A bank extends its balance sheet by lending the money deposited with it to others, who in turn lend to others, who lend

---

[41] Ibid., chap. 12, on the peculiarly 'non-democratic' City of London Corporation and the power of the Lord Mayor of London. Generally on money, finance and capitalism, see Geoff Ingham, *Capitalism* (Cambridge: Polity, 2008).

[42] Trevor Evans, 'Money makes the world go round', *Capital and Class*, 24 (1985): 99–124, at p. 109; Warren Hogan and Ivor Pearce, *The Incredible Eurodollar* (London: Unwin, 1984); Lash and Urry, *The End of Organized Capitalism*, pp. 204–5.

[43] Shaxson, *Treasure Islands*, p. 101; see chaps 5, 6.

[44] Hogan and Pearce, *The Incredible Eurodollar*, pp. 158–60.

[45] See Mary Mellor, *The Future of Money* (London: Pluto Press, 2010), pp. 26–7. See Lash and Urry, *The End of Organized Capitalism*.

to others, and so on. This process of creating money through credit is full of danger, since banks may lend money to which they cannot gain access. During the era of organised capitalism in the 'West', which lasted roughly from the 1940s until the 1970s, this process of creating money was highly regulated. There was control by each national state of what its banks were able to do, especially through the state setting firm and reasonably high reserve requirements. Avoiding bank failure was seen as a central concern of the state. The Glass–Steagall Act of 1933 was key to the US enforcing the distinction between commercial banks and investment finance.

But, with 'disorganised' or neo-liberal capitalism developing from the 1970s onwards, many of these firewalls disappeared and the conditions were set for offshoring income, wealth and much else. Writing as early as 1982, Aglietta described the emergence of 'a fully fledged international credit system, deterritorialised and beyond regulation by any sovereign state'.[46] As that deterritorialised system extended, there was increasing competition between places around the world to provide and regularise accounts that would offer secrecy, lower tax rates and less regulation. The establishment of many new tax havens and the escalation of offshoring became central to finance as it was unleashed and spun off from national regulations that had been core to organised capitalism. And, with the growth of global inequality, many individuals and corporations increasingly provided rich pickings for some developing societies that were induced to move into providing offshored financial services for the ever more powerful rich class.

Palan, Murphy and Chavagneux show how tax havens are core to developing this world of finance. Although each haven is not especially significant on its own: 'combined, they play a central role in the world economy . . . one of the key pillars of . . . "neo-liberal globalization".'[47] Significantly the US Glass–Steagal Act was overthrown in 1999, so creating an even more permissive lending environment without appropriate firewalls. This repeal helped to generate an exceptional concentration of US banks over a very short period, such that the share of the top three banks'

---

[46] Michel Aglietta, 'World capitalism in the eighties', *New Left Review*, 136 (1982): 5–41, at p. 25; see Mellor, *The Future of Money*, chap. 2.
[47] Palan, Murphy and Chavagneux, *Tax Havens: How Globalization Really Works*, p. 236.

assets doubled over the seven to eight years before the economic collapse of 2007–8.[48]

Sometimes it seems that money staying onshore is now the exception to the rule, suitable only for the 'little people' with little money who are still paying tax. In 2007, one-third of the UK's largest companies had paid no taxes in the previous boom year.[49] Most big money is partially offshored, with offshore including all mainstream banks and financial institutions. Palan points out that, through various regulatory changes, there has been 'the embedding of offshore in the global political economy', a mainstreaming such that offshore does not literally mean having to go 'abroad'.[50]

Indeed, Shaxson describes how the US is – 'by a mile – the world's most important secrecy jurisdiction'.[51] In the little state of Delaware there is a single building housing 217,000 companies – in a way the largest building in the world! Nearly two-thirds of the Fortune 500 top US companies are incorporated in Delaware, among them GM, Walmart, Ford, Boeing and Coca-Cola. There is a laissez-faire attitude to corporate governance, with shareholders and stakeholders possessing few rights. This is a place of secrecy which emphasises the importance of the 'corporate veil'.[52] Caletrio writes how, in this world of finance, 'privacy, silence and secrecy routinely define business interactions'.[53]

Moreover, as money is moved 'offshore', so it uses the same accounts, instruments and devices that are also deployed by money that is laundered, or corrupt, or criminal, or which finances terrorism. Kochan drily observes that, when one takes out a bank loan, 'it is very likely the money you borrow will have at one time

---

[48] See Andrew Haldane and Robert May, 'Systemic risk in banking ecosystems', *Nature*, 469 (2011): 351–5, at p. 354; as well as the YouTube video 'Who repealed the Glass–Steagall Act?', www.youtube.com/watch?v=x0k2PmF-o5Q (accessed 4.1.2013).

[49] Shaxson, *Treasure Islands*, pp. 12–13.

[50] Palan, *The Offshore World*, p. 135.

[51] Shaxson, *Treasure Islands*, p. 146.

[52] See how to incorporate your company in Delaware, www.incnow.com/?gclid=CMi1rs2uw7gCFfMQtAoddUYAPg (accessed 22.7.2013).

[53] Javier Caletrio, 'Global elites, privilege and mobilities in post-organized capitalism', *Theory, Culture and Society*, 29 (2012): 135–49, at p. 139; see Brittain-Catlin, *Offshore*, chap. 4.

passed through a bank account belonging to a dictator or a major drug dealer.'[54] Estimates from the mid-2000s suggest that these forms of 'illegal' money amount to a colossal US$1.1 to 2.5 trillion per year.[55] This fast-moving money evades the generally weak forms of regulation that rely upon implementation by banks, many of which are serial tax avoiders. Poachers and gamekeepers are one and the same!

Such banks regularly fail to prevent corrupt, laundered, terrorist and criminal money moving through their accounts. In the 1990s the once respectable Bank of New York was a conduit for 'spinning' vast amounts of laundered Russian money such that no state was able to catch hold of it. Kochan documents how offshore accounts have made possible extensive money laundering.[56] Likewise the bank BCCI, originally set up in 1972, developed as the world's fastest-growing bank only because of the offshored worlds established over the previous two decades. BCCI was exposed as a vast fraudulent conspiracy in 1991. No regulator had been able to see the whole picture. As Brittain-Catlin argues, this bank was 'a monster that had grown up in the gaps between national financial systems and authorities'.[57]

In July 2012 the Senate Permanent Subcommittee on Investigations described how banking giant HSBC and its US affiliate exposed the US financial system to money laundering, drug trafficking and terrorist financing. HSBC has 7,200 offices in more than eighty countries and earned profits of $22 billion in 2011. But it now faces fines of up to $1billion, which shows the scale of its mobile and illegal money movement. This was a systemic failure resulting from poor money-laundering controls. The 330-page report from the Senate Permanent Subcommittee witheringly detailed the significance of 'correspondent banking' whereby

---

[54]Nick Kochan, *The Washing Machine* (London: Duckworth, 2006), p. 157.

[55]See estimates in Raymond Baker, *Capitalism's Achilles Heel* (Hoboken, NJ: John Wiley, 2005); Kochan, *The Washing Machine*, p. xxxiv; and 'Magnitudes: dirty money, lost taxes and offshore', www.taxjustice.net/cms/front_content.php?client=1&lang=1&parent=91&subid=91&idcat=103&idart=114 (accessed 1.8.2012).

[56]See Kochan, *The Washing Machine*, especially chap. 2.

[57]Brittain-Catlin, *Offshore*, p. 177.

various agents acted on behalf of a major bank. This proved to be a crucial route for illicit money flows, especially from vast Mexican drug empires. HSBC did not implement laws to prevent this large-scale laundering of drugs money, which some calculate as globally worth twice the value of the world's car industry.[58] Overall, Petras summarises how the 'ascendancy of a criminal financial elite and its complicit, accommodating state has led to the breakdown of law and order, the degradation and discrediting of the entire regulatory network and judicial system. This has led to a national system of "unequal injustice" where critical citizens are prosecuted for exercising their constitutional rights while criminal elites operate with impunity.'[59]

This world of offshoring and frequent illegality is thus central to the enormous shadow banking system and the imbalance between 'financialisation' and the 'real economy'. Almost all of the world economy is now 'financialised'.[60] Thus by 2010 the total annual value of foreign currency transactions was US$955 trillion – more than fifteen times the value of world GDP at a mere US$63 trillion.[61] These huge circulations of finance generated what has been called the 'dictatorship of financial markets', as this scale of circulation redistributes income and rights away from the 'real economy'.[62] Moreover, much financial trading now occurs through algorithmic trading, with, it is said, 70 per cent of all US stock-market trade taking place via computer-aided high-frequency trading.[63]

[58] Kochan, *The Washing Machine*, p. 124.
[59] James Petras, 'The two faces of a police state: sheltering tax evaders, financial swindlers and money launderers while policing the citizens', http://axisoflogic.com/artman/publish/Article_64836.shtml (accessed 14.8.2012).
[60] See Joseph Stiglitz, *Making Globalization Work* (Harmondsworth: Penguin, 2007); Paul Krugman, *The Return of Depression Economics* (Harmondsworth: Penguin, 2008); George Soros, *The New Paradigm for Financial Markets* (London: Public Affairs, 2008).
[61] www.spiegel.de/international/business/out-of-control-the-destructive-power-of-the-financial-markets-a-781590.html (accessed 12.4.2013).
[62] Serge Latouche, *Farewell to Growth* (Cambridge: Polity, 2009).
[63] Felix Salmon and Jon Stokes, 'Algorithms take control of Wall Street', www.wired.com/magazine/2010/12/ff_ai_flashtrading/ (accessed 9.2.2013).

Economies are thus restructured with a shift in power and wealth, from organisations that manage others to produce goods and services to organisations involved principally in financial circulation or intermediation. We have seen how much of this intermediation occurs offshore and is directed by various new interdependent financial elites that emerged over the past three to four decades.[64] This power of financial intermediation runs counter to the interests of a productive economy made up of smaller companies that are innovating new products and related services.

Centrally important in the power of finance, circulation and debt are private equity buyouts. The latter involve a private equity firm putting up a small proportion of the purchase cost, with the rest coming from institutional investors or borrowed using the future company's assets as collateral. Once the public company has been bought, it will then be made 'private' and hidden out of sight. There are far fewer restrictions on what activities private entity firms undertake. Evidence shows that, through exemptions in securities laws, most private equity funds avoid regulatory oversight. And yet private equity-owned firms are more likely to reduce employment levels, to have slower growth rates and to go bankrupt. Private equity-owned firms, being registered and operating offshore, are also more likely to deploy tax avoidance/evasion strategies.[65]

The world of offshore has been generated by and favours large corporations. The offshore world makes it hard for 'innovative minnows' to compete and, if they do prosper, they will become parts of large multinational corporate bureaucracies whose income flows will be significantly offshored.[66] It is increasingly realised just how the world of offshore systemically weakens local, smaller companies, which face nothing like a level playing field in competing with large offshored companies.

Such an offshore world is thus core to the development of a significantly untaxed, ungovernable and out-of-control 'casino

[64] See on this shift, Mike Savage and Karel Williams (eds), *Remembering Elites* (Oxford: Blackwell, 2008).
[65] See Eileen Appelbaum and Rosemary Batt, *A Primer on Private Equity at Work: Management, Employment, and Sustainability*, www.cepr.net/documents/publications/private-equity-2012-02.pdf (accessed 4.1.2013).
[66] Shaxson, *Treasure Islands*, pp. 190–1.

capitalism', a capitalism more like gambling than banking and which has helped to magnify economic, social and property inequalities in most countries across the globe.[67] Finance now generates about 41 per cent of operating profits in the US, compared with 16 per cent in 1980, although it produces less than 10 per cent of value added.[68] In the UK, while banks' assets remained about half the size of the GDP for a hundred years, they have increased tenfold over the past few decades. By 2006 the assets of British banks were ten times the size of Britain's GDP and resulted in a huge rise in systemic risk.[69] The dominance of finance developed through offshoring thus involves a profound structural transformation of economy and society, one element of the 'new spirit of capitalism' described by Boltanski and Chiapello.[70]

Politics of tax

But this offshored tax system is not simply settled once and for all. Until a couple of decades back in the 'West', income and taxation were generally regarded as private matters, not anyone else's business except for one's accountant or lawyer. No one knew how much (or little) major figures or corporations paid in tax; it was their business. One feature of a celebrity life was to be remunerated in ways which avoided paying much tax. Likewise

---

[67] See Susan Strange, *Casino Capitalism* (Manchester: Manchester University Press, 1997); Nouriel Roubini and Stephen Mihm, *Crisis Economics* (London: Penguin, 2011), p. 231; Robert Holton, *Global Finance* (London: Routledge, 2012).

[68] Kathleen Madigan, 'Like the phoenix, U.S. finance profits soar', http://blogs.wsj.com/economics/2011/03/25/like-the-phoenix-u-s-finance-profits-soar/ (accessed 4.1.2012); http://www.spiegel.de/international/business/out-of-control-the-destructive-power-of-the-financial-markets-a-781590.html (accessed 28.7.2012).

[69] See John Thompson, 'The metamorphosis of a crisis', in Manuel Castells, João Caraça and Gustavo Cardoso (eds), *Aftermath* (Oxford: Oxford University Press, 2012), pp. 68–9.

[70] See Luc Boltanski and Eve Chiapello, *The New Spirit of Capitalism* (London: Verso, 2005), who maintain that the ideal figure of this new capitalism is a nomadic 'network-extender', light and mobile, tolerant of difference and ambivalence, informal and friendly.

corporations often paid very small proportions of their profits in corporation-type tax, and this was often not seen as a problem, since it meant that more money was thereby available for 'investing' by the company concerned.

Thus taxation was more or less secret, not really on most people's agenda, and it did not relate to the status of people in wider society. Indeed, in the UK Shaxson notes the insidious way in which even 'serial tax avoiders are made knights of the realm. . . . Bit by bit, offshore's corrupted morality becomes accepted into our societies.'[71] Especially significant were the ways in which professional accountants and lawyers were allowed, and indeed expected, to treat as personal and private the actions of their clients, even if those actions were illegal or unethical. The key notion was that the client's confidential relationship with the professional was sacrosanct.

One important politics of taxation has concerned the refusal to pay taxes because a particular group did not have the vote or because of conscientious objections to government policies, including waging war.[72] During the 1970s, a taxpayer revolt in the US led to Reagan's election to the US presidency in 1980. A powerful politics of taxation was pioneered in California. Particularly important was Proposition 13, which involved limiting property taxation and future tax rises through constitutional amendments which were then endorsed by the US Supreme Court. From 2009 the Tea Party movement in the US strenuously campaigned against future tax increases and endorsed candidates opposing government expenditure programmes and taxation.[73]

However, since around 2000, issues of tax evasion by the rich and powerful and the role of tax havens have also become central to the emerging counter-politics of taxation. From the turn of the millennium a new array of taxation politics emerged. There are now many critical reports (by Oxfam on how tax havens contribute to global poverty); media stories (even in the pro-business *Wall Street Journal* or *The Economist*); new campaigning NGOs (such

---

[71] Shaxson, *Treasure Islands*, p. 31.
[72] See the exhaustive David M. Gross (ed.), *We Won't Pay!: A Tax Resistance Reader* (Create.Space, 2008).
[73] The term Tea Party refers to the Boston Tea Party, the iconic protest by US colonists objecting to the British tax on tea in 1773.

as Offshore Watch); interventions by the World Social Forum (establishing a global campaign against tax havens); new kinds of research capability (such as the International Consortium of Investigative Journalists); a greater role for the OECD (to curb 'unfair tax competition'); an increased rate of leakage of financial data to the media (thirty-eight media organisations received such data in March 2013); and the raised public identification and critique of corporations 'scandalously' involved in aggressive tax avoidance/ evasion.[74]

This taxation counter-politics is now a torrent. Much direct action, NGO activities, official government reports, and a new activism have exposed and denigrated many different forms and aspects of 'tax dodging'. Such dodging is seen as reducing the capacity to tax revenues where income and wealth are generated and as undermining a level playing field, since local companies pay full taxes while transnational corporations do not.[75] UK Uncut has especially targeted as a 'scandal' tax dodging by major British-based companies such as Vodafone, Topshop, Boots, Fortnum and Mason, Barclays, HSBC and RBS. Similarly, Occupy Wall Street campaigners in New York dressed in 'Tax Dodgers' uniforms protested on tax day, 17 April 2012, against Bank of America, Wells Fargo, GE, Bain Capital and J. P. Morgan Chase. Tax shaming is now a major political issue in many countries and is rapidly developing into a global movement.[76]

This was strikingly shown in early 2013 through research conducted by the International Consortium of Investigative Journalists after a computer hard drive packed with corporate data and personal information and e-mails arrived in their mail.[77] The offshore information totalled more than 260 gigabytes of data, with about 2.5 million files and more than 2 million e-mails. The drive

---

[74] Hampton and Christensen, 'A provocative dependence?', p. 204.
[75] See www.ukuncut.org.uk/ (accessed 27.1.2012). The terms 'dodging' and 'limitation' do not distinguish between tax avoidance (legal) and evasion (illegal), treating both as indefensible.
[76] See Vanessa Barford and Gerry Holt, 'Google, Amazon, Starbucks: the rise of "tax shaming"', www.bbc.co.uk/news/magazine-20560359 (accessed 31.12.2012).
[77] See www.icij.org/offshore/how-icijs-project-team-analyzed-offshore-files (accessed 4.4.2013).

contained four large databases plus half a million pages of text, PDFs, spreadsheets, images and web files.

The data originated in ten offshore jurisdictions, among them the British Virgin Islands, the Cook Islands, Cyprus and Singapore, and included details of more than 122,000 offshore companies or trusts, nearly 12,000 intermediaries (agents or 'introducers'), and about 130,000 records relating to the people and agents who run, own, benefit from or hide behind offshore companies. The extensive data showed that those setting up offshore entities most often lived in China, Hong Kong, Russia and former Soviet republics. The International Consortium of Investigative Journalists' analysis reveals the many structures designed to conceal the true ownership and control of assets placed offshore. Many positions in companies are held by so-called nominee directors, whose names sometimes appear in hundreds of companies. Nominee directors are people who, for a fee, lend their names as office holders of companies that they know little about (this device is widely used in the offshore world). Their addresses in this data are spread across more than 170 countries and territories.

Another organisation that has helped to make a politics out of the private behaviour of tax dodging is the Tax Justice Network. This opposes all those mechanisms that enable owners and controllers of wealth to escape responsibilities to the societies upon which they and their wealth depend.[78] While the secrecy jurisdiction of Delaware proclaims that 'Delaware can protect you from politics', the Tax Justice Network seeks to ensure that there can be no such protection, emphasising the importance of compliance, openness and transparency.

Other authors have begun to generalise this issue of tax, some claiming, for example, that 'tax is a feminist issue'.[79] In many countries it is now thought scandalous and a matter of legitimate protest that companies and individuals pay low or zero amounts of taxation, that façades enable tax payments to be systemically

---

[78] 'Tax havens cause poverty', www.taxjustice.net/cms/front_content .php?idcatart=2&lang=1 (accessed 24.7.2012).

[79] Sylvia Walby, *The Future of Feminism* (Cambridge: Polity, 2011); and see the Women's Budget Group, 'Gender budget analysis', www.wbg.org .uk/GBA.htm (accessed 24.7.2012).

avoided, and that others have to pay more or services are poorer than they really should be. Large corporations and rich individuals are increasingly forced to defend their tax position, often seeking a 'taxwash' to keep the scandal-hungry media and protestors at bay.

This problem of taxation increasingly threatens many of the world's major brands, which are critiqued for their insatiable pursuit of profit, aggressive tax avoidance and deliberate evading of transparency and public scrutiny. One example is Barclays Bank, which has engaged in much scandalous behaviour and routinely tries to gag newspaper inquiries. Barclays seems to have made around £1 billion a year from its tax-avoidance factory run on 'fear and macho excess'.[80] Its scandalous character led Barclays to begin closing it down in February 2013. Its 'highly lucrative dark arts' were threatening the entire Barclays brand rather than just the Structured Capital Markets Division, which is where this 'industrial-scale' tax avoidance had been located.

Similarly, Goldman Sachs is increasingly characterised as a vampire brand, with its insatiable thirst for infinite growth and public and private debt. The secretive, nocturnal life of the vampire is seen to echo the dark pools of financial offshoring, shadow banking, many toxic liabilities hidden off balance sheet, and the deep opacity of derivatives markets. Freund and Jacobi develop the concept of 'brand monsters' to capture the way that many brands are now unmasked, crystallised, dramatised, and intensify the putative evil that many see lurking at the heart of the scandalising corporation. Matt Taibbi, in a July 2009 *Rolling Stone* article, used a powerful image that went viral: 'The first thing you need to know about Goldman Sachs is that it's everywhere. The world's most powerful investment bank is a great vampire squid wrapped around the face of humanity, relentlessly jamming its blood funnel into anything that smells like money!'[81]

---

[80] See Felicity Lawrence, 'Barclays secret tax avoidance factory that made £1bn a year profit disbanded', www.guardian.co.uk/business/2013/feb/11/barclays-investment-banking-tax-avoidance (accessed 18.2.2013).
[81] See, on this paragraph, James Freund and Erik Jacobi, 'Revenge of the brand monsters: How Goldman Sachs' doppelgänger turned monstrous', *Journal of Marketing Management*, 29/1–2 (2013): 175–94, doi:10.108 0/0267257X.2013.764347; and see chap. 1 above.

Conclusion

This chapter shows that offshore is an endlessly shifting ecosystem, with different concentrations of legal, financial and taxation expertise, diverse modes of secrecy, and varied balances of legal and illegal activities. Offshore services partly developed to avoid double taxation, so that monies earned in one country were not taxed both in that country and in the country where the individual or corporation is based. But offshoring in fact enables 'double non-taxation', often through so-called laddering or salami-slicing, so as to increase the secrecy and complexity of financial flows. It is often now impossible for authorities to see the detail, and this enables taxation to be systematically avoided. The loss of taxation from this offshoring world of finance is minimally calculated as hundreds of billions of US dollars per annum.[82]

It is further shown that offshore does not have to be literally offshore from centres of economic power. Offshore, we might say, is everywhere. One company's onshore is another's offshore. And this is a powerful world which is, in a way, located nowhere as such, its power stemming from its ethereal character. Murphy powerfully writes how 'illicit financial flows . . . do not flow through locations as such, but do instead flow through the secrecy space that secrecy jurisdictions create . . . They float over and around the locations which are used to facilitate their existence as if in an unregulated ether.'[83]

As a consequence, this overlapping 'secrecy world', this unregulated ether', cannot be regulated by single national states and, indeed, may not be regulatable at all. A world of secrecy has developed on such a scale and taking the form of an 'unregulated ether' that it is almost impossible to nail down, let alone to tame, but where excesses do sometimes get to be made public and subject to dramatised shaming.

---

[82] 'Revealed: global super-rich has at least $21 trillion hidden in secret tax havens'.

[83] Richard Murphy, *Defining the Secrecy World* (London: Tax Justice Network, 2009), p. 7.

This secret offshore world derives from the power of finance especially over states and industry. The dictatorship of financial markets means that money is thought of not as a public resource but as private and allowed to expand for profit. This 'privatisation' of money into finance occurs in various ways: through the competitive proliferation of new financial products and services; through how most finance (at least 95 per cent) is market speculation; through the ways in which finance searches out low or zero tax locations; and through competition between taxing authorities, so providing ever more attractive tax and related arrangements to potential 'investors'. Large corporations and HNWIs have certainly prospered beyond their wildest dreams through the growth of a vast, unregulated offshored world of 'privatised' finance.

The money system is thus turned into an object for capitalist speculation, no longer functional for industry and other services but often in effect becoming the economy. Mellor describes this as 'turbo-capitalism', where money is invested in financial assets so as to create more money. Shareholder value is core to offshoring.[84] The useful public role of money has been lost through the dominance of finance and its troublesome interests, and this is further reflected in many other offshoring processes examined below.

Capital within the contemporary world does not flow to where it is more 'productive', let alone most socially useful. Even the chairman of what was the UK Financial Services Authority (Adair Turner) argued that many of the 'products' developed by the clever young men working in the financial centres of New York or London are 'socially useless', indeed often socially harmful.[85] Thus finance moves to where it is most secret, gets the lowest tax rates, can evade as many regulations and laws as possible, and travels the world finding ever laxer regulatory forms. Finance does not provide financial energy for the economy.

---

[84] See Mellor, *The Future of Money*, chap. 4.
[85] www.spiegel.de/international/business/out-of-control-the-destructive -power-of-the-financial-markets-a-781590.html (accessed 28.7.2012). The FSA no longer exists (2013). See Gillian Tett, *Fool's Gold* (London: Little, Brown, 2009), on disastrous innovation at J.P. Morgan.

Moreover, because of networks of nodes and linkages and insufficient firewalls, finance is particularly vulnerable to extreme events which can make history jump backwards as well as forwards, as for example with the economic and financial collapse of 2007–8, the cost of which is thought to be at least US$20 trillion.[86]

[86] See Philip Ball, *Why Society is a Complex Matter* (Heidelberg: Springer, 2012), p. 57.

5

Leisure Offshored

Pirates

It was noted in the last chapter that many tax havens are also places of leisure and pleasure. Krane writes, for example, of Dubai: 'It's the earth's most barren landscape, a land with nothing in the way of historic sights, and big spending visitors fly half way around the world to see it' – and also to open tax-avoiding bank accounts.[1] In this chapter I consider how places for consumption and leisure developed offshore and became especially significant within the neo-liberal period. Over the past half century the off-shoring of pleasure enables onshore laws or norms to be wholly or partially avoided. Many visitors have been seduced by the allure of journeys to places of fun and freedom, so escaping laws and norms back home.

An early example of offshoring pleasure, although one that now seems rather tame, was the 1960s development of pirate radio stations playing continuous pop music.[2] Previously in Britain the BBC had delivered programmes designed to boost

---

[1] Jim Krane, *City of Gold* (London: Picador, 2010), p. 117.
[2] Kimberley Peters, 'Taking more-than-human geographies to sea: ocean natures and offshore radio piracy', in Jon Anderson and Kimberley Peters (eds), *Water Worlds* (Farnham: Ashgate, 2013).

morale and keep industry running with 'sing along' music pro-grammes and comedy, often broadcast over factory tannoy systems. But during the 1950s the cult of the 'teenager' began developing, along with the availability of new forms of Ameri-can music. Opportunities for hearing and participating in this new fashion on BBC radio were limited, as shows were hosted mostly by established presenters and recording companies pre-vented the unregulated playing of records. New American popular music could be heard only on Radio Luxembourg, the main cross-border broadcaster.

During the early 1960s, various Dutch radio stations began broadcasting offshore, although Dutch radio law was as restrictive as that of Britain. But in both cases the law extended only 3 miles from the coast. Beyond that lay international waters, where there was no law other than that defined by the flag states of ships. While in international waters, a ship registered in Panama needed to recognise only Panamanian law. If the law of the flag state did not make international marine broadcasting illegal, then the ship could so broadcast.

With a burgeoning youth culture and pop industry in the early 1960s, Britain had potential to develop a new musical popular culture. A couple of counter-cultural entrepreneurs devised the idea for Radio Caroline. Radio studios were built on the upper decks of the ship while AC generators were connected to transmit-ters in the hold. On Easter Sunday 1964 it announced: 'This is Radio Caroline on 199, your all day music station.' The monopo-lies of the BBC and the record companies were thereby broken and radio and TV broadcasting transformed. An audience of mil-lions, new music and youth fashion accelerated as bands were given visibility on this offshored broadcasting space. Radio Caro-line led to other offshored music stations being set up to overcome onshore restrictions and what was seen as a pre-existing cultural conservatism.

But the Marine Offences Act of 1967 outlawed unlicensed off-shore broadcasting, at more or less the same time that BBC initi-ated Radio 1, which copied the format of offshored pirate radio. Subsequent UK legislation made it harder to broadcast offshore. British governments sought to regulate offshore 'pirate' broadcasts emanating from outside territorial boundaries through managing the extra-territorial international space of the high seas. This was, though, problematic, as it challenged Britain's long-held ideology of maritime freedom.[3]

Consuming elsewhere

By the 1970s the offshore music industry had moved onshore. Young people rapidly became mass consumers of music, clothes, holidays and fashion, but where these were increasingly derived from elsewhere, from beyond their neighbourhood. The pirate radio stations symbolised the broader cultural shift from 'neighbourhood lives' to 'lives beyond neighbourhood' generated through new forms and experiences of leisure, popular music, consumer goods, travel, information, drink and drugs.

With neighbourhood lives, the scale of most work and leisure practices was a few miles. Most consumption, family and friendship experiences were accessed through mainly slow modes of mobility, especially walking and cycling. Life centred upon groups of known streets, on a complex and active group, work and social life. The disciplining of young men and women took place inside these neighbourhoods. Consumption involved conforming to the norms present and reinforced within each locality. There was relatively little separation of production and consumption.[4]

Many agricultural communities and industrial-urban communities were based upon these normatively sanctioned neighbourhood lives, with limited consumption of goods made elsewhere or of services obtained from afar. Even when extensive working-class holidays developed, these were often neighbourhood based, involving groups of employees or neighbours journeying together and using collective forms of travel, with much mutual regulation of the experience.[5] Consumption patterns were regulated through family and neighbourhood.

---

[3] See Kimberley Peters, 'Sinking the radio "pirates": exploring British strategies of governance in the North Sea, 1964–1991', *Area*, 43 (2011): 281–7, on developing a 'geography of the sea'.
[4] Richard Hoggart, *The Uses of Literacy* (London: Penguin, [1957] 2009), p. 49; Barry Smart, *Consumer Society* (London: Sage, 2010).
[5] See John Urry and Jonas Larsen, *The Tourist Gaze 3.0* (London: Sage, 2011), chap. 2; John Walton, *Riding on Rainbows* (St Albans: Skelter, 2007), on the history of Blackpool.

However, twentieth-century consumerism increasingly involved social practices that moved beyond neighbourhoods, generated through offshore radio, film, TV, foreign holidays, magazines, advertising, the World Wide Web, and so on. The systems linking production and consumption became extended in time and space, made possible especially through the spreading of new socio-technical systems. The most important systems were electricity and the national grid, automobility, radio and television broad-casting, and aeromobility.[6] The consumption of goods and services occurred over much greater distances. Goods were mass produced within large-scale factories. Shops, malls, theme parks and other sites of leisure developed which were travelled to, often over sig-nificant distances, and increasingly stocked with items sourced from around the world.[7]

Social practices thus developed that were more varied and involved travelling often much greater distances.[8] Such practices often necessitated multiple movements, often requiring people to purchase, use and display goods that travelled long distances and to consume services from beyond their neighbourhood. New social practices involved people and objects moving about on an enhanced scale, including what Ossman describes as 'serial migration'.[9] Peo-ple's lives were dependent upon consumer goods and services produced 'elsewhere' and then often moved significant distances. Family and friendship patterns were significantly lived at a dis-tance and sometimes offshored.

Such processes extended the comparisons that people made, and these often heightened dissatisfaction with the goods and services purchased. Schwartz notes that, in the case of neighbour-hood lives,

---

[6] David Nye, *Consuming Power* (Cambridge, MA: MIT Press, 1998), p. 182; Ben Fine, *The World of Consumption* (London: Routledge, 2002), chaps 5, 6.
[7] Smart, *Consumer Society*, pp. 160–1; John Urry, *Societies beyond Oil* (London: Zed, 2013).
[8] On social practices, see Elizabeth Shove, Mika Pantzar and Matt Watson, *The Dynamics of Social Practice* (London: Sage, 2012).
[9] Susan Ossman, *Moving Matters* (Stanford, CA: Stanford University Press, 2013).

We looked around at our neighbours and family members. We did not have access to information about people outside our immediate social circle. But with the explosion of telecommunications [and of travel we could add] . . . almost everyone has access to information about almost everyone else . . . This essentially universal and unrealistically high standard of comparison decreases the satisfaction of those who are in the middle or below.[10]

People were increasingly confronted by choices that often made them anxious and reduced wellbeing. The proliferation of choice takes time, involves uncertainty and produces concern that the wrong choices have been made. Schwartz argues that consumers of goods and services frequently express regret about the consumer items they did not choose as well as frustration with what they have purchased.[11] This is especially the case with children, as a veritable cornucopia of goods is produced for their entertainment, pleasure, convenience and education. And yet those children seem less content, more stressed and less healthy than those in previous generations. Beder argues that the decline in children's wellbeing was largely caused by corporations increasingly targeting ever younger children, who are thought to be no longer 'off-limits'.[12]

This frustration with goods and services consumed is heightened by global advertising. Such advertising presented enticing opportunities often derived from, or available within, locations well away from a person's neighbourhood.[13] It seems that the more radio and TV listened to or watched, the greater the consumption of goods and services from distant places.[14] Overall, the

---

[10] Barry Schwartz, *The Paradox of Choice* (New York: Harper, 2004), p. 191; Anthony Elliott and John Urry, *Mobile Lives* (London: Routledge, 2010); Fred Hirsch, *Social Limits to Growth* (London: Routledge & Kegan Paul, 1977), pp. 39–40.

[11] Schwartz, *The Paradox of Choice*, p. 191.

[12] Sharon Beder, *This Little Kiddy Went to Market* (London: Pluto Press, 2009).

[13] Advertising expenditures amounted to $643 billion in 2008. See Worldwatch Institute, *2010 State of the World* (New York: W. W. Norton, 2010), p. 11.

[14] Ibid., p. 13.

proliferation of choice involved multiple mobilities, having available cuisines, products, places, services, friends, family members and gambling from elsewhere. This flow of novelty under 'affluence' undermines many existing commitments and conventions, producing the 'freedom to be addicted', including 'shopping addiction' via the web, where there is little neighbourhood regulation of what a person is purchasing.[15] Many potential addictions lie beyond one's neighbourhood and its forms of proximate regulation.

Places of offshore excess

I turn now to examine the more specific offshoring of pleasure. From around 1990, finance flowed especially into property development, generating in the late 1990s and early 2000s real-estate 'bubbles'. Central in neo-liberalism is a speculative intertwining of finance and property development, with the extravagant building of suburbs, apartments, second homes, hotels, leisure complexes, gated communities, sports stadia, office blocks, universities, shopping centres and casinos. Many developments were built offshore, such as the almost literal 'construction' of Dubai in an otherwise wholly inhospitable desert. There is an overlapping indebtedness of governments, developers and purchasers. The debts were often parcelled up, sliced and diced into financial packages, and then sold on, on the presupposition that property could only rise in value. This created a financially complex house of cards resting upon the 'bet' that property values will increase.

Vast new consumption centres developed with spectacular buildings designed by celebrity architects. As discussed in the next chapter, much oil is used to transport people and objects in and out of such places. These places are themed with connotations of leisure and illicit pleasures. Newly constructed sites of consumption excess include Arg-e Jadid, a Californian oasis in the Iranian desert, Palm Springs gated community in Hong Kong, Sandton in

---

[15] Avner Offer, *The Challenge of Affluence* (Oxford: Oxford University Press, 2006); Smart, *Consumer Society*, pp. 149–51.

Johannesburg, Dubai, Sentosa in Singapore, Paseo Cayala in Gua-
temala, and Macao.[16] Many of these were developed or promoted
by global brands with enormous marketing, design, sponsorship,
public relations and advertising expenditures, such as Sandals,
Gap, Jumeirah, easyJet, Club 18–30, Ibiza, Hilton, Virgin, Club
Med, Sands and so on. Klein argues: 'liberated from the real-world
burdens of stores and product manufacturing, these brands are
free to soar . . . as collective hallucinations.'[17]

Especially significant here are the offshored 'collective hallucinations' of 'sex, drugs and rock and roll', which include 'pleasures'
that are illegal back home or normatively disapproved of, such as
drug taking, gambling, over-drinking or teenage sex. Many places
developed offshore, providing sites for consuming illicit products
or services but around which new kinds of offshore zone emerged,
and indeed are often part of that place's 'image', sometimes being
characterised as 'alternative'. Not all these places are literally
offshore, of course.

A striking example of such trends is the vast billion-dollar
investment in Macao providing leisured gambling especially for
Chinese visitors – Macao being the only place where Chinese
nationals are legally allowed to gamble in casinos. Macao is becoming the world centre of casino gambling, or 'gambling tourism',
after the breakup of its previous gambling monopoly. This tiny
island of around half a million people attracts 25 million tourists
a year, more than half from mainland China.[18] Macao is a place
for teaching newly prosperous Chinese how to behave as purchasers and users of goods, and especially services such as those implicated in a 'café culture'. It is described as a laboratory of
consumption, as the Chinese learn to be individualised consumers

---

[16] Mike Davis and Daniel Bertrand Monk (eds), *Evil Paradises* (New
York: New Press, 2007).

[17] Naomi Klein, *No Logo* (London: Flamingo, 2000), p. 22.

[18] www.macaudailytimes.com.mo/macau/27277-Over-million-tourists
-may-visit-Macau.html (accessed 26.8.2012); Tim Simpson, 'Macao,
capital of the 21st century', *Environment and Planning D: Society and
Space*, 26 (2008): 1053–79; Tim Simpson, 'Neo-liberalism with Chinese
characteristics: consumer pedagogy in Macao', in Heiko Schmid, Wolf-
Dietrich Sahr and John Urry (eds), *Cities and Fascination* (Aldershot:
Ashgate, 2011).

of goods and services being generated on an extraordinary scale. A huge 'Fisherman's Wharf' has been built, with themed reproductions of the Roman Coliseum, reproduced buildings from Amsterdam, Lisbon, Cape Town and Miami, and a simulated exploding volcano.

Such offshore sites are highly commercialised, with many simulated environments more 'real' than the original from which they are copied. Gates, often digitised, prevent the entry and exit of local people and those visitors without signs of good credit. Norms of behaviour are unregulated by family/neighbourhood, with bodies being subject to many commodifying experiences. Such themed places are beyond control by neighbourhood groups, and there are many unregulated modes of consumption and pleasure. Indeed these places are sites of potential mass addiction of gambling, alcohol, drug taking, shopping, over-eating, and so on. These all presuppose 'choice', with high potential for people to become addicted.[19] Such zones come to be globally recognised for their consumption excess and the huge flows of visitors having fun and pleasure in places of apparent escape and freedom, but which are nothing of the sort.[20]

The offshoring of leisurely consumption can also be seen with cruise ships, which are like floating islands, mostly moving around literally offshore. These floating gated communities are based on consuming to excess without being observed or disapproved of by family or neighbourhood. The offshore consumption zone is based upon the strict separation of local people, except as employees, and mobile visitors. These offshored visitors are allowed onto special zones of, for example, Caribbean islands reserved solely for them. Most of those travelling on cruises stay offshore. They contribute little to local economies or societies that they sail by, waving down to the 'locals', whose patterns of life they consume visually as the cruise ships pass off the shore.

The world's largest ever cruise ship was recently launched by Royal Caribbean Cruise Lines; it has nearly 2,000 guest rooms,

---

[19] These are well illustrated in Michael Moore's 2009 movie *Capitalism: A Love Story*.

[20] See Jennie Germann Molz, *Travel Connections* (London: Routledge, 2012), chap. 7.

an ice rink, the first ever surf park at sea, cantilevered whirlpools extending 12 feet over the sides of the ship, a waterpark with fountains, geysers and a waterfall, a rock-climbing wall and the Royal Promenade.[21] Some super-rich people are planning permanent, self-governing ocean-based seasteads. The Seasteading Institute has sponsored studies on how to construct ocean-based colonies on the high seas that would be 'independent' of states.[22]

These places of fun and separation are also places of work for the service providers, with many migrants travelling to build the attractions and to 'service' consumers. Especially significant is the sex industry, involving the trafficking of women by crime networks. Methods for trafficking range from promises of a holiday or a visa to abduction and rape.[23] Many trafficked women are subject to regular sexual violence before the journey and end up in offshore zones of consumption excess. Victims of trafficking are transported from their country of origin, put under surveillance and housed by traffickers, and then often left without money, passports or permits. They are immobilised once they arrive, with the lack of neighbourhood regulation leaving them vulnerable to organised male power. A significant proportion of those trafficked will be under the legal age of consent.

Moreover, some of the 'business' undertaken by the offshore rich class is conducted within those locations where trafficked women are on display or form part of the service provided in order to 'smooth' negotiations. Major business deals may be completed in brothels, bars or lap-dancing clubs, where displayed women have been forced to move from elsewhere.[24] There has been an astonishing increase in the scale of the 'global sex industry', which has become a routinised part of the allure or place-image of many places, including in the Caribbean, Dubai, Thailand and the

---

[21] www.royalcaribbean.co.uk/our-ships/features-comparison/   (accessed 25.8.2012).
[22] 'Cities on the ocean', www.economist.com/node/21540395 (accessed 13.5.2013).
[23] Sietske Altink, *Stolen Lives* (London: Scarlet Press, 1995).
[24] Kathryn Hopkins, 'City bankers "regularly offer prostitutes to clients"', www.guardian.co.uk/business/2009/oct/14/banking-prostitution (accessed 9.11.2009).

Philippines.[25] In neo-liberalism almost everything and anyone is commodifiable, without boundaries, especially if the consuming and exploitation takes place offshore and out of sight.

More generally, many places of sexual 'pleasure' lie almost offshore, on or near beaches. Rachel Carson once described the edge of the sea as a strange and wonderful place because it is never the same from one moment to the next.[26] It is an in-between place, not quite land or sea, not quite on- or offshore. Over the past two centuries the beach moved from being a place of repulsion and danger to one of attraction and desire, and increasingly one that is built and designed. It became a place to be dwelt upon by visitors, for leisure rather than work, a place especially for mobile visitors rather than locals. Beaches are where visitors place themselves temporarily in a state of undress and reveal how their body matches up to a designed tanned ideal revealing a life of pleasure.

For many in the rich North, the beach is a zone of affect signifying a symbolic other to factories, offices and domestic life. This thin line between sea and land is central for multiple performances of contemporary pleasure-making. The beach as the emblematic space for a life of leisure is especially attractive if it is offshore and has to be visited from far away. Although Australia possesses many iconic beaches, Australians still travel in very large numbers to beaches elsewhere.[27]

The Caribbean possesses many such beaches of paradise.[28] Here 'all-inclusive resorts' are common, providing a space for 'offshore' consumption largely cut off from the surrounding territory and from local people, apart from those providing 'excess services'. Gated and often fortified, they secure temporary consumption away from the prying eyes of locals and of those 'back home' who might disapprove.

On occasions whole islands provide secure sites for engaging in excess. Islands need not be literally 'gated', since they can provide

---

[25] Dennis Altman, *Global Sex* (Chicago: University of Chicago Press, 2001).

[26] Rachel Carson, *The Sea Around Us* (New York: Oxford University Press, 1961), p. 2.

[27] I am grateful to Adrian Franklin for pointing this out.

[28] Mimi Sheller, *Consuming the Caribbean* (London: Routledge, 2003).

a 'natural' barrier to the outside world. Various Caribbean islands are curated into exclusive resorts for the super-rich and removed from control and governance by local communities and their governments. Sheller describes their development; these are 'amalgams of infrastructure, architecture, and software . . . unbundled from local communities, citizenries, and publics, and repackaged as intensely capitalised destinations of luxury tourism and foreign ownership'.[29]

Some developments are aimed at the 'private jet-set', those who accumulate planes, houses and servants as others accumulate cars. Budd shows how private jets enable users to bypass conventional forms of transport and timetabled spaces of flow and create personalised and bespoke geographies of movement. By effectively separating the trajectories of the super-rich away from those of the less affluent, the private jet system creates and reproduces exclusionary spaces of corporeal mobility.[30]

One example of an offshored island normally accessed by private jet is St Barts, a French territory in the northern part of the Antilles and one of the most exclusive places in the world. It has been transformed from insular destitution into a place of elite pleasure-seeking, especially after 1957 when David Rockefeller bought a promontory of land. Other very wealthy offshore visitors arrived and purchased land. St Barts was transmuted into a place of casual elite privilege. Exclusiveness has been sustained through the way it can be accessed only by small private aircraft, by the harbour being inaccessible to liners, by there being no public transport, and by an almost total freeze on building permits.

The super-rich can be offshore at St Barts and spatially segregated from the merely rich. Central to the appeal is that St Barts is an offshore place where the 'rich class' socialise, let their hair down together and develop trust towards each other, especially as

---

[29] Mimi Sheller, 'Infrastructures of the imagined island: software, mobilities, and the new architecture of cyberspatial paradise', *Environment and Planning A*, 41 (2008): 1386–403, at p. 1399; Mimi Sheller, 'The new Caribbean complexity: mobility systems and the re-scaling of development', *Singapore Journal of Tropical Geography*, 14 (2008): 373–84.
[30] Lucy Budd, 'Aeromobile elites: private business aviation and the global economy', in Thomas Birtchnell and Javier Caletrio (eds), *Elite Mobilities* (London: Routledge, 2013).

their super yachts nestle up against each other in one or other of the select coves.[31] The offshored brand of St Barts signifies island exclusiveness, Caribbean exoticism, French taste and gastronomy, and luxury yachting. More generally, the Luxury Brands Club expresses this well: 'For high net worth individuals, luxury is not a lifestyle but a prerequisite.'[32]

Haseler describes the various offshored mobilities of the super-rich. He says they are the world's global citizens:

> owing loyalty to themselves, their families and their money . . . Their money is highly mobile, and so are they themselves, moving between their various homes around the world – in London, Paris and New York; large houses in the Hamptons in the United States, in the English and French countryside, and in gated communities in sun-belt America . . . and for the global super-rich the literal mobility of yachts in tropical paradises not scarred by local poverty.[33]

Likewise, Elliott describes the 'elsewhere' lives of 'globals' and how their movement space is created through rootless, moving, liquid lives.[34] One commentator reports how, for billionaires at least, 'you don't live anywhere, and neither does your money. Or rather you live everywhere, and so does your money.'[35] This world involves homes dotted throughout the world, endless business

---

[31] See Bruno Cousin and Sébastian Chauvin, 'Islanders, immigrants, and millionaires: the dynamics of upper-class segregation in St. Barts, French West Indies', in Iain Hay (ed.), *Geographies of the Super-Rich* (Cheltenham: Edward Elgar, 2013).

[32] Mike Featherstone, 'Super-rich lifestyles', in Birtchnell and Caletrio (eds), *Elite Mobilities*, p. 99; and see many studies in this collection.

[33] Stephen Haseler, *The Super-Rich: The Unjust New World of Global Capitalism* (Basingstoke: Macmillan, 2000), p. 3. See Mike Featherstone on the importance of luxury houses for the super-rich: 'Super-rich lifestyles', in Birtchnell and Caletrio (eds), *Elite Mobilities*, pp. 109–10.

[34] Anthony Elliott, 'Elsewhere: tracking the mobile lives of globals', in Birtchnell and Caletrio (eds), *Elite Mobilities*. Elliott and Urry, *Mobile Lives*.

[35] Quoted by Mike Featherstone, 'Super-rich lifestyles', in Birtchnell and Caletrio (eds), *Elite Mobilities*, p. 115.

travel, private schools, family life structured around episodic get-togethers, private leisure clubs, luxury ground transport, airport lounges, private jets, luxury destinations, and places of distinction and luxury for encountering other super-rich and extending one's 'network capital'. Carroll describes how a global offshore class has been secured through networked relations between directors who are based in major urban centres of North-West Europe and north-east North America, with London, New York and Paris enjoying pride of place.[36] Place, property and power are intertwined in forming and sustaining such a networked rich class.

These offshore elite places establish models of the good life, of which developers then develop mass-market copies, such as cheaper cruise ships, downmarket resorts, mass-market islands and suburban shopping malls. What is imagined and constructed for elites 'moves' elsewhere, or the same development itself travels downmarket, as is currently occurring in Dubai. Offshore worlds for the super-rich provide ideals of embodied lives that through multiple media and global travel enflame desires for similar kinds of mass experience, for consumption, exclusion and security by those a bit less well-off.[37]

There are of course very varied kinds of consumption, exclusion and security. Many 'youngish' people put their body into 'playful risk' when chemically raving through the night (as in Goa and Ibiza) or drinking to excess (as in package tours targeted at 'partying' youth). Especially significant is the role played by 'expressive expatriates' in developing leisure sites in many other alternative places. D'Andrea especially examines the social and ritual life of such expressive expatriates who live, travel and experiment within the global circuits of what he terms New Age and Techno countercultural practices. He describes Ibiza 'as a node of transnational flows of exoticized peoples, practices and imaginaries whose circulation and hybridization across remote locations suggest a globalized phenomenon'.[38] These risky practices of young people in

---

[36] William K. Carroll, *The Making of a Transnational Capitalist Class: Corporate Power in the 21st Century* (London: Zed, 2010), pp. 224–5.
[37] Davis and Monk, 'Introduction', in *Evil Paradises*, p. xv.
[38] Anthony D'Andrea, *Global Nomads* (London: Routledge, 2007), pp. 2–3, and more generally on 'nomadic ethnography'.

Koh Phangan, Byron Bay, Goa or Ibiza remain out of sight from those back home (except when Facebooked). Such leisure seekers and counter-cultural entrepreneurs experience lives offshored from home. Their globalised circuits are in a way just as offshored as those of the super-rich.

So far I have described people travelling to zones of obvious pleasure and excess. But another feature of offshoring is to find pleasure in places of danger, where crime and fears about personal safety are central. Part of the allure of the Caribbean is said to be that 'danger' is just around the corner, just beneath the veneer. Tales of pirates, Rastas, drugs and Yardies contribute to the performing of 'dangerous tourism' in the paradise islands of the Caribbean. There are even guidebooks for 'dangerous travel', as well as a former BBC TV series on 'Holidays in the Danger Zone', to help visitors to get dangerously offshore.

In Rio there is a hyper-concentration of tourism and criminality within so-called favela tours. Touring poverty has recently become really big business. Freire-Medeiros establishes how very different social actors and institutions orchestrate, perform and consume 'touristic poverty' in Rocinha in Rio, as well as in Cape Town, Soweto and Mumbai. Growing inequalities present new opportunities for commodifying tourism, especially for visitors seeking an extreme other. She argues that 'poverty tours are all about crossing the ocean and heading to destinations in the global south which are advertised and uncritically consumed in the tourist market as the iconic loci of poverty.'[39] Even poverty can be consumed offshore from the rich North, with places of extreme danger facilitating the relatively smooth consumption of the 'poverty experience'.

There are also other performances of bodily extremes without observation or monitoring by family or friends from back home. These extremes include bungee jumping, off-piste skiing, paragliding, skydiving, white-water rafting, and high-altitude walking. New Zealand provides many zones for such extremes: 'Nature provides a site in which tourists indulge their dreams of mastery over the earth; of being adventure heroes starring in their own

---

[39] Bianca Freire-Medeiros, *Touring Poverty* (London: Routledge, 2013), p. 167.

movies', as young people seek to cheat death in ever new more dangerous ways.[40] New Zealand packages landscape for consumption by youngish people away from the prying eyes of the concerned 'folks back home'.[41] But while offshoring may be beyond the eyes of one's neighbours, it will not necessarily be beyond Facebook or the mobile phone camera of any person who happens to be paragliding past.[42]

Many of these characteristics of offshored leisure and pleasure have come together in the strange story of contemporary Dubai.

Dubai

Up to around 1960, Dubai was one of the poorest places on earth. It was a series of small mud villages located by the sea and sitting on the edge of a vast inhospitable desert without a single river. No one thought it could ever become a city. It used virtually no energy. The main means of travel was by camel and there was no electricity.[43] Dubai became independent from Britain only in 1971 as one of the United Arab Emirates. At the time illiteracy was over 70 per cent and there were no universities.

By the 2000s Dubai had become the eighth most visited city on earth and the world's largest building site. The exceptional growth of this 'city of gold', located in the most desolate corner of a desolate land without historic sites, illustrates many extraordinary characteristics of contemporary offshoring.

Pumping oil commenced in 1966 but, unlike much of the surrounding area, Dubai is now only a small oil producer. But it nevertheless took advantage of that oil being found elsewhere and constructed a vast visitor, real-estate, transport, tax-avoiding and consumption-based economy. Dubai consumes oil to build islands,

---

[40] Claudia Bell and John Lyall, 'The accelerated sublime: thrill-seeking adventure heroes in the commodified landscape', in Simon Coleman and Mike Crang (eds), *Tourism: Between Place and Performance* (New York: Berghahn, 2002), p. 22.

[41] Ibid., p. 36.

[42] See Jennie Germann Molz, *Travel Connections* (London: Routledge, 2012), on new kinds of 'digital' travellers' tales.

[43] See Krane, *City of Gold*, chap. 1.

hotels and exceptional attractions; to transport very large numbers of visitors, construction workers and sex workers via its modern airport (eighth largest in the world) and leading airline (Emirates); to import via the world's largest man-made harbour enormous quantities of food and goods sold in the many shopping malls; to become a global centre for transportation, with one of the ten largest container ports worldwide; to generate the highest water consumption rate in the world, based upon many desalination plants; and to use enormous amounts of energy providing thermal monotony through climate control in the desert.[44]

More quickly than anywhere else, Dubai developed the infrastructures of a modern society, eliminating much of its 'heritage' almost overnight. This infrastructural modernisation occurred within an Islamic society ruled by an unelected patriarchal tribal dynasty.[45] Dubai developed especially into a leading global site for consuming Western goods and services. During the 2000s it was perhaps the number one global site for ostentatious shopping, eating, drinking, gambling and prostitution (with thousands of victims of human trafficking). And this was principally male consumption – women make up only a quarter of the official Dubai population. Guilt is not to consume beyond the limit in this Islamic country. There are over seventy shopping malls, although the population is only 2 million. Dubai's official national holiday is the month-long Shopping Festival.

Property developments in Dubai include two palm islands that extend the coastline by 120 kilometres; a string of new islands shaped like the countries of the world; a domed ski resort and many major sports venues; the world's tallest building – the Burj Khalifa, at 818 metres; the world's largest hotel – the Asia-Asia, with 6,500 rooms; the world's only seven-star hotel – the Burj Al Arab, with hundred-mile views; and the world's largest party at the opening of the Atlantis hotel complex.[46] There are many

---

[44] See Urry, *Societies beyond Oil*.

[45] This is well brought out in Krane, *City of Gold*, chaps 5, 6.

[46] See www.burj-al-arab.com/. See Christopher Davidson, *Dubai: The Vulnerability of Success* (London: Hurst, 2008); Heiko Schmid, *Economy of Fascination* (Berlin: Gebrüder Borntraeger, 2009); Krane, *City of Gold*.

places for play: the Hanging Gardens of Babylon, the Taj Mahal, the Pyramids, and a snow mountain. These copies of the 'real' are more perfect than the originals, what Eco terms the 'hyper-real'.[47] Until the 2008 collapse, Dubai's annual rate of growth was 18 per cent as it strove for visual and environmental excess.[48]

Locals boast that Dubai is a place for 'supreme lifestyles'. Dubai displays its excess; it is a place to learn what luxury really is and how it is embodied. Hotel guests in the Burj Al Arab hotel find an excess of fresh water – in taps, power showers, oversized bath tubs, private jacuzzis, fountains, waterfalls, canals and artificial lakes. But almost all of this water comes from incredibly energy-intensive water desalination plants. A surfeit of water signifies utter luxury and excess.[49]

This place of excess also became from the beginning of the twenty-first century a place for buying real estate. This generated a gold rush: it became the world's fastest-growing city, with the speculative building of houses and apartments on a vast scale.[50] For example, the Jumeirah Beach Residence is the largest single-phase residential development anywhere in the world, with forty towers accommodating about 15,000 people, almost all of whom bought property being based outside Dubai.

Overall Dubai is an oasis of free enterprise, without income taxes, trade unions, corporation taxes, planning laws, opposition parties or elections, or environmental regulation. It is, for some at least, the offshore paradise. But this is only possible because most of the work undertaken there is carried out by migrant contract labourers from Pakistan and India. These labourers are typically bound to a single employer and have their passports removed upon entry. They are forced to live in distant labour camps, the best known being Sonapur, located in a far corner of Dubai next

---

[47] Umberto Eco, *Travels in Hyper-Reality* (London: Pan, 1987).
[48] Mike Davis, 'Sand, fear, and money in Dubai', in Davis and Monk (eds), *Evil Paradises*, p. 52.
[49] See, on learning to luxuriate, Crispin Thurlow and Adam Jaworski, 'Visible-invisible: the social semiotics of labour in luxury tourism', in Birtchnell and Caletrio (eds), *Elite Mobilities*.
[50] See Krane, *City of Gold*, chap. 6.

to the refuse area and with major sewage problems.[51] Up to 300,000 people live in such hugely overcrowded conditions. The labourers are transported by cattle truck or bus to construction sites on journeys of at least an hour each way and then work fourteen-hour shifts in the unrelenting heat. Good leisure and bad work are normally in close juxtaposition in offshore 'paradises' such as Dubai.

Offshoring leisure zones

This chapter has so far presumed that offshore means literally offshore. However, there are certain legal entities that are able to create areas onshore but which function as offshore zones. I have already noted special economic zones, but there are also 'special leisure zones' possessing specific legal and taxation status. Olympic Games parks are like this. According to the rules of the International Olympic Committee (IOC), such parks must be constituted as tax-exempt enclaves. This reflects how the IOC, like many other governing bodies of major sports, is registered as a 'non-profit sports organisation' in Switzerland. It possesses tax-exempt status even though its 'business' is worth billions of dollars and the IOC employs hundreds of workers.[52] Even manifestly corrupt international sports organisations are granted tax-exempt status in Switzerland, which finds itself hosting many sports events 'in exchange'.

The 2012 London Olympic and Paralympic Games were tax exempt and offshored although clearly held in East London.[53] One precondition for London hosting the games was that legislation should be passed making organisations and individuals involved exempt from UK income and corporation tax during a specified period (actually longer than the Games themselves). Those within

---

[51] Davis, 'Sand, fear, and money in Dubai', pp. 64–6; Krane, *City of Gold*, chap. 11; Matilde Gattonni, 'Sonapur – Dubai's city of gold', http://invisiblephotographer.asia/2011/09/15/photoessay-sonapurdubai -matildegattoni/ (accessed 26.8.2012).
[52] See the website www.playthegame.org for further discussion.
[53] See 'Tax exemptions for the 2012 games', www.hmrc.gov.uk/2012games/ tax-exemptions/index.htm (accessed 15.7.2012).

this temporary tax haven included competitors, media workers, representatives of official Olympic bodies, foreign governments, technicians, team officials, judges, Olympic partners such as McDonald's, Coca-Cola and Visa, performers at the official ceremonies, and the London Organising Committee. The loss of taxation resulting from this area of East London going offshore for some months was £600 to 700 million.[54]

More generally, any country seeking to host an Olympic Games must sign up to the entirety of the Olympic Charter, which is based on the value not of exercise or casual sport or play, but of 'competitive sport'. This has its own logic and practice, a world of records, performances, daily training, drug testing, national competition, specialised medicine and international management.[55] This is a monopoly of governance, since the Olympic Games is the exclusive property of the IOC, which owns all rights and data. In relation to the 2012 Olympic Games, the UK government guaranteed the Games' total monopoly by extending

> legal protection to all properties associated with the London 2012 Olympic and Paralympic Games. Moreover, it forbids any entity from associating itself, or its products or services, with the Olympic Games to gain a commercial advantage . . . The law also provides local authorities and LOCOG with the means to fight ambush marketing efficiently, and to prevent the unauthorized sale of Olympic tickets and other ambush marketing activities at an Olympic venue or in the air space surrounding it.[56]

Sport more generally is increasingly offshored. For example, eleven out of the twenty English Premier League football clubs are owned by foreign individuals and companies, many of which

---

[54] Tim Hunt, 'The great Olympic tax swindle', www.ethicalconsumer.org/commentanalysis/corporatewatch/thegreatolympictaxswindle.aspx (accessed 15.7.2012).

[55] Marc Perelman, *Barbaric Sport: A Global Plague* (London: Verso, 2012), p. 27.

[56] Marianne Chappuis, 'The Olympic properties', www.wipo.int/wipo_magazine/en/2012/03/article_0003.html (accessed 25.8.2012).

are registered in tax havens (as in 2012). These havens offer investors secrecy, the avoidance of British capital gains tax and sometimes income tax. This offshore status is paradoxical, since the specific brand appeal of such clubs is to supporters, who are locked into highly localist or regional identities, seeing themselves as the 'soul' of the clubs, many of which are one hundred or more years old.[57]

More or less the best-known brand in world sport is Manchester United. Currently this 'club', while playing in Manchester, is owned by Americans and registered in the Cayman Islands, and has sponsors in Europe, Africa, Asia and the Middle East.[58] Many football and other sports stars are also in a way 'offshore', with tax-avoidance schemes provided as part of the payment structure agreed by their clubs and negotiated through highly influential agents. This is different in some parts of the world, as some successful clubs in Germany and Spain, for example, are owned by their members. There are thus alternatives to the offshoring of leisure ownership.

Security

Another significant feature of the Olympic zone in East London was its material form. The main zone or camp in East London was a 500-acre site of land previously open to the public. But it has now been enclosed. The park was surrounded by an 11-mile-long steel security cordon topped with 5,000-volt electrical razor wire and 'protected' by at least 900 surveillance cameras. The Olympic Park appeared like a prison camp. This fencing off of the zone has been critically described as a modern-day 'enclosure' of land, something which also happened in the case of the

---

[57] See many articles by David Conn, such as 'Reading, tax havens, secrecy and the sale of homely football clubs', www.guardian.co.uk/football/david-conn-inside-sport-blog/2012/aug/21/reading-zingarevich-offshore-tax-havens, on the offshoring of Reading, a club founded in 1871 at a public meeting (accessed 24.8.2012).

[58] Bill Wilson, 'Sir Alex Ferguson's retirement: will it hurt Man Utd?', www.bbc.co.uk/news/business-22445807 (accessed 9.5.2013).

Beijing Olympics, where it is thought that over 1 million people were displaced by building its 'park'.[59]

Overall sports stadia, international hotels, shopping malls and theme parks increasingly deploy an architecture of security designed to isolate consumers within the camp. The Olympic village was a self-contained 'camp', rather similar in design to a contemporary airport with its necessary movement through an initial ring of 'retail opportunities' (Westfield Stratford City in the case of the Olympic Park).

Airspaces are typical of 'places' in the emerging global order.[60] The exceptional camp of airspace is becoming the rule, especially where newly constructed zones of pleasure and leisure are constructed. Not only do passengers increasingly go offshore, but the systems of movement and securitisation also move around the world, landing in many towns, cities and especially leisure sites. Fuller and Harley argue that 'the airport is the city of the future', especially when cities are full of people from elsewhere who 'need' to be subjected to 'security', at least according to the security industry.[61] At the 2008 Beijing Olympics, 80,000 security staff put into practice fifty-two different security plans, while there was a security force of 23,700 at the London Olympics, a mix of military, private security guards and unpaid volunteers.[62]

Anonymity in such sites is illusory because of the pervasive gaze within such pleasure zones as Olympic parks. There are not only many security staff but also continuously running digitally based surveillance cameras. Thus:

[59] Stephen Graham, *Cities under Siege* (London: Verso, 2011), p. 125; and see Jacquelin Magnay, 'One year on', www.telegraph.co.uk/sport/olympics/10127550/One-year-on-the-transformation-of-Londons-Olympic-park.html (accessed 24.7.2013).
[60] Saolo Cwerner, Sven Kesselring and John Urry (eds), *Aeromobilities* (London: Routledge, 2009).
[61] Gillian Fuller and Ross Harley, *Aviopolis: A Book about Airports* (London: Black Dog, 2005), p. 48.
[62] See Perelman, *Barbaric Sport: A Global Plague*, p. 6; Ben Quinn and Conal Urquhart, 'G4S boss discovered Olympic security guard shortfall only a few days ago', www.guardian.co.uk/sport/2012/jul/14/london-2012-olympic-security-g4s (accessed 25.8.2012).

the all-seeing, pervasive gaze of the camera puts at risk the opportunities for anonymity that the public sphere has traditionally aimed to provide. Sophisticated CCTV systems . . . coupled with databases and/or automatic identification software, unobtrusively register individuals and their movements – even in spaces and situations wherein one may legitimately expect to be an anonymous, unidentified member of the public.[63]

Tourists and visitors to sports events are routinely captured by and subject to a powerful digital panoptic machine justified by the perceived risks of crime, violence and terrorism. Even if one is onshore, the techniques of offshore move out and subject most people to the security gaze of an offshore kind of world.

There are thus many examples of leisure being offshored, with various strange places developing as neighbourhood lives are extensively replaced by lives experienced beyond neighbourhood. In the next chapter I turn directly to the issue of energy, which, as seen in many of these sites of leisure and pleasure, is crucial to offshoring.

---

[63] Lynsey Dubbeld, 'Observing bodies: camera surveillance and the significance of the body', *Ethics and Information Technology*, 5 (2003): 151–62, at p. 158. And see chap. 8.

6

Energy Offshored

The problem of energy

How societies are 'energised' is crucial for how they are organised across space and over time. There are many different systems of energy production, distribution and consumption, generating varied and sometimes very unequal economic, social and political patterns within different societies. Energy in a way provides oxygen for societies, since without the right energy in the right places societies can die.

Up to the mid-eighteenth century the muscle power of animals and humans accounted for 80 to 85 per cent of energy, the rest being made up of wind, water power, the sun and the burning of wood and peat. These forms of energy were mostly used in situ and not transported significant distances. They were localised and fixed, low-energy forms with a very limited 'energy surplus'.[1] There were no ways of transporting these materials far or of moving the energy produced, which was used more or less next to where the power was generated. Before fossil fuels, energy was localised and with little or no distance of time/space between production and consumption.

---

[1] See the classic Fred Cottrell, *Energy and Society* (Bloomington, IN: McGraw-Hill, [1955] 2009).

This chapter explores the long-term shift from localised energy sources to those more distant and mobile, to various forms of 'mobile energy', and especially to energy that is offshored. Moreover, 'mobile energy' has to be transported from producers to consumers, and this transportation itself requires significant energy. Societies have become much more dependent upon distant energy sources, partly because the global population grew during the twentieth century from 2 to 6 billion. Cities, towns, villages and houses all became high-consuming energy centres dependent upon novel 'energy converters', all presupposing the long-distance movement of various energy resources. The next section briefly examines earlier processes over the last two to three centuries of human history by which fossil fuels transformed the energising of societies.

Fossil fuel energy

The fossil fuels of coal, gas and oil account for over four-fifths of the world's current energy.[2] Their burning has constituted the most important single transformation of the world economy and society over the past three centuries. These fuels enabled many novel 'energy converters' to be developed and extensively used.

Especially significant was coal-based steam power, which emerged in the 'West' during the eighteenth and nineteenth centuries. Before fossil fuel-based energy converters developed, China and India were the world's two largest economies.[3] But soon the paths of East and West diverged. Although coal found on the earth's surface had long been used for heating, two eighteenth-century innovations led to new energy converters as coal set societies onto a distinct trajectory. First, novel techniques for mining developed, including the use of wooden pit props that could reinforce tunnels dug underground. Pit props meant that the coalfields of northern England and Wales could develop on a major scale, so enabling coal to be the source of energy for fuelling the world's

---

[2] Matthew Huber, 'Energizing historical materialism: fossil fuels, space and the capitalist mode of production', *Geoforum*, 40 (2009): 105–15; see Cottrell, *Energy and Society*, pp. 13–14, on energy converters.
[3] Giovanni Arrighi, *Adam Smith in Beijing* (London: Verso, 2007).

first industrial revolution. With coal as the source of energy, societies came to be organised around factory-based production and
steam-based transportation. New patterns of living signalled the
break with the pre-industrial world. Crutzen argues that these
eighteenth-century innovations initiated a new geological period
of human history, the 'anthropocene', during which humans transformed the state, dynamics and future of the earth system. These
human activities have been equivalent to a great force of nature.[4]

Second, steam engines engendered huge increases in the scale
of power. These coal-fired steam engines helped to generate
increasingly large factories, new industries and products, and new
cities, as well as the railway network. Working in combination,
these new systems transformed much of the physical world.[5]
Especially significant was how burning coal could be used to
generate mechanical movement – the steam railways that grew
so rapidly beginning in mid-nineteenth-century England. By 1901,
H. G. Wells predicted that future historians would take 'a steam
engine running on a railway' as the nineteenth century's central
symbol.[6]

But 1901 also saw the world's first oil gusher, at Spindletop in
Texas. From then onwards the scale and impact of power and
movement were transformed by the increased burning of energy-
dense oil. An oil civilisation developed, with the spreading of cars,
trucks, aircraft, oil-fired shipping, diesel-based trains and oil-
based heating.[7] In this new civilisation much was newly powered
up or was now on the move, including people, companies, objects,
money and waste. Over the twentieth century many new structures and activities developed while old ones were 'creatively'
destroyed.

Oil is energy-dense, storable, mobile, versatile, convenient and,
for most of the twentieth century, exceptionally cheap. In today's
world it is the single resource that makes possible friendship, business life, professions and much family life. Oil also transports

---

[4] See www.anthropocene.info/en/anthropocene (accessed 18.9.2012).
[5] Ian Morris, *How the West Rules – for Now* (London: Profile, 2010),
chap. 10.
[6] Cited in Ian Carter, *Railways and Culture in Britain* (Manchester:
Manchester University Press, 2001), p. 8.
[7] See John Urry, *Societies beyond Oil* (London: Zed, 2013).

components, commodities and food around the world. Almost all activities that presuppose movement rely upon oil; and few activities significant in the modern world do not entail movement of some kind.[8] Offshoring rests upon plentiful supplies of the resource of oil.

This oil civilisation began in the US, with mobile energy converters carrying their own energy source. Given the denseness and historic cheapness of oil, this system laid the foundation for the US's 'addiction to oil'.[9] Cheap plentiful oil became central to twentieth-century American economic, cultural and military power. Cottrell argued: 'the American rather than the British pattern must be taken as the prototype of high-energy society.'[10] The US drives almost a third of the world's cars (and still most of the larger ones) and produces nearly half the world's transport-generated carbon emissions.[11]

It seemed that there would be unlimited energy from oil, with decreasing costs as many huge fields came on stream, especially up to around 1970. It is calculated that the total value of the worldwide oil industry is greater than that of all banks; at $100 a barrel, the world's known oil reserves are worth $104 trillion, or 50 per cent more than the annual GDP of the world.[12] However, if one rewinds back to 1901, then the last thing that should have been done with all this oil was to burn it up in powering cars, trucks, trains, ships and planes. Rubin notes how: 'there is a lot more value in producing products like plastics from oil than there is from turning oil into gasoline or diesel . . . You can make five times as much by turning oil or natural gas into a petrochemical as you can from selling it as a transport fuel.'[13]

[8] David Owen, *Green Metropolis* (London: Penguin, 2011), chap. 2; Urry, *Societies beyond Oil*.
[9] Ian Rutledge, *Addicted to Oil* (London: I. B. Tauris, 2005), pp. 2–3.
[10] Cottrell, *Energy and Society*, p. 120.
[11] John DeCicco and Freda Fung, *Global Warming on the Road* (Washington, DC: Environmental Defense, 2006).
[12] Manraaj Singh, 'What's all the oil in the world worth?', http://daily-reckoning.co.uk/oil/oil-outlook/oil-world-worth-00027.html (accessed 4.9.2013).
[13] Jeff Rubin, *Why your World is about to Get a Whole Lot Smaller* (London: Virgin, 2009), pp. 76–7.

The US between the wars also saw the striking development of electricity, national grids and suburban houses full of electricity-using consumer goods. Electrical power is generated by electro-mechanical generators driven by steam produced from fossil-fuel combustion, or from the heat released from nuclear reactions, or from kinetic energy extracted from wind power or flowing water. The steam turbine invented by Charles Parsons in 1884 is still used for generating about four-fifths of electric power. Coal-generated electricity expanded greatly, with the average American household of 1970 using more energy than that of an eighteenth-century American small town.[14]

Increases in the generation and consumption of energy for lighting, power and transportation turned the US into the most 'high-powered society' in human history. Nye summarises how, in the American twentieth century, the 'high-energy regime touched every aspect of daily life. It promised a future of miracle fabrics, inexpensive food, larger suburban houses, faster travel, cheaper fuels, climate control, and limitless growth.'[15]

Energy, it seemed, did not have to be factored in to 'economic calculations'. The fossil fuels of coal, gas and oil were so plentiful that their use was not seen as generating relative rates of economic growth across different societies.[16] There was an energy surplus, an energy goldmine at the end of the capitalist rainbow. This led to an overexploitation of the earth's energy resources throughout the twentieth century, especially by the richest and most energy-intensive one-tenth of the world's population. McNeill reports that humans have deployed more energy since 1900 than all of human history before 1900.[17] The rapid burning of fossil fuel generated CO_2 emissions that remain in the atmosphere for hundreds of years and seem to be changing the world's climate. In May 2013 the CO_2 level in the earth's atmosphere topped 400 parts per million for the first time for 3 to 5 million years. This

---

[14] David Nye, *Consuming Power* (Cambridge, MA: MIT Press, 1998), p. 202.

[15] Ibid., p. 215.

[16] See Timothy Mitchell, *Carbon Democracy* (London: Verso, 2011), pp. 139–42.

[17] John R. McNeill, *Something New Under the Sun* (New York: W. W. Norton, 2000), p. 15.

reading was taken at the Keeling laboratory on Hawaii, which provides the longest, continuous readings of CO_2 stretching back to 1958.[18]

The generation of CO_2 emissions is also an issue of global inequality. The *2010 State of the World* report notes how

> the world's richest 500 million people (roughly 7 percent of the world's population) are currently responsible for 50 percent of the world's carbon dioxide emissions, while the poorest 3 billion are responsible for just 6 percent . . . it is the rich who have the largest homes, drive cars, jet around the world, use large amounts of electricity, eat more meat and processed foods, and buy more stuff.[19]

Eliminating these 500 million richest consumers and their emissions would halve the world's CO_2 emissions.

'Western civilisation', we can note, was not inherently superior to civilisations in the rest of the world. Rather, the rapid exploitation of the contingent and climate-changing carbon resources of coal, oil and gas enabled energy converters in the 'West' to dominate the last three centuries. It was not just the Enlightenment or Western science or liberalism that ensured Western civilisation; it was also made possible by the West's carbon-based energy resources, which were increasingly delivered at a distance and burnt remarkably unequally.

I now examine three forms in which the offshoring of energy developed over recent decades and further exaggerate many of these features of energy dependence.

Distant energy

We have noted that, for almost all human history, heating and power were localised and decentralised. Energy converters were

---

[18] 'Carbon dioxide passes symbolic mark', www.bbc.co.uk/news/science-environment-22486153 (accessed 10.5.2013); Aradhna Tripati, 'Last time carbon dioxide levels were this high', www.sciencedaily.com/releases/2009/10/091008152242.htm (accessed 22.3.2013).
[19] Worldwatch Institute, *2010 State of the World* (New York: W. W. Norton, 2010), p. 6.

found in the home or workshop, such as the coal fire, the wood-burning stove, the water heating/cooking system or the small turbine. And most of the fuel being burnt was accessed from nearby. This localised pattern was found in much of Europe even as late as the 1950s and was widespread throughout most of the world. Transportation energy was dependent upon animal muscle power (horse-drawn coaches, oxen) or human muscle power (walking, cycling).

Only in the second half of that century did most societies come to be locked into high-energy systems where power was accessed and delivered from often very distant and specialised locations. Freudenberg and Gramling refer to the unending search for 'weapons of mass consumption', of using distant and often off-shore oil and gas.[20] The US federal government facilitates these sources of energy through charging oil and gas companies less than almost any other country for rights to drill on its territory.[21]

Most societies now depend upon large-scale delivery systems of energy that are distant and 'just-in-time'. China, the world's second largest importer of oil, has barely a fortnight's strategic reserve and hence must ensure that the oil tankers keep on arriving; about 80 per cent of this slow-moving oil passes through the South China Sea.[22] China would cease to be the cheap labour workshop of the world if this oil supply were to cease even for a brief period. Globalisation is now focused more upon movement within the South China Sea than within the North Atlantic airspace.

Apart from 5,500 oil tankers and 6,000 coal carriers, energy is also transported through two kinds of 'tubes'. First, there are pipes through which gas or oil is pumped; and, second, there are cables for delivering electricity generated using coal, gas, oil, hydro-electric, geo-thermal and nuclear converters. Energy is

---

[20] See William Freudenberg and Robert Gramling, *Blowout in the Gulf* (Cambridge, MA: MIT Press, 2011).
[21] The US federal government take from oil drilling was reduced in 1995 and further relief was granted in 2005.
[22] www.iea.org/publications/freepublications/publication/key_world_energy _stats.pdf (accessed 15.8.2012). See Paul French and Sam Chambers, *Oil on Water* (London: Zed, 2010), on the precarious character of uninterrupted energy supplies for almost all societies in the world.

delivered along these 'tubes', so enabling very large 'energy converters' to be built far away gaining significant economies of scale. Vast global offshore systems developed, combining ship- or tube-like mobile delivery of power that is generated by coal, gas, oil, hydro-electric, geo-thermal and nuclear reactions.

Marriott and Minio-Paluello describe the oil (and gas) road whereby energy sources are pumped from under the Caspian Sea, not for local consumers but to 'power up' the economies of Western Europe and especially the car-building plants of Germany.[23] The oil and gas are pumped and shipped thousands of miles to a battery of refineries to provide high levels of income and consumption for Central and Western Europe and for people travelling through Europe. That the oil from the Caspian arrives in the 'West' results from an assemblage of arrangements developed between the energy companies, states, lawyers and the EU. This assemblage is designed to ensure that 'natural resources' are removed from extracting countries and forced along pipelines and occasionally tankers powering up the consumers of Western Europe. These tubes are often described as 'energy corridors', but the contents travel only in one direction.

Almost all societies depend upon offshore sources of energy, although nowhere reaches the offshoring of Taiwan, which imports 98 per cent of its energy.[24] Most societies depend upon energy supplies and prices effectively determined elsewhere. Japan and France import all their oil and gas, and South Korea 97 per cent of its oil. The world's third largest oil producer, the US, imports three-quarters of its crude oil.[25]

Economies and societies are locked in to high-energy use, and yet most of these energy resources are obtained from elsewhere. The recent dash to develop so-called biofuels or agrofuels is a good example of energy offshoring. Agricultural land is used to grow crops which are then converted into a fuel to be used by car-drivers from elsewhere. The discourse of 'sustainability' is often deployed to justify such agrofuel development, but using agricultural crops

---

[23] See James Marriott and Mika Minio-Paluello, *The Oil Road* (London: Verso, 2012).
[24] http://en.wikipedia.org/wiki/Energy_in_Taiwan (accessed 6.8.2012).
[25] Charles Hugh Smith, 'We're no. 1 (and no. 3)!', www.dailyfinance.com/2011/02/28/surprising-facts-about-us-and-oil/ (accessed 17.8.2012).

and land as an offshore replacement for oil has very negative consequences. These include reduced food production and higher prices, the undermining of local agriculture and interests of women farmers, overdependence upon a single crop, deforestation and higher emissions.[26]

Much energy such as biofuel is imported by large private or public corporations that may be located and/or owned and/or managed elsewhere. These offshore corporations will often pursue the 'national' agendas of those other states. The largest oil companies are all state-owned: Saudi Aramco, the National Iranian Oil Company, the Iraq National Oil Company and the Kuwait Petroleum Company account for one-half of the world's official oil reserves. Saudi Aramco is the world's largest oil-producing company, while the largest 'Western' company is Exxon, which is ranked only twelfth.[27]

There are very significant limits on future supplies of cheap and accessible energy, which in the case of oil may have peaked. Extracting oil reserves has a beginning, a middle and an end. The oil reaches maximum output when half the potential oil has been extracted. As each field passes the mid-point of its life, oil becomes more troublesome and expensive to extract.[28] As the output moves down the energy slope after passing its peak, oil becomes increasingly difficult to acquire. Oil extraction is less profitable and more energy is expended to obtain the same supply. At present a colossal US$1 billion per day is spent on oil imports by the US and 'Europe'.[29]

The world's largest oilfields were discovered over half a century ago, with 1965 the peak year of discovery. There have been no really vast discoveries of oil since the 1970s. At least four barrels

---

[26] Les Levidow and Helena Paul, 'Global agrofuel crops as contested sustainability, Part 1: sustaining what development?', *Capitalism, Nature, Socialism*, 21 (2010): 64–86.

[27] See Vaclav Smil, *Oil: A Beginner's Guide* (Oxford: One World, 2008), chap. 1.

[28] In 1956, M. King Hubbert, a Shell Oil geologist, predicted that the peaking of US oil would take place between 1965 and 1970 (the actual peak was 1970, although the level was higher than predicted).

[29] James Murray and David King, 'Climate policy: oil's tipping point has passed', *Nature*, 481 (2012): 1–19, at p. 8.

of oil are consumed for every new one discovered, and some people suggest that this ratio will soon rise to 10:1.[30] The chief economist of the International Energy Authority argues that the existing fields are declining so rapidly that, in order to stay where the world is in terms of extraction rates over the next twenty-five years, it will be necessary to develop four new Saudi Arabias. Peak oil occurred around 2006.[31] Somewhat similarly, Lloyd's of London suggests that maintaining current extraction levels of oil production requires a new Saudi Arabia coming on stream every three years.[32] Because of growing population, and the high proportion who are new 'consumers' of oil, there are already large reductions in the oil that can be consumed *per person* across the world. BP has calculated that world oil production per capita peaked over a generation ago in 1979.[33]

Views contrary to those of the 'peak oilists' have been emphasised by cornucopiasts such as Helm, who maintains that 'the peak oil brigade is leading us into bad policymaking on energy', since there is in fact too much and not too little fossil fuel.[34] Despite this claim, many official and semi-official bodies are increasingly concerned about energy insecurity. Most countries are dependent upon uncertain offshored supplies. The UK Industry Taskforce on Peak Oil and Energy Security reported on the growing danger of an 'oil crunch' whose effects would be as catastrophic for world incomes and for expanding offshoring as was the credit crunch of

---

[30] Report cited in Michael C. Ruppert, *Confronting Collapse* (White River Junction, VT: Chelsea Green, 2009), p. 19. See summary in James Morgan, 'Peak oil', www.scienceomega.com/article/1135/peak-oil-preparing-for-the-extinction-of-petroleum-man (accessed 11.10.2013).

[31] 'The age of cheap oil is now over – and that's official', www.irishtimes.com/newspaper/world/2011/0429/1224295673147.html (accessed 13.9.2013).

[32] Antony Froggatt and Glada Lahn, *Sustainable Energy Security* (London: Lloyd's and Chatham House, 2010), p. 13; see the authoritative UKERC report at www.ukerc.ac.uk/support/tiki-index.php?page=0910GlobalOil Release (accessed 3.6.2012).

[33] Jeremy Rifkin, *The Hydrogen Economy* (New York: Penguin Putnam, 2002), p. 174.

[34] Dieter Helm, 'The peak oil brigade is leading us into bad policymaking on energy', *The Guardian*, 11 October 2011.

2007–8.[35] It should be noted that coal now accounts for nearly one-third of global energy use, a figure growing significantly.[36] But many consider that world coal production will peak as early as 2025, with increasingly frequent downward estimates of known world reserves.[37]

Extreme energy

These uncertainties are reinforced by the second consideration here, that alternative twenty-first-century energy sources are located within 'extreme' environments characterised by very dangerous conditions for workers and relevant ecosystems. Much 'extreme energy' is literally 'offshore' and often found under the sea. The sea and its dark secrets are key to many future energy developments. Importing or exporting energy generally means being on, in or crossing oceans through offshore wind power, deepwater drilling, the laying of undersea cables, and the building of tankers and pipelines. These forms of extreme energy generate excessive costs, uncertainties and risks, especially as they are often also owned by entities that are offshore.

In addition, there are various choke points in the world's oceans where oil and other supplies can be disrupted by piracy and terrorism. The most important is the Strait of Hormuz leading out of the Persian Gulf. This is only 21 miles across, and yet one-fifth of the oil traded each day passes through it. The second most significant is the Strait of Malacca lying between Indonesia, Malaysia and Singapore, through which oil tankers pass travelling especially to China and other Asian societies. At its narrowest point it is only 1.7 miles across.[38]

---

[35] UK Industry Taskforce on Peak Oil and Energy Security, *The Oil Crunch* (London: Ove Arup, 2010).

[36] www.worldcoal.org/coal/market-amp-transportation/ (accessed 15.8. 2012).

[37] See Murray and King, 'Climate policy: oil's tipping point has passed', pp. 6–7.

[38] See Gus Lubin, 'A brief tour of the 7 oil chokepoints that are crucial to the world economy', www.businessinsider.com/oil-chokepoints-suez -canal-2011-1?op=1 (accessed 27.12.2012); see chapter 9 below on piracy.

There are various forms of extreme energy, including the deep-water extraction of oil and gas in the Gulf of Mexico, Alaska, Nigeria, Brazil and, ultimately, the Arctic. Deepwater wells are made possible by significant increases in the depth at which drilling can now take place.

The explosion on BP's Deepwater Horizon rig on 20 April 2010 in the Gulf of Mexico generated much debate about such extreme energy.[39] The Deepwater Horizon was a vast semi-submersible oil rig drilling off Louisiana, where the offshore oil industry was really invented, in water 1 mile deep, with the 'oil reservoir' another 2.5 miles below the seabed. Such reservoirs contain rock, water, oil and gas, the last of these producing the danger of a blowout. The cement for the blowout preventer was put in place by Halliburton, part of the system of fragmented authority established by BP. The rig itself was owned by Transocean, which was subject to less regulation and lower staffing levels, since its registration had been offshored to the Marshall Islands, one of the world's three largest flags of convenience registries (see chapter 9 below).

BP was also known for its draconian cost saving. It has been referred to as the 'renegade refiner', although there had been over 12,000 oil-related safety incidents in the Gulf of Mexico over the previous five years. The major companies involved in this incident, BP, Halliburton and Transocean, brought about an explosion killing eleven workers and resulting in the world's largest marine oil spill, with almost 5 million barrels of crude oil deposited in the Gulf. Three years later the claims from this oil spill are continuing to grow, and these are on such a scale that they threaten the long-term viability of BP.[40]

In Brazil billions of barrels of oil were recently 'discovered', but they are located in sub-salt fields more than 200 miles off the southern coast where the sea is more than 5 miles deep. This pushes beyond where drilling and extraction are currently safe. Such deepwater exploration, drilling and exploitation presuppose exceptional technological and human coordination between the companies and technologies that are involved.

---

[39] See Freudenberg and Gramling, *Blowout in the Gulf*.
[40] See 'BP to seek Cameron's help as oil spill costs escalate', www.bbc.co.uk/news/business-22549710 (accessed 16.5.2013).

It is hard to imagine what further disasters would occur if extensive oil drilling does develop in the most taxing of environments, the Arctic. There are many challenges: there is no relevant infrastructure, especially to transport any resulting oil/gas. Its development rests upon temperatures rising further to melt more ice. The drilling period will last for only a few months of the year and must not conflict with the whale-hunting season. There is much conflict over the ownership of this vast area, and likely fields are widely dispersed, with the total amount of oil thought to be limited. Overall this requires deepwater extraction in uniquely challenging conditions.[41] It also seems that current technology would be unable to deal adequately with a major oil spill, since the infrastructure to mount a large-scale response is absent. Moreover, the well-containment equipment has not been tested. Shell recently confirmed that it will not test the capping system in the icy conditions that would prevail. If extracting occurs on any scale in the Arctic, there will be a much lower energy return on the resulting oil, as well as huge dangers of spillage and explosions. There is as yet no knowledge as to how any spillages would be cleared up and no estimates of the costs to the companies concerned.[42]

Some commentators estimate that, by 2015, these deepwater projects in the Gulf of Mexico, the Arctic and off Brazil would have to provide almost one-third of new oil capacity. If these sources do not deliver, the likely global energy shortfall is further compounded.[43]

Tar or oil sands are a further source of extreme energy. This extraction was initiated in 1999 when Shell established the Athabasca oil sands project in Alberta, Canada. Other big deposits of

---

[41] Recent drilling off Greenland by Cairn Energy cost $1 billion but resulted in no significant finds: www.thetimes.co.uk/tto/business/industries/naturalresources/article3243624.ece (accessed 13.9.2013); Yereth Rosen, 'Time running out for Shell drilling in Arctic', http://uk.reuters.com/article/2012/08/13/uk-shell-alaska-drilling-idUKBRE87C14R20120813 (accessed 15.8.2012).
[42] See Platform's recent report, http://platformlondon.org/wp-content/uploads/2012/05/Shell-Arctic-investor-briefing.pdf (accessed 16.8.2012).
[43] Industry Taskforce on Peak Oil and Energy Security, *Briefing Note on Deepwater Oil Production* (London: ITPOES, November 2010).

tar sands are in Venezuela and Siberia. These sands are deposits
of sand and clay saturated with bitumen. The bitumen is solid, or
semi-solid, and getting it to flow requires injecting it with up to
1,000°F of heat. The resulting 'oil' has then to be converted into
crude oil, which in turn is refined into various oil products. This
heavy oil is not nearly as valuable as 'light crude' oil. Two tons
of tar sands results in only one barrel of refined oil. Extracting
tar-sands oil is subject to many technological difficulties, much
political contestation because of its environmental effects, and
huge economic uncertainty because of the long-term investment
needed.[44] Canadian tar sands will at most generate 4.7 million
barrels per day by 2035.[45] Extracting this oil generates at least
three times the greenhouse gas emissions of normal oil extraction.
It also uses huge amounts of energy, especially natural gas and
much water. The natural gas now used in Alberta tar-sands extraction would heat half the homes in Canada.

Another extreme energy is shale oil, especially within the US.
There is in fact no oil in shale but a solid material called kerogen,
which is not-quite-yet oil. After an extensive recovery process, 1
ton of shale oil can produce the petrol needed to fuel one car for
a two-week period. This recovery involves mining, transportation,
accessing vast amounts of water, heating up to more than 480°C,
adding hydrogen, and disposing of the waste. No company has
yet managed to develop a large-scale long-term shale oil industry
because the energy return is so low.

But there are huge 'reserves' in remote parts of the US and there
is much incentive for companies to develop viable extraction,
especially in the Colorado desert. Maugeri maintains that US
shale oil could be a paradigm shifter, with North Dakota and
Montana becoming a big oil-producing area within the US, which
has more than twenty big shale oil formations. Most is profitable
at a price of oil of $50 to $65 per barrel, thus making these formations sufficiently resilient to a significant downturn of oil

---

[44] See the report by the campaigning group Platform, *BP and Shell:
Rising Risks in Tar Sands Investments*, http://platformlondon.org/p
-publications/risingrisks/, as well as http://platformlondon.org/about-us
(accessed 4.9.2013); Morgan Downey, *Oil 101* (New York: Wooden
Table Press, 2009), pp. 43–6.
[45] Murray and King, 'Climate policy: oil's tipping point has passed'.

prices.[46] The combined additional production from the aggregate shale/tight oil formations could at most reach 6.6 million barrels per day by 2020 (out of current global oil consumption of around 85 million barrels per day).

However, there are massive obstacles: the inadequate oil transportation system, the country's refining structure, the amount of associated gas produced along with shale oil, environmental doubts about hydraulic fracturing, and the fact that Shell has for four decades been trying to extract shale oil without much financial success. The major difficulty is the effect of hydraulic fracturing, or fracking, upon the environment, which produces water and land contamination, natural gas infiltration into fresh water aquifers, the poisoning of the subsoil, even minor earthquakes, and very much opposition.[47] This shale oil revolution cannot be easily replicated in societies other than the US, even according to its enthusiastic advocate, Maugeri.[48]

Desertec – a vast network of solar and wind farms stretching across the Mena region of the Sahara and intended to connect to Europe via high-voltage direct current transmission cables – is a further form of extreme energy. This idea has gained momentum over the past few years with especially German corporations. The first phase of construction is set to begin in Morocco. Most energy would come from concentrated solar power plants that use both natural gas and solar panels. The fluid is heated to 400°C and then used to heat steam in a standard turbine generator. By 2050 it is projected that this could provide 15 to 20 per cent of Europe's electricity. One huge difficulty is the harsh desert itself; its high winds and dusty conditions mean that the vast panels need daily cleaning. It is also expensive, as well as being politically controversial. The Mena region lacks universal access to electricity, and so much of this energy could and should be locally used.[49]

[46] See Leonardo Maugeri, *Oil: The Next Revolution* (Cambridge, MA: Harvard Kennedy School, 2012).
[47] See http://platformlondon.org/wp-content/uploads/2013/06/Pages-from -Shell-Global-Megafrackers.jpg (accessed 26.6.2013).
[48] Maugeri, *Oil: The Next Revolution*.
[49] http://inhabitat.com/solar-energy-from-sahara-will-be-imported-to-europe -within-5-years/ (accessed 11.10.2013).

Finally, these extreme energy sources are mostly made more risky because of increasing extreme weather events. Many such events have been experienced in the last two to three years, even in resource-rich societies such as Australia, with frequent wildfires and floods, or the US, with New York suffering a US$50 billion bill for the effects of Frankenstorm Sandy in 2012.[50] These extreme weather patterns necessitate extra energy resources to provide heating, shelter, food and lighting for often desperate dispossessed populations at the same time that much energy will have gone offline.

Such extreme weather occurred in 2005 when hurricanes Katrina and Rita hit the Louisiana coastline. They destroyed billions of dollars of gas and oil infrastructures when the Mississippi delta was flooded. Other oil refineries around the world were working to full capacity and were unable to raise production. These hurricanes showed the vulnerability of the world's supplies of oil and of the main resource that underpins offshoring. Without capacity to replace Gulf of Mexico supplies, the price of oil skyrocketed, and this was a major factor generating the financial crash in sub-prime American suburbs during 2007–8.[51]

Financialisation

As well as distanciation and extreme energy, there is the financialising of energy. Both energy and financial markets were deregulated during the previous two to three decades, and this increasingly led to energy being subject to significant financial speculation.

The effects of deregulation were revealed in the dramatic rise and fall of the US energy giant Enron a decade or so ago. Enron president and chief operating officer Jeffrey Skilling argued that the company did not really need any assets and could make money just by speculating on energy markets. It was believed that anything and everything could be financialised. During the late 1990s Enron created various offshore entities, so freeing up its movement

---

[50] Louise Boyle, 'After the storm', www.dailymail.co.uk/news/article -2225112/Superstorm-Sandy-Death-toll-hits-FIFTY-damage-set-50BIL LION.html (accessed 6.11.2012).
[51] See my analysis in *Societies beyond Oil*, chap. 2.

of currencies and other sources of finance, with at one stage 692 subsidiaries incorporated in the Cayman Islands.[52] These offshore entities made Enron look more profitable than it really was, and created a spiral in which the corporation performed ever more deception so as to sustain an illusion of profits. Enron hid mounting losses through a tangle of offshored accounts.

Under Skilling, Enron adopted 'mark to market' accounting, in which anticipated future profits from deals were recorded as if those profits had already been realised. Enron recorded gains on its accounts from what over time might turn out to be losses, as the company's fiscal health was deemed secondary to its share price. Enron's actions were often gambles to keep the deception going, so pushing up the share price and sustaining shareholder value, which was seen as paramount. For six years running Enron was named as the 'most admired' corporation by *Fortune* magazine, and it rose to become the US's seventh largest company.

Enron traders significantly contributed to the 2000 and 2001 energy crises in California when there were severe electricity outages. There were rolling blackouts, although energy demand was lower than California's installed capacity, caused by market manipulation and illegal shutdowns of pipelines by various energy consortia. Drought, delays in approval of new power plants, and supply manipulation decreased supply and brought about an 800 percentage increase in wholesale prices between April and December 2000. This gap was created by the energy companies, mainly Enron. Energy traders took power plants offline for maintenance at the time of peak demand so that power was sold at premium prices, sometimes twenty times its normal value. This financial and energy crisis resulted from the partial energy deregulation that occurred in 1996 and cost California $40 to $45 billion. In the end it turned out that Enron, as well as paying almost no taxes, was a vast fraudulent conspiracy, and it collapsed with huge debts in 2001.[53]

---

[52] See William Brittain-Catlin, *Offshore: The Dark Side of the Global Economy* (New York: Picador, 2005), chap. 3, on the following.
[53] See the 2005 documentary *Enron: The Smartest Guys in the Room*, www.imdb.com/title/tt1016268/ (accessed 4.1.2013).

More recently, financial derivatives based around the future prices of oil, gas and electricity have been developed. There are now over seventy-five crude oil financial derivatives, compared with only one just fifteen years ago. A derivative is a financial instrument whose value depends on other, more basic, underlying variables such as the future price of oil. These involve secondary markets for finance which separate the financially offshored ownership of energy and the management of energy. These financial innovations do not involve 'investing' in new plant and machinery to develop extra energy provision.

Thus there is the intertwining of new kinds of finance with supplies of oil. Oil's price movements stem as much from speculation as from changes in the supply and demand of oil for transportation and manufacturing. A major report for Lloyd's of London shows that speculation destabilises supply and price, so further reducing energy security.[54] This report shows how financial trading makes oil prices higher and more unstable, oil prices being exceptionally sensitive even to small changes in demand.[55] There are also said to be 'oil sharks', tankers that are instructed not to load their cargo until prices are significantly higher. They lie offshore. In the UK, Paul Watters of the AA commented that 'Tankers are off the UK coast and also off the US. They are acting as storage tanks. As always, motorists are the victims in this. They are at the end of the food chain.'[56]

The US government allows speculation and manipulation of energy prices by big banks and major funds. One commentator reports how 'There are 50 studies showing that speculation adds an incredible premium to the price of oil, but somehow that hasn't seeped into the conventional wisdom. Once you have the market

---

[54] Froggatt and Lahn, *Sustainable Energy Security*, pp. 13–15. Extensive derivative markets are essentially unregulated and contributed greatly to the economic collapse of 2007–8.

[55] See Dan Dicker, *Oil's Endless Bid* (New York: Wiley, 2011).

[56] David Derbyshire, Andrew Levy and Ray Massey, 'Revealed: 50 oil tankers loitering off British coast as they lie in wait for fuel price hikes', www.dailymail.co.uk/news/article-1229337/Petrol-prices-Oil-tan kers-loitering-British-coast-lie-wait-price-hikes.html#ixzz23hTeT8Dd (accessed 16.8.2012).

dominated by speculators, what you really have is a gambling casino.'[57]

This permissive regulation of oil markets enabled a handful of banks, financial institutions and energy companies to manipulate huge short-term swings in the price paid for oil. Futures traders such as banks and hedge funds, with no intention of taking physical delivery of energy but only of turning a paper profit, today control around 80 per cent of the energy futures market. This is up from 30 per cent a decade ago. Thus more and more tankers will be laid up offshore, waiting to speculate. They are literally offshore and betting against future prices. In May 2013, the EU accused leading European oil and gas companies of acting as a price-fixing cartel, so keeping prices for consumers much higher than they should have been.[58]

Financialisation is aided by the fact that many of the world's energy companies are partly registered offshore. For example, the company Caymans 97, based in the Cayman Islands, pools in one place the controlling ownership of many of BP's worldwide operations. BP is a public company and so theoretically transparent, but behind the scenes there are networks of offshore subsidiaries that few know about and which prevent governments and the public from seeing what they really do. Secrecy is at the heart of this process, to avoid the scrutiny of regulators over exactly how much tax gets paid within the different countries where BP operates.[59] Many Russian energy companies, as well as its Central Bank, especially developed offshored accounts in Cyprus as oil and gas companies moved offshore from Russia in the early 1990s onwards.[60]

---

[57] Quoted in F. William Engdahl, 'Behind oil price rise: peak oil or Wall Street speculation?', http://axisoflogic.com/artman/publish/Article_64370.shtml (accessed 14.8.2012).
[58] www.bbc.co.uk/news/business-22533993 (accessed 15.5.2013).
[59] 'Offshore: tax havens, secrecy, financial manipulation, and the offshore economy', www.multinationalmonitor.org/mm2005/072005/interview-brittain-catlin.html (accessed 15.5.2013).
[60] See Brittain-Catlin, *Offshore*, pp. 42–3, 191–2. This offshoring of tax is part of the context for the collapse of the Cyprus economy in early 2013.

Conclusion

This chapter has revealed long-term shifts from local and decentralised energy to that which is increasingly offshored, literally, financially and metaphorically. As energy is offshored, it is often interconnected with other offshoring processes. It is extremely hard to reverse energy mobility, extreme energy and financialisation.

Also most major energy innovations take a very long time to develop, often decades. This is partly because a new 'technology' is not just a single technology but involves an array of elements that take decades to be so assembled, such that it constitutes a new 'socio-technical' system. A new system involving a complex combination of existing elements to reverse offshoring would have to be assembled over decades.[61] An energy transition from one type of energy resource to another may happen only once a century but then with momentous consequences.[62] Switching from a fossil-fuels offshoring civilisation is a gigantic task which could take most of this century. But it is not realised that there may be insufficient energy to extend the many forms of offshoring examined in this book, offshore worlds being exceptionally carbon-intensive.

Indeed many books, reports and articles now maintain that the remaining fossil fuel needs to be left underground in order to have a good chance of limiting temperature increases within 2°C.[63] Climates have been transformed through burning all this fossil fuel. Two thousand billion tons of CO_2 have been spewed into the atmosphere and will remain there for hundreds of years.[64] Such emissions increased exponentially from 1850 to the present and show no signs of slowing down, let alone reversing.[65] There is no benign solution unfolding here.

---

[61] Brian Arthur, *The Nature of Technology* (New York: Free Press, 2009); Frank Geels and Wim Smit, 'Failed technology futures: pitfalls and lessons from a historical survey', *Futures*, 32 (2000): 867–85.

[62] Vaclav Smil, *Energy Transitions* (Santa Barbara, CA: Praeger, 2010).

[63] James Hansen, *Storms of my Grandchildren* (London: Bloomsbury, 2011).

[64] Mike Berners-Lee and Duncan Clark, *The Burning Question* (London: Profile, 2013), p. 26.

[65] Ibid., p. 12.

A related problem is the huge size of the financial assets that are valued on the basis of the ability to burn these fossil fuels. Stock markets value the energy companies' reserves of fossil fuels as if this is the case, even though maybe only 40 per cent could ever be used if global temperature increases are to be limited to 2°C over this coming century. According to Will Hutton, there is either a vast carbon bubble, with investors and companies wildly over-speculating on the value of fuel reserves that can never be burnt, or no major corporation believes that there is any chance of keeping to the limits on fossil fuel use that would contain global warming to a 2°C increase. Burning all these carbon reserves would increase global temperatures by at least 6°C. But if they are not burnt, then US$4 trillion of stock market value would be halved and there would be further financial crashes easily as significant as that which occurred from 2007–8 onwards.[66]

Some argue that, in order to overcome such an enormous contradiction, an even more extreme form of offshoring should be developed, which can be called 'off-earthing'. This involves developing utterly massive geo-engineering projects that various Cold War scientists have been trying to get implemented. Geo-engineering would not reverse fossil-fuel dependence but involves planetary approaches to deal with its continuing deleterious consequences.

There are two main forms of such geo-engineering. In the first, carbon dioxide is removed from the atmosphere by using giant chemical vents to scrub the atmosphere or by fertilising the oceans with particles of iron sulphate so as to stimulate algal blooms which better absorb carbon dioxide. The second is known as solar radiation management and is designed to reflect a small percentage of the sun's light and heat back into space away from the earth. This would be achieved by placing trillions of tiny 'sunshades' in

---

[66] Will Hutton, 'Burn our planet or face financial meltdown', www .guardian.co.uk/commentisfree/2013/apr/21/carbon-problems-financial -crisis-hutton (accessed 3.5.2013); Carbon Tracker, *Unburnable Carbon 2013: Wasted Capital and Stranded Assets* (London: Carbon Tracker/ Grantham Research Institute on Climate Change and the Environment, LSE, 2013).

orbit around the planet.[67] Such global off-earthing schemes presuppose astonishing financial, organisational and scientific collaboration. This kind of 'global social experiment' would probably engender a whole new scale of geopolitical conflict. As a 'Plan B', it is a Faustian bargain that trumps democratic politics and depends upon a globalist imaginary bypassing national and democratic processes.

But if the scale of climate change comes to be seen as 'catastrophic', then powerful interests may mobilise behind a planetary technological fix of this nature so as to develop a 'climate capitalism'.[68] Such a global social experiment could get presented as absolutely the only way of keeping the fossil-fuel fires burning away. Never let a crisis go to waste, as neo-liberalism proclaims.

---

[67] Royal Society, *Geoengineering the Climate: Science, Governance and Uncertainty* (London: Science Policy Centre Report 10/09, 2009); for social science analysis, see Phil Macnaghten and Bron Szerszynski, 'Living the global social experiment: an analysis of solar radiation management and its implications for governance', *Global Environmental Change*, 23/2 (2013): 465–74.
[68] See more general analysis in Peter Newell and Matthew Paterson, *Climate Capitalism: Global Warming and the Transformation of the Global Economy* (Cambridge: Cambridge University Press, 2010).

7

Waste Offshored

Introducing waste

The neo-liberal world examined in previous chapters is one of shiny palaces glinting in former deserts, astonishing treasure troves of goods sourced from across the world, an array of personal services people had no idea they needed, and technological arte-facts that enable unexpected links, connections and surveillance around the globe. I describe and analyse these remarkable devel-opments in this book. I also try to identify their dark side, although this is often hard to do, as products, services and experiences which go offshore move out of sight of the humble researcher.

Revealing the dark side is indeed difficult in relationship to the vast topic of waste. Neo-liberalism engenders a tremendous scale of waste products through the planned obsolescence of products and places; these waste products are moved around the world often secretly; they land up in some extraordinarily dangerous waste centres offshore from where they were initially 'wasted'; certain societies and places become specialists at dealing with this offshore waste; and waste is sometimes recycled into different products which return to centres of capitalist consumption, so recommencing the great chain of 'capitalist being'.

Waste has always been central to societies, with some being exceptionally skilful at reusing waste products. Chinese agricul-ture relied on human excrement, or night soil, as a fertiliser.

Outhouses in rural China were often placed near pigsties and waste was collected from both. The morning distribution of night soil was a common sight. Every day Shanghai produced over 10,000 tons of human excrement which was gathered up, put in barrels, and then transported to the fields surrounding the city. In the twentieth century the 'rag and bone man' was a common sight in many rural areas and cities, collecting, selling and partially recycling various materials from households and workshops within a neighbourhood.[1]

More recently, many industrial products such as glass, timber, wood pulp, plastics, tyres and paper are partially recycled. Both in wartime and more recently, complex systems have been developed by which households and industries reuse what appears to be various 'wastes'. Some of this recycling is enshrined in law and local regulations, while other waste products are deemed toxic or dangerous, with strict rules theoretically applied to their disposal. Whole areas of land can be left contaminated and unusable for years through legal or illegal dumping of toxic materials. Some waste products from the chemical or nuclear industries remain dangerous for long periods and are 'out of sight', housed in supposedly secure locations for tens or hundreds of years.

Much of the difficulty in recycling stems from how most products are not designed such that all components can be effectively recycled. Industrial ecologists maintain that products should have a complete 'closed-loop' life cycle that is mapped out and certified for each component. Some cities are trying to develop strategies that would turn them into 'zero waste cities' based upon 100 per cent recycling and recovery. But this is astonishingly difficult to achieve because of how today's 'consumption-driven society' produces such an enormous amount of waste, while waste management has received insufficient attention in city and regional planning.[2]

---

[1] This even led to a BBC comedy classic series, *Steptoe and Son*, first broadcast fifty years ago (1962–74): www.bbc.co.uk/comedy/steptoeandson/ (accessed 27.8.2012).
[2] Atiq Uz Zaman and Steffan Lehmann, 'Urban growth and waste management optimization towards "zero waste city"', *City, Culture and Society*, 2 (2011): 177–87.

For all these systems of recycling and waste management, an immense 'global waste mountain' is building up around the world. This mountain is a dramatic indicator of contemporary globalisation. A recent World Bank report estimates that the annual scale of municipal solid waste will soon rise from 1.3 billion to 2.2 billion tons, with much of the increase deriving from rapidly growing cities within developing countries. The annual cost of waste management is projected to increase from US$205 billion to US$375 billion.[3] This cost is rising faster in lower-income countries partly because some waste being recycled has been 'imported' from offshore. Generally the rich produce more waste; but after a certain level of development there is some decoupling of economic growth from the rate of waste production.

Finally, 'waste' is not always thought undesirable. This is partly because money can often be made out of waste, as shown in the developing world, where rubbish dumps are full of scavengers picking over vast waste mountains. But it is also because, according to Veblen, wasteful consumption can demonstrate that one is really wealthy.[4] People attempt to impress others and gain status advantage through 'conspicuous consumption'. In some societies, the conspicuous waste of time, effort and goods shows that a person is wealthy and possesses high status. This thesis was elaborated in Veblen's *The Theory of the Leisure Class*, published in 1899, and it is salutary to think what he would have made of twentieth-century capitalism, which so scaled up consumption, leisure and waste.

Making waste

This scaling up is partly the result of the emergence of whole new industries producing goods and services that no one knew they needed. Huge consumer industries have developed meeting unknown 'needs'. Examples include the $60 billion bottled water industry, the $120 billion fast-food industry, the $42 billion pet

---

[3] Secretariat of the Basel Convention, *Vital Waste Graphics 3* (Basel: Secretariat of the Basel Convention, 2012).

[4] Thorsten Veblen, *The Theory of the Leisure Class* (New York: Macmillan, [1899] 1912), pp. 85, 96.

food industry, and the $40 billion cosmetic surgery industry.[5] These are all wasteful energy-intensive industries. In particular, the principal value promulgated by neo-liberalism has been 'to inspire us all to consume, consume, consume. Every opportunity is taken to convince us that purchasing things is our civic duty, that pillaging the earth is good for the economy.'[6]

And yet obsolescence is built into products, as well as into services and places. This process of planned obsolescence was first critiqued fifty years ago in Vance Packard's *The Waste Makers*.[7] This analysis showed how business seeks to make people wasteful, debt-ridden and discontented with their current consumer purchases. Waste-makers aim to reduce the time between consumer purchases. Packard claimed that shortening the replacement cycle generates waste, exploits customers and uses up resources through cosmetic changes that are of little value. His analysis was especially prescient, and he would no doubt be surprised at the industrial scale of contemporary 'waste-making' since he wrote in the 1960s.

There are many ways in which 'designed obsolescence', or pointless waste, is built into most products and services.[8] They are meant to waste, to become out of date and be replaced. Products and services are built around such wastefulness, including products that are designed to be disposed of, such as tissue paper, paper tableware, packaging, disposable cameras, medical gloves, syringes, cups, razors, nappies and some clothing.[9]

Cars are a good example of a product that quickly appears unfashionable, although their core concept has changed little since the late nineteenth century. Cars are subject to the most intense advertising, branding, display and dating processes so as to ensure

[5] Worldwatch Institute, *2010 State of the World* (New York: W. W. Norton, 2010), p. 14; Barry Smart, *Consumer Society* (London: Sage, 2010), p. 67; personal communication from Anthony Elliott re the cosmetics industry.
[6] John Perkins, *Confessions of an Economic Hit Man* (London: Ebury Press, 2005), p. xiii; Avner Offer, *The Challenge of Affluence* (Oxford: Oxford University Press, 2006).
[7] Vance Packard, *The Waste Makers* (New York: D. McKay, 1960).
[8] Smart, *Consumer Society*, chap. 4.
[9] Secretariat of the Basel Convention, *Vital Waste Graphics 3*, pp. 10–11.

that old models quickly look obsolescent. This process ensures that car owners are induced to spend disproportionate amounts of money on the latest 'must-have' model. Glossy sexualised motor shows played a significant role in engendering an annual obsession with tiny modifications of the design, function or look of a car then advertised and marketed as 'innovative' or 'revolutionary' or simply 'the future'.

This 'producing the obsolete' is also found in towns and cities that become obsolescent, that go out of fashion. Places seem worn out and exhausted, and consumers and related investment moves elsewhere. There is the periodic reconstruction or theming of place: 'a motivated form of geographical representation in which meaningful connections are made amongst unifying ideas, symbols, or discourses'.[10] Theming is common around the world, with businesses and places having little alternative to being themed and re-themed. The previous theme rapidly turns into waste and is literally and metaphorically dumped in the ubiquitous skips that populate towns and cities across the world. This old theme will be mostly left in a landfill site containing various other dead themes. Much re-theming involves a designed reconstruction through themes imported from elsewhere, especially from the 'global centres' of the contemporary world.

Particularly significant is the role of advertising, also critiqued by Vance Packard half a century ago. Global advertising expenditures can account for up to 2 per cent of a country's national income.[11] Advertising is designed to make obsolescent recently purchased products, services and places. Adverts present enticing opportunities for very new goods and services often available only from elsewhere or within locations that have to be travelled to using high carbon transportation.

Especially noteworthy has been the growing corporate interference in children's lives. Beder shows how corporations target ever

---

[10] Scott A. Lukas (ed.), *The Themed Space* (Lanham, MD: Lexington Books, 2007), p. 2.
[11] See Vance Packard, *The Hidden Persuaders* (Harmondsworth: Penguin, 1960); Avner Offer, *The Challenge of Affluence* (Oxford: Oxford University Press, 2006), pp. 68, 70, 123; Smart, *Consumer Society*, chap. 4, on 'designing obsolescence'. See chap. 10 on its implications for climate change.

younger children with advertising and marketing designed to foster discontent and turn them into hyper-consumers being defined by what they have rather than who they are. Children's play has been transformed into a commercial opportunity. A decline in such play seems to generate deteriorating wellbeing. Even schools are no longer a haven from these commercial pressures that bear in upon small children.[12]

More generally, the world's media circulate images of the good mobile life and the importance of the newest global brands, products and services. High-carbon advertising constructs many perfectly functional products and services as 'waste'. This industry persuades people that functional objects and services are really past it, old-fashioned and indicative that a person's or place's life needs reimagining.

Previous chapters demonstrated how hyper-high-carbon societies developed in the late twentieth century. These involved the planned obsolescence of products, services and places, gigantic buildings, the profligate use of energy and water, huge indebtedness, and an industrial scale of wastefulness of food, water, materials and energy.[13] I noted that the *2010 State of the World* reported that this vast production of waste stemmed from global inequality.[14] Much of that stuff bought directly as goods or indirectly as services and places ends up as waste.

Indeed, it seems that the greater the inequalities in a society, the more waste that gets generated. This is demonstrated especially by the escalating problem of food waste, with a recent report claiming that Americans throw away up to 40 per cent of their food, cramming landfills with food valued as at least $165 billion a year. These wasteful tendencies have worsened over time, with the average American dumping ten times as much food as consumers in South-East Asia. Overall as much as half of the world's food, amounting to 2 billion tons' worth, is wasted as a result of poor storage, strict sell-by dates, bulk offers and consumer fussiness. Food is the largest component of solid waste in

---

[12] Sharon Beder, *This Little Kiddy Went to Market* (London: Pluto Press, 2009).
[13] See details in Clive Hamilton, *Requiem for a Species* (London: Earthscan, 2010), chap. 3.
[14] Worldwatch Institute, *2010 State of the World*, p. 6.

landfill sites.[15] And this results in the comparable wasting of the water which has been used to irrigate the growing of what turns out to be wasted food.

And waste is the classic offshore problem. The waste is binned, whether literally in a smart plastic bin in a Western society or more metaphorically onto a tip in a developing society. And once it is binned it is mostly forgotten about. As de Castella writes: 'we put things in the bin and expect them to be taken away. Where it all goes few of us know, or care.'[16] Across the globe most goes into landfill sites normally located out of sight, on the wrong side of the tracks, while much of the rest is placed in incinerators. Some is recycled or composted and a little is turned into bio-energy through super-heating. In Britain a vast area the size of the county of Warwickshire is taken up with landfilled waste.

Overall waste is a global problem, and in many societies it is dealt with by waste pickers, who sort through by hand and reuse waste materials. Across the world there are at least 15 million people scavenging waste, mainly in developing countries, where waste is mostly not collected through formal, organised channels. Up to 1 to 2 per cent of city populations informally recycle materials, generating an economic value of several hundred million dollars. In Brazil the formal recycling industry relies on such waste pickers, or *catadores*, who recover up to 90 per cent of material.[17] There are of course huge health and environmental downsides to waste picking.

Moreover, there will be large increases in the scale of scavenging as developing economies adopt more 'Western'-style products, packaging and wasting. Especially significant is how many materials are increasingly replaced by plastic counterparts produced from oil. Plastic absorbs persistent organic pollutants (POPs) from

[15] 'UK supermarkets reject "wasted food" report claims', www.bbc.co.uk/news/uk-20968076 (accessed 10.1.2013); Dina ElBoghdady, 'In U.S., food is wasted from farm to fork',www.washingtonpost.com/business/economy/in-us-food-is-wasted-from-farm-to-fork/2012/08/21/2d5fed94-ebdb-11e1-9ddc-340d5efb1e9c_story.html (accessed 14.9.2012).
[16] See Tom de Castella, 'The tipping point', www.tomdecastella.com/?p=429 (accessed 13.9.2012), and for this paragraph.
[17] Secretariat of the Basel Convention, *Vital Waste Graphics 3*, p. 19.

the environment and eventually transfers them back to the environment. POPs are organic (carbon-based) chemical substances and include pesticides, industrial chemicals or by-products of industrial processes that are toxic to humans and wildlife.[18] Places of waste are often places of high toxicity.

Moving waste

Certain places have developed into specialist places of waste. Gille notes how Soviet-style Eastern Europe was once seen as a 'wasteland', both figuratively and literally. The countries of Eastern Europe were out of date, unfashionable, left behind in the slow lane and inefficient. Certain places in such a wasteland became dumping grounds for waste from the Soviet regime, such as the small village of Garé in Hungary, where leaking toxic waste made animals sick and farm products hard to sell.

After the implosion of the Soviet system, things changed, but only partially. Eastern Europe is again a wasteland through receiving increasing amounts of toxic waste from Western economies, at least up to 2007–8. Gille examines the location of a possible new incinerator plant to be built in Hungary, reflecting the increase in the method of incineration to deal with global waste. Especially hazardous waste tends to be sent to societies possessing weaker regulatory regimes and looser emission standards.[19]

Gille demonstrates how the villagers of Garé embraced the idea of a large incinerator to deal with this toxic waste being imported from Western Europe. The villagers allied themselves with the global incinerator industry to take advantage of this rush to burn and hence to become part of an emerging new Europe. Local opponents to the building of the incinerator aligned themselves with the Green movement. Both sides, for or against the building of the incinerator, were thus affected much by global forces and less by debates within Hungary. Issues of waste became structured

---

[18] Ibid., pp. 7–8, and more generally on consumerism, waste and inequality.
[19] Zsuzsa Gille, 'Cognitive cartography in a European wasteland', in Michael Burawoy et al. (eds), *Global Ethnography* (Berkeley: University of California Press, 2000), pp. 242–5.

through conflicts between two global forces, the world's waste industry and global environmentalism.

Related conflicts can be seen with regard to issues of waste travelling across the oceans. One example involved the oil-trading company Trafigura, convicted of criminal charges in 2006 when many people in the Ivory Coast became ill. This mass illness was apparently caused by a ship leased by Trafigura dumping 500 tons of toxic waste in the Ivory Coast rather than reprocessing it in Amsterdam, which had been the original plan. According to a UN report posted by Wikileaks, this toxic dumping led 108,000 people in the Ivory Coast to seek medical attention. A BBC *Newsnight* broadcast claimed that Trafigura knew the waste that it was dumping was hazardous.

Another kind of offshore dumping is of ships themselves. Various specialised places in the developing world have become established for breaking up and partially recycling 'dead' ships, such as Alang in Gujarat in India and Chittagong in Bangladesh. Before ship breaking began in Alang in June 1983 the beach was pristine and unspoiled. Now an astonishing gargantuan landscape has evolved, with hundreds of 'dead' ships driven onto the beach waiting to be dis-assembled on these nautical killing fields. Langewiesche describes contemporary Alang: it 'was barely recognisable as a beach. It was a narrow, smoke-choked industrial zone six miles long, where nearly two hundred ships stood side by side in progressive stages of dissection.'[20]

Previously ships were dismantled using cranes and heavy equipment located in large-scale shipyards in North America and Europe. Now, though, regulation and much higher pay in the global North has led to this industry being offshored away from formal shipyards, to these beaches in India, Bangladesh and Pakistan. Local entrepreneurs realised that ships could be more or less entirely dismantled by hand. There was no need for expensive docks because many men living on or below the poverty line would work for a dollar or two a day. The ships were just beached and then swarms of poor workers began their dis-assembly.

---

[20] William Langewiesche, *The Outlaw Sea* (London: Granta, 2004), p. 201.

These workers at Alang recycle approximately half the ships salvaged each year around the world. Large supertankers, car ferries, container ships and some ocean liners are beached during high tide. As the tide recedes, hundreds of manual labourers begin dismantling each ship, salvaging what they can while reducing the rest to scrap. Thousands of local men are now expert in this large-scale scavenging. There are 40,000 workers, with millions of tons of steel being recovered and used locally. Such work is immensely dangerous, since ships contain many toxic and hazardous materials. The workforces are subject to often brutal regimes in order to get the dead ship stripped down as fast as possible, thus enabling each stretch of beach to be occupied by another vast ship. In Chittagong at least one worker dies each week – workers often work barefoot and wear no protective clothing.[21]

The EU has recently proposed that ships registered in Europe should be broken up only in licensed yards meeting strict environmental guidelines. Toxic materials would have to be removed from the ships before being sent for recycling. However, there is much opposition to these new rules within Asian countries, which have come to rely upon this work and the recycled materials for their rapidly growing manufacturing industry. Also better regulation, as Greenpeace and others have especially campaigned for, would mean that some ships would not be dismantled at all but would mysteriously sink in the middle of the ocean out of sight. Further, most ships are not in fact registered in Europe but with various flag of convenience registries. Thus the outlaw sea makes it hard to bring onshore what has powerfully escaped offshore.

Another aspect of offshoring is how the developing country where a waste activity occurs often becomes dependent upon the waste arriving from the developed world. For example, there are 160,000 waste collectors in Beijing who recycle huge amounts of plastic sheeting, office printouts, bottles, radiators and scraps of cardboard.[22] Indeed, China is the largest importer of the world's

---

[21] See John Vidal, 'Bangladesh's gigantic graveyard for ships, where workers risk their lives for scrap', *The Observer*, 6 May 2012.
[22] Tania Branigan, 'From east to west, a chain collapses', www.guardian.co.uk/environment/2009/jan/09/recycling-global-recession-china (accessed 14.9.2012).

waste materials, importing a third of Britain's recyclables, for example.[23] But the economic collapse of 2008 led to a loss of consumer demand in the West for many products of recycling. As a result, the Chinese recycling industry was severely damaged by collapsing demand, and four-fifths of China's recycling units closing during this period. This in turn left the UK, the US and others grappling with growing volumes of waste, with nowhere now to send it. Each link in the chain disintegrated, from factories to scrapyards to collectors.

A newer kind of waste has recently become especially important. Up to around 1990 two kinds of objects provided the background to human life – the natural world of plants and animals and the industrial world of manufactured objects. But from around 1990 a third background to life emerged, of 'virtual' or 'digital' objects, including screens, cables, smartphones, batteries, satellites, tablets, social media, sensors, routers, software, networks and so on.[24] These digital objects came into the background of human experience and transformed how life is mundanely experienced minute by minute, day to day. This became true around the world, albeit with many inequalities in the distribution of digital access and power.

One distinct feature of what once was called a 'weightless' world is that digital connections are actually only possible because of very material bases – of computer products made up of metals, especially aluminium, plastics, rare earth metals, wiring, cables, glass, and so on. Digital objects are built of some distinct and dangerous materials. When they go out of fashion, these dead machines are then dumped in landfill sites and incinerators. But their disposal is increasingly offshored, as 'Western' societies have become aware of the dangerous materials embedded within e-waste and hence prevented dumping within their own territories. Particularly significant in the new world order are places that concentrate upon the disposal and dis-assembling of these dangerous materials.

---

[23] This might be characterised as 'high carbon recycling'.
[24] See Nigel Thrift and Sean French, 'The automatic production of space', *Transactions of the Institute of British Geographers*, new series, 29 (2002): 309–35.

Guiyu on the coast of the South China Sea is the 'e-waste capital of the world'.[25] Something like four-fifths of computer waste from the US and much from elsewhere is exported to this one small location in China. Many materials ending up here began their journey in the rich North when handed in to be 'recycled'. Recyclers often charge a fee for recycling and get a tax break for being 'green'; they then double their money by selling materials to the Chinese, with the e-waste eventually arriving in Guiyu. The Chinese workers subject the waste to a breakdown or scavenging of the digital waste. The owner who dropped off the dead computer at their 'recyclers' thousands of miles away knows nothing of this. The exporting of e-waste is illegal from EU countries, though it is not from the US, which has not signed the Basel Convention.[26] Guiyu is also a major destination for unwanted parts and defective materials in new computers, as well as computers and parts returned for warranty repair to major manufacturers, such as Panasonic, Samsung and HP.[27]

Businesses in Guiyu earn over US$75 million a year from processing 1.5 million tons of e-waste. China officially bans its import but most authorities look the other way. Raw materials are in short supply, with Chinese factories clamouring for these materials from scavenging. Guiyu's entire economy is centred on this 'dis-assembling' industry, initially generated by the disposal of computers in the rich North but also now from China and the rest of the developing world. It is said that the US throws away about 30,000 computers each day, while an astonishing 100 million cellular phones are 'wasted' across Europe every year.[28] Yet by 2016 the number of unwanted computers from developing countries will exceed those from the developed world.[29]

---

[25] See 'Electronic waste dump of the world: Guiyu, China', http://sometimes-interesting.com/2011/07/17/electronic-waste-dump-of -the-world/ and 'Where does e-waste end up?', www.greenpeace.org/international/en/campaigns/toxics/electronics/the-e-waste-problem/where-does-e-waste-end-up/ (accessed 12.9.2012) for the next few paragraphs.

[26] Secretariat of the Basel Convention, *Vital Waste Graphics 3*.

[27] See the blog of the Shanghai Scrap.

[28] See Wikipedia entry on Electronic Waste (13.9.2012).

[29] Secretariat of the Basel Convention, *Vital Waste Graphics 3*, p. 9.

Some 150,000 workers in Guiyu toil through sixteen-hour days dis-assembling old computers, printers and phones, recapturing metals and parts to be reused or sold. Within thousands of small workshops, labourers cut cables, pry chips from circuit boards, grind plastic computer cases into particles, and dip circuit boards in acid baths to dissolve the lead, cadmium and other metals. Thousands more strip insulation from wire so as to salvage tiny amounts of copper. The air in Guiyu reeks of burning plastic and toxic metals. Workers burn circuit boards and components over coal fires so as to melt the lead solder and separate out the various metals. Noxious gases are released into the air and toxic materials seep into the ground. Workers use bare hands for an intricate dis-assembly of parts. The higher than average wage keeps people working in Guiyu, since these dis-assemblers earn almost five times what they would get as peasant farmers. Some workers move to Guiyu to earn what are viewed as high wages.

The environmental and health effects are highly damaging. The air is not safe to breathe. The water cannot be drunk, as excess printer toner is swept from the streets into the river. Drinking water is trucked in. Over ten heavy (and some poisonous) metals are everywhere, including lead, mercury, tin, aluminium and cadmium. The residents are only partially aware of negative health effects. Guiyu has the highest level of cancer-causing dioxins in the world; pregnancies are six times more likely to end in miscarriage, and seven out of ten children are born with levels of lead in their blood 50 per cent higher than children elsewhere. Guiyu is cited as the second most polluted location in the world. Thus the waste of digital worlds ends up in places which in their appearance and design are the exact opposite of shiny Apple retail stores. But they are both key nodes in the digital worlds that have developed so extensively since 1990.

There are many reasons why there is so much digital waste, including the speed of technical innovation, the effect of Moore's law and built-in planned obsolescence. Key is the ability of 'digital capital' to invent new applications for computer hardware that users never knew they needed and which can only be run on new machines, not the old. There is also the power of advertising to convince consumers that existing machines should be for the scrapheap after just a few years, although almost all machines are under-employed.

Moreover, we may have seen nothing yet with such e-wasting because of the astonishing scale of dead machines that 4G promises to deliver over the next few years. 4G will enable up to 100Mbps for users on the move. It will displace not only 3G but also much fixed-line broadband. And this means that almost all existing hardware will be obsolete, since existing sets cannot run on 4G and many will get thrown out. 4G could involve the replacement of all hardware, including the 5 billion mobile phones now working around the world.[30] Guiyu and other centres of e-waste, especially in India and Ghana, will have much future business – with every cloud having an 'aluminium' lining, we might wonder.

Moving emissions

Another major source of offshored 'waste' also depends upon movement across the oceans. Chapter 3 documented the offshoring of manufacturing from major production centres in the US and Western Europe to Mexico, China, India, Vietnam and other developing countries. These offshore sites offered low-income labour for assembly-line work as well as supplies of cheap local energy, mostly coal. Mass production by poorly paid and generally unskilled labourers in the global South was directly linked with mass consumerism and consumer fantasies in the global North. This linking was brought about through the slow but steady movement of very large numbers of container ships. We saw in chapter 3 how the cargo container was key in the wider socio-technical system shaped by global production, consumption, provision, investment, inequality and wealth. The oceans came to be organised around vast container ships, massive ports and exceptional flows of global trade.

This containerised transport of goods manufactured offshore also brings about the worldwide redistribution of CO_2 emissions. For example, Britain claims to have reduced its emissions by about

---

[30]I am grateful for analyses of 4G futures provided by Michael Hulme at Lancaster; and see Lucy Siegle, 'What is the lifespan of a laptop?', www.guardian.co.uk/environment/2013/jan/13/lifespan-laptop-pc -planned-obsolescence?INTCMP=SRCH (accessed 16.1.2013).

18 per cent since 1990. The Department for Energy and Climate
Change (DECC) maintains that emissions of goods manufactured
in China and exported to Britain should count as China's emissions and not Britain's. However, this is increasingly disputed, and
some commentators now argue for 'consumption-based emissions
reporting' rather than what is normally used, 'production-based
emissions reporting'.[31] Once imports, exports and international
transport are taken into account, UK emissions actually increased
by 20 per cent over this period. In 2004, 30 per cent of global
consumption-based emissions were generated by manufactured
goods imported into developed countries from other societies.[32]

I discussed in chapter 5 the extraordinary rise of Dubai as a
centre for high-carbon consumption of services. It has a world-
beating carbon footprint based on cheap energy and government-
subsidised electricity. And yet in some ways many of those
emissions ought to be recorded in the societies from which all
those passengers and property owners arrived and to which they
returned.[33]

This international trade of goods and services reverses the trend
of apparently decreasing emissions generated within developed
countries. CO_2 emissions from consuming goods and services
manufactured elsewhere are under-counted. When net embodied
carbon imports to developed countries are taken into account,
emissions increased in those countries from 400 million tons in
1990 to 1.6 billion tons in 2008, a faster growth than the global
economy or of global carbon emissions in general.[34] Also, if production and transportation of objects are factored in, then emissions from 'stuff' considerably dwarf other sources of greenhouse
gases.[35] Offshored emissions are swept under the carpet.

---

[31] Mike Berners-Lee and Duncan Clark, *The Burning Question* (London:
Profile, 2013), chap. 6.
[32] Stephen Davis and Ken Caldeira, 'Consumption-based accounting of
CO_2 emissions', *Proceedings of the National Academy of Sciences*, 107
(2010): 5687–92.
[33] See Jim Krane, *City of Gold* (London: Picador, 2010), chap. 13.
[34] 'The cost of trade', www.economist.com/blogs/dailychart/2011/04/
greenhouse_gases (accessed 5.19.2012).
[35] David MacKay, *Sustainable Energy – Without the Hot Air* (Cambridge:
UIT, 2008), p. 94; available at www.withouthotair.com.

These 'offshored emissions' were a significant issue at COP15, the 2009 Copenhagen Climate Change Conference. The shift in high-carbon-intensive production to China, India and other manufacturing hubs allowed high-consumption countries to claim they have reduced their greenhouse gas emissions and can criticise developing countries for not meeting their targets. Countries in the South were placed in a difficult situation, to commit to stringent emissions reductions while continuing to produce goods to satisfy consumers in the rich North. The real problem emerges when lobbying to make targets legally binding under Kyoto and international protocols results in countries in the global South facing financial penalties that fundamentally stem from the rich North's consumption of goods manufactured offshore.

Just before the COP15 event in 2009, the author of the *Stern Review*, Nicholas Stern, made a dramatic break from British government policy, arguing that Britain should compromise and meet developing countries halfway through recognising the scale of the export and import of emissions occurring between different countries.[36] This was an interesting move to recognise and deal with how emissions have been significantly offshored.

Conclusion

This chapter examined some processes generating an astonishing production and movement of waste products across the world. This 'waste-making' was anticipated over fifty years ago but has grown dramatically since then. Especially significant is the designed obsolescence of products, peoples and places. These are all reimagined and rebuilt. An industrial scale of planned obsolescence characterises the neo-liberal world. Much waste is generated, and one problem for the world economy is how to organise its disposal over time and across space.

Once some waste was seen as useful. Now even the waste which can be recycled is often secretly moved offshore. Vast container ships of waste patrol the world's seaways and deposit their often

---

[36] See George Monbiot: 'Stern proposes radical break with British government policy', www.youtube.com/watch?v=wm6teQ4eLhM&feature=youtube_gdata_player (accessed 9.2.2012).

toxic materials in some extraordinarily dangerous centres of waste. Certain societies and places are specialists at dealing with these wastes, including ships themselves and bright shiny digital objects. Some of the time, waste is recycled into different products that are returned to centres of capitalist consumption. But often it is just wasted away, though in places very distant from where it appeared to originate. And its toxic consequences are often offshored to those whose rights to good health are deemed less significant than the rights of those people generating that waste.

One way of documenting this travelling waste deploys ubiquitous computing and will itself generate e-waste. In 2008, Greenpeace investigated electronic waste exporting, which is legal in the US but outlawed in most countries. Greenpeace embedded GPS sensors into TV sets that were broken beyond repair and took them to a recycling centre in the UK. Despite legislation banning the movement of e-waste, many of the defunct TVs were tracked through GPS to Nigeria, where they had been illegally dumped.[37]

---

[37] See 'Urban digestive systems', http://senseable.mit.edu/papers/pdf/2011_Offenhuber_et_al_Urban_digestive_Sentient_City.pdf (accessed 28.12.2012), p. 4.

8

Security Offshored

Security at a distance

This chapter is concerned with secret worlds, many of which overlap with and help to sustain other secret worlds. Secrets are all about closure and exposure, hiding and revealing, the covert and the overt. Implicated in security are multiple worlds moving in and out of visibility, including those of states, corporations, violent and peaceful oppositional groups, researchers, journalists, and so on. There are complex connections between each of these, often stretching across national borders and involving multiple efforts to keep secrets from 'enemies' and to win over 'friends'. How this distinction between friends and enemies is drawn has many implications for the nature and consequences of secrets and, in particular, for what gets offshored and what remains onshore.

Writing in the 1920s Weimar Republic in Germany, Carl Schmitt distinguished between friend and enemy. This distinction has animated much contemporary political thought and politics, with escalating citations and references to Schmitt's antithesis between 'friend' and 'enemy'. He viewed the political as primordial, coming before the state and its mundane policies. Schmitt argues that 'The distinction of friend and enemy denotes the utmost degree of intensity of a union or separation . . . the other, the stranger . . . is, in a specially intense way, existentially something different and alien.'[1] The justification for wars does not, he says, reside in their being fought for ideals or justice or economic prosperity, but in preserving the very existence of the primordial polity. Each political entity and its war-making properties presuppose the existence of real enemies.

Schmitt's argument was directed against a false universalism, which obscured the existential nature of politics and replaced it with the struggle for formal rights. He maintains that a world state embracing the entire globe and all humanity could not exist. The political world is a pluriverse, not a universe. Schmitt holds that commitment to politics is not rational and calculative, but 'primordial'.

This argument can of course be used to justify some extraordinarily discriminatory and violent treatments of those deemed to be one's enemies – Schmitt being himself notorious for his pro-Nazi anti-Semitism during the mid-1930s. His work has been used to justify policies where the 'ends justify the means', where those means involve surveillance, torture, murder and extermination of those deemed to be one's enemies. There is also the danger that the number of one's real friends shrinks and those of one's enemies grow, as is common in many post-revolutionary situations. And Schmitt omits to consider the danger that violence can get built into societies so that both friends and enemies are caught up in sets of violent relationships, so reinforcing the primordial antagonism of friend and enemy which might otherwise dissipate. In addition, in the contemporary world there are examples of 'truth and reconciliation' where enemies can be 'rebooted' as friends, often through systematically forgetting what had previously animated the primordial antagonism. Post-apartheid South Africa shows that enemies and friends can find common purpose, with unexpected new friends arising from those who were once one's bitterest enemies.

For all these critical points, the global flows of people have made the determination of who are friends and enemies especially troublesome. Those movements across borders intensify the fear that one does not really know who are one's friends and who will remain as friends. And who is a friend as such, since in a more

---

[1] Carl Schmitt, *The Concept of the Political* (Chicago: University of Chicago Press, [1927] 1996), pp. 26–7.

mobile world there are countless semi-friends with multiple attach-
ments and loyalties – here today, gone tomorrow, back the day
after? Are they still a friend and, if so, how do the members of a
society know this?

These systemic uncertainties are part of the context for how the
contemporary world has seen large increases in the range, scale
and reach of 'security', such that many now talk of 'security states'
and 'security capital'. Determining friend and enemy is big business for corporations, and 'security' is one of the largest areas of
corporate and research activity, especially involving new forms of
cyber-surveillance.[2] As more people, objects and information are
moving physically and virtually, so it is no simple matter to determine who is and who remains a friend. Much contemporary politics rests upon the simplifying stereotypes of them and us, of foe
or friend. Much military training also employs Hollywood techniques of mediatised and virtual images to emphasise just who the
'bad guys' are – those who are not to be trusted and whose lives
often count for (much) less.[3]

In the last century, national states developed extensive security
services as they sought to determine who their friends were and
thus who were their enemies. This was crucial both during actual
wars and during conflicts often characterised as 'wars', such as
the Cold War from the 1950s to the 1980s. The real and fictional
exploits of multiple spies were of course central to much popular
culture, especially during this Cold War between the West and the
Soviet Union.

Determining who was a friend turned out to be immensely difficult, particularly as each 'side' developed increasing expertise,
both in the surveillance of others and in being able to conceal their
own espionage practices. Secret photographs or written-down
information were key in the pre-digital world. Especially important were those agents who travelled elsewhere and used their

---

[2] See documentation in Stephen Graham, *Cities under Siege* (London:
Verso, 2011). In Britain, 'security' has engendered many new research
projects and centres at a time when most areas of research are under-
funded. See the latest revelations about the US's National Security
Agency, www.guardian.co.uk/world/nsa (accessed 26.6.2013).
[3] See James der Derian, *Virtuous War: Mapping the Military–Industrial
–Media–Entertainment Network* (London: Routledge, 2009).

'eyes' to see for themselves the situation and especially to determine who was still a friend.

Much effort was involved in establishing and sustaining secret agents, as well as to turn the enemy's agents into double agents, or to turn double agents into 'triple' agents.[4] And in this period the security services were themselves often 'secret', with maps failing to register the location of buildings and large areas that housed these secret services and their experiments in surveillance and weaponry. It was often impossible even for elected members of parliaments to question and challenge the behaviour of the agents of their own state, since the various security sites did not officially exist.

Paglen writes of the continuing distinction between 'white' and 'black' worlds, the latter including the enormous range of security work carried out secretly. He writes: 'The black-world consists of massive landscapes, corporations and privately-held firms, workers sworn to lifelong secrecy . . . It is a landscape produced through secrecy and compartmentalisation. And much of this world . . . is hidden behind remote desert mountains', such as the Nellis Range Complex in Nevada, said to be the world's largest single piece of real estate.[5] It is clear that, in all states, very many people and organisations are formally or informally members of such secret worlds.

On occasions these secret services even spy on their own rulers, as was the case with Prime Minister Harold Wilson, who was deemed 'not one of us' during 1960s Britain. Porter summarises how, in this period, 'Government secrecy . . . blanketed vast areas of British public life for most of the last century, upheld by a fierce and undiscriminating Official Secrets Act . . . the rest of us weren't even told what was being kept secret.'[6] Similar processes have been found in almost all societies, with some collecting extensive paper files not only about foreigners thought to be the enemy but also

---

[4]This is the theme of the 2012 movie set in 1990s Belfast entitled *Shadow Dancer*.
[5]Trevor Paglen, 'Groom Lake and the imperial production of nowhere', in Derek Gregory and Allan Pred (eds), *Violent Geographies* (London: Routledge, 2007).
[6]Bernard Porter, book review, www.guardian.co.uk/books/2013/jan/10/ classified-secrecy-state-christopher-moran-review (accessed 16.1.2013).

about many of their own citizens also viewed with systematic suspicion (as by the Stasi in East Germany or the KGB in the USSR).

The security services often ran agents who were elsewhere, offshore, and with whom complex communications were sustained often involving elaborate codes. These offshore (and sometimes 'sleeping') agents were especially troublesome, since it was often difficult to know if they remained an asset or had been 'turned' by the overseas state. This led to many efforts by security services to crack the communication systems of the enemy so as to determine if that agent was now an enemy. If they had been turned then they became particularly dangerous double agents. Such secret service agents were 'masters' at establishing and maintaining secrets through fraudulent documentation, appearances, and lying on an industrial scale. Theirs was a world of secrets, with aliases, alibis, lives, and documentation to keep those secrets from exposure. In pre-digital days this almost always involved more travel and direct observation and questioning, or indeed torturing, of agents, even by their own side. Some assets were dispensed with in order to sustain the larger secret or to access the highly valued secrets of others.

Security is thus a set of state and corporate activities organised around discovering, revealing, selling and exchanging secrets. These secrets pertain to individuals, other states, corporations, and oppositional groups, both legal and illegal. Many lives are subordinated to secrets, or to certain classes of secret, including agents deliberately forming long-term relationships with the 'enemy' so as to conceal their real interests.[7]

This chapter explores various aspects of these complexities of contemporary security at a distance, and in particular how some of this security work has been and is offshored. First, I deal with the fighting of wars elsewhere, offshore from a society's core territory, made more likely especially by rapidly miniaturising drone technology. Second, there is the offshoring of torture through the concept of 'extraordinary rendition'. Third, I examine a general

---

[7]See Rob Evans, 'Undercover spy allegations cast campaigner verdict in doubt', www.theguardian.com/uk-news/2013/aug/01/undercover-spy -environmental-campaigner-verdict (accessed 5.8.2013), on infiltration into environmental campaign groups.

offshoring of surveillance with the growth of large security companies that hide some secrets while revealing others. Much money can be made in both; indeed, the greater the secrecy, the more money that can be made through what we might call the digital book of revelations. In the twenty-first century, what is crucial is not so much the informational economy as the 'secrecy economy' and its deployment of big data.

Fighting offshore

There are many ways in which states fight wars 'offshore', and indeed have done so for centuries. Imperial wars were typically conducted elsewhere, on or close to the territory that the imperial power was seeking to annex, exploit or subjugate. Imperial powers mostly fought wars not at home but offshore, and often out at sea, with powerful navies being key to their success.

This fighting and military occupation involved the transport of, and fighting by, very many young men, mostly from poor, rural or working-class families. They mainly fought wars elsewhere for colonial powers. Such imperial powers also persuaded men from dominated territories to fight for them, even though these forces were often poorly treated by the colonial power.[8]

When wars were predominantly army-based, very large numbers of men were deployed in action and many ended up dead. Their bodies were placed in mass or individual graves or returned in secret. Such large armies were generally slow in their rate of progress. Armies moved, but they often moved painfully slowly and relied upon supply chains that were lengthy and often difficult to sustain, especially because of the vast amounts of food and water required (an army marches on its 'stomach', according to Napoleon).

Armies typically experienced factory-scale killing fields. The most notorious of these was during the First World War, when 8.5 million men were killed in just four years. Overall an unbelievable

---

[8] See 'Lumley is target of "Gurkha town" Facebook hate campaign', www.dailymail.co.uk/news/article-2038377/Joanna-Lumley-target -Gurkha-town-Facebook-hate-campaign.html (accessed 19.1.2013), on the treatment of Gurkhas in Britain.

37 million men were injured, taken prisoner, killed, or simply disappeared during this relatively short war fought by young men mostly on European or Russian soil.[9]

This pattern changed somewhat with air power, which transformed twentieth-century military mobility. The first airflight was made at Kill Devil Hills, North Carolina, in 1903 by the Wright brothers.[10] Flying machines enabled a new realm of air power to develop, including aircraft that were able to bomb from the air while moving rapidly over the airspace of other countries. Although aircraft played a role in the First World War, it was a few decades later that air power radically changed warfare and the ability of nation-states to fight elsewhere. Especially significant was the way that air power changed perspective.

Beginning with the hot-air balloon, Kaplan describes how the cosmic view enabled by air power developed.[11] Nature was seen from above as a separate vast space. Distant objects appeared with clarity. This cosmic view entailed a mastering of the world and was drawn upon for waging war from above, as fighters, helicopters, bombs and missiles appeared out of the sky, blitzing the poor enemy stuck on the ground.

This has been part of the more general process by which the environment above the earth has become militarised and contested by many different kinds of flying machines. There has been a belief that the air above one's national territory is a kind of national airspace. US citizens especially believed that the air over their land was 'theirs', while the air above many other territories was often made 'American' and not seen as similarly legitimately possessed by other countries.

In particular, Kaplan brings out the importance of Major De Seversky's 1942 *Victory through Air Power*, which was instrumental in the US developing unified, strategic air power to prevent other nations from entering or contesting US airspace.[12] Air power

---

[9] 'WWI casualty and death tables', www.pbs.org/greatwar/resources/casdeath_pop.html (accessed 1.9.2013).

[10] See here Saolo Cwerner, Sven Kesselring and John Urry (eds), *Aeromobilities* (London: Routledge, 2009).

[11] Caren Kaplan, 'Mobility and war: the cosmic view of US "air power"', *Environment and Planning A*, 38 (2006): 395–407.

[12] See ibid., pp. 399–403.

came to be central to US domination during the second half of the twentieth century. It enabled the country to intimidate the rest of the world from entering its own airspace (not breached until September 2001), while making it possible for US air power from hundreds of bases to develop swift aerial warfare to move rapidly into the airspace of others. The superiority of air power, especially in offshoring relationships, was highly fateful for the trajectory of the last century. During the Cold War the US managed to ensure that, had there been a major war with the Soviet Union, that theatre of war would be offshored to Europe and not within the US.

And the new century has seen further development of aerial warfare. First, the US's 'Revolution in Military Affairs' involved developing a 'network-centric' use of new technology, with fast-moving troops, extensive air power and the widespread deployment of satellites to enable effective real-time communications. These were all designed to enable the much faster speed of troop movement. Satellites were key to the systems of surveillance from afar, although their accuracy in the backstreets of Baghdad turned out to be imperfect, leading to many bloody errors. The satellite images were often inaccurate, but overall the RMA was effective at fighting wars offshore and hence in reducing American fatalities.

More recently a different kind of seeing at a distance was developed through the growth of what the defence industry termed unmanned aerial vehicles (UAVs) or remotely piloted air systems (RPAS). There are thought to be some 10,000 such drones in service, as they have swept the global arms market, being the very big new thing. There are around 1,000 armed drones, while the rest are used in search and rescue, reconnaissance and surveillance. These thousands of drones are now flying tens of thousands of missions.[13]

Under pressure from the arms industry, Barack Obama and most other world leaders have been persuaded that drones represent the war of the future, a war that is safe, easy, clean and

---

[13] See documentation in 'Drones by country: who has all the UAVs?', www.guardian.co.uk/news/datablog/2012/aug/03/drone-stocks-by -country (accessed 23.1.2013).

involves 'precision targeting'.[14] No one on one's own side, one's 'friends', need get hurt, since it is said that drones keep 'boots off the ground'. These smart and increasingly small mobile machines use many technologies initially developed for use in laptops and smartphones.

Drones do the dirty work of surveillance and killing at a distance. They are normally operated by 'desk pilots' based in their 'home' territory and often dressed in 'flight suits'. Indeed, such drone pilots normally live close to their homes and loved ones. These 'pilots', brought up on a childhood of video games and screened efforts to kill as many 'enemies' as possible, can surveil and kill for real and then return home for a refreshing beer.[15]

Drones thus offshore the human consequences of killing in what has been called a 'post-heroic' age. Drones make war invisible for some, and hence make it easier to kill, since enemies are physically and ethically distant and screened – similar to how enemies appear on video games. The face of the enemy is screened and distant, so no responsibility need be felt for his or her gory death.

The location of drone bases is often secret, increasing the lack of accountability of contemporary warfare. In February 2013 it was revealed that the US had been using a drone base in Saudi Arabia for assassinating al-Qaeda leaders in Yemen. This base was kept secret for two years, although it was known to the US press, which accepted informal censorship by the Obama administration.[16] The British Ministry of Defence has recently admitted that armed Reaper drones are flying within Afghanistan but remotely operated from RAF Wallington in Lincolnshire.[17]

Drones, together with unaccountable 'special forces', make war easier to initiate. Wars do not literally have to be declared upon

---

[14]See Simon Jenkins, 'Drones are fool's gold: they prolong wars we can't win', www.guardian.co.uk/commentisfree/2013/jan/10/drones-fools -gold-prolong-wars (accessed 19.1.2013); and Nick Turse, *The Changing Face of Empire* (Chicago: Haymarket, 2012), on the following.

[15]See 'Attack of the drones', www.aljazeera.com/programmes/people andpower/2012/07/201271872041648814.html (accessed 21.1.2013); Turse, *The Changing Face of Empire*, pp. 24–6.

[16]'CIA operating drone base in Saudi Arabia, US media reveal', www .bbc.co.uk/news/world-middle-east-21350437 (accessed 8.2.2013).

[17]'Armed drones operated from RAF base in UK, says MOD', www .bbc.co.uk/news/uk-england-lincolnshire-22320275 (accessed 9.3.2013).

specific enemies. Drone and special operations attacks on foreigners are 'warlike', but neither the enemy nor one's own side may have declared war. There is no mutually recognised 'enemy', and yet drones search out and destroy many apparent 'enemies'.

Civilian deaths from drone strikes are often described by military spokespersons as 'collateral damage'. But it has been calculated that the world's drones have killed more non-combatant civilians than died in the 'terror' attacks of 11 September. Moreover, ever more drones in the world almost certainly mean more wars, as well as unaccountable offshore killings of 'enemy' combatants and especially civilians.[18] Drones are normally illegal in the territories within which they operate, partly because of their killing of civilians and children.

However, drones can be counterproductive. The journalist Simon Jenkins describes drones as fool's gold. In Afghanistan, which has been the test-bed for US drone or UAV technology since about 2008, there has been no decline in Taliban or al-Qaeda activity resulting from deploying drones. The Afghan president, Hamid Karzai, characterised drone attacks as 'in no way justifiable'. The Pakistan government, at whose people the drones are increasingly directed, has withdrawn permission for their use, while Yemenis face al-Qaeda recruiters waving pictures of drone-killed women and children. Membership of al-Qaeda in Yemen is thought to have grown threefold since around 2009. Overall former US President Jimmy Carter declared that America's violation of international human rights through widespread drone use greatly aids the US's enemies and alienates its friends.[19]

Drones are cheap and rapidly spreading. Chris Anderson, from *Wired* magazine, talks of how there will be $200 drones in the near future.[20] Already at least forty-five states deploy them, including Iran. The US is selling drones to Japan for potential use in their escalating conflict with China. China is building drone bases

---

[18] See Zygmunt Bauman, 'On never being alone again', www.social-europe.eu/2011/06/on-never-being-alone-again/ (accessed 21.1.2013).

[19] See for documentation, Simon Jenkins, 'Drones are fool's gold'. A drone attack on an Islamic school and the death of a particular young boy is the key event in the TV series *Homeland*, a series said to be regularly watched in the Obama White House.

[20] 'Attack of the drones'.

along its coast. The Pentagon is now training more drone opera-
tors than pilots. Bumiller and Shanker point to the 'sheer size,
variety and audaciousness of a rapidly expanding drone universe'.[21] For example, nearly 19,000 4-pound 'Ravens' are already
used by at least eighteen countries. These appear more like toy
planes than weapons of war.[22]

Indeed, drones are getting smaller, and some are even designed
to mimic the flight characteristics of insects such as hawk moths.
These micro-drones or spy flies have come in from the pages of
science fiction and are getting up close and personal, even being
able to land on a window sill. Drones will also increasingly be
able to swarm. The surveillance drones now generate vast amounts
of data, as they can move in and through many environments
without being observed or attacked. Automatically operating
algorithms interpret this data, so in theory separating friend from
enemy, but in practice making many mistakes. There is too much
big data. These micro-drones can surveil enemies in foreign deserts
but also increasingly domestically. They are part of a new military
urbanism, with cities being regarded as 'under siege'.[23]

Bridle thus summarises how drones

> are just the latest in a long line of military technologies augmenting
> the process of death-dealing, but they are among the most efficient,
> the most distancing, the most invisible. These qualities allow them
> to do what they do unseen, and create the context for secret, unac-
> countable, endless wars. Whether you think these killings are
> immoral or not, most of them are by any international standard
> illegal.[24]

---

[21] See Elisabeth Bumiller and Thom Shanker, 'War evolves with drones,
some tiny as bugs', www.nytimes.com/2011/06/20/world/20drones.
html? (accessed 11.10.2013), on the following.
[22] See http://en.wikipedia.org/wiki/AeroVironment_RQ-11_Raven (accessed
21.1.2013).
[23] Graham, *Cities under Siege*, p. 174, on the sci-fi breeding of insects with
electronics embedded inside them, so enabling them to be controlled!
[24] See James Bridle, 'Dronestagram: the locations behind America's secret
drone war', www.newstatesman.com/politics/2012/11/dronestagram
-locations-behind-americas-secret-drone-war (accessed 21.1.2013), as
well as the web resources known as Dronestagram and TomDispatch.com.

We might say that the drone genie has been let out of the bottle. What will happen when every country possesses thousands of drones and each border is buzzing with them? Jenkins indeed argues that the greatest threat to world peace is not now from nuclear weapons but from the exceedingly rapid proliferation of drone warfare, which cannot be easily reined in or put into reverse.[25] To some degree even guided missiles were regulated by international law and protocol. But drones are ungoverned by law or protocol and their use is mostly illegal. Their proliferation constitutes a major threat to world peace, as they are so far the ultimate in offshored warfare. However, the possibility for the future is of armed robots that kill 'automatically' without any human decision or piloting. This would be the literal outsourcing of killing to machines and their software.[26]

We have noted that, within the US, drones developed alongside the growth of 'special ops' following the formation of SOCOM (US Special Operations Command) in 1987. It is thought that US secret operations occur each day in around seventy countries engaging an astonishing 60,000 personnel. These ops entail illegal killing, assassinations, kidnapping, training and surveillance. They are mostly conducted in secret and involve an almost industrial-scale counter-terrorism killing machine.[27]

The most striking example of the operation of this machine was in 'assassinating' bin Laden and his family members in a compound in Abbottabad in Pakistan in 2011.[28] Operation Neptune Spear was conducted by Navy SEALs of the Naval Special Warfare Development Group. This killing by special ops forces was contrary to US, Pakistan and international law. And yet no one has been charged with any offence. More generally, US Admiral Olson says that the military's secret military wants 'to get back into the

---

[25] See Jenkins, 'Drones are fool's gold'; Turse, *The Changing Face of Empire*.
[26] Charli Carpenter, 'How scared are people of "killer robots" and why does it matter?', www.opendemocracy.net/charli-carpenter/how-scared-are-people-of-%E2%80%9Ckiller-robots%E2%80%9D-and-why-does-it-matter (accessed 5.7.2013).
[27] Turse, *The Changing Face of Empire*, p. 13.
[28] For detail, see http://en.wikipedia.org/wiki/Death_of_Osama_bin_Laden#Objective (accessed 30.1.2013).

shadows and do what they came to do', without visibility, responsibility and legality.[29] Special operations and drone wars are mostly offshore, lurking in some very murky shadows.

Torturing offshore

One particularly significant activity of many militaries is extracting secrets from the enemy without the enemy, or indeed the military's 'friends', knowing what they are up to, why, and where the extracting of information occurs. Such torturing is mostly secret, with all forces trying to keep it well hidden from view.

Torture is prohibited by the United Nations Convention Against Torture (UNCAT), a convention ratified by 147 countries. National and international legal prohibitions on torturing suspects or third parties derive from the view that torture is illegal, immoral and impractical. But torture is in fact found in almost all societies, either onshore or offshore. Organisations monitoring abuses of human rights report the widespread use of torture, which is condoned by many states even if they do not themselves employ torture. Amnesty International estimates that at least eighty-one states currently use torture, some openly but many secretly.[30]

Those who may be tortured often have an idea of what will be involved and, indeed, may be trained to resist the torturing or to kill themselves so as to take their secrets to the grave. Recently there has been an increasing tendency for torturing offshore, away from legal regulation which prohibits torturing suspects, and especially torturing those who have not as yet been charged with an offence. What developed since 2001 has been 'extraordinary rendition'.[31] This rendition is extralegal, outside the law, and involves the transfer of suspected terrorists to countries known to use torture or that employ harsh interrogation techniques amounting to torture. Those capturing the suspect, such as the US, release the

---

[29] Quoted in Turse, *The Changing Face of Empire*, p. 19.
[30] 'Human rights violations', www.humanrights.com/what-are-human-rights/violations-of-human-rights/article-3.html (accessed 4.2.2013).
[31] See www.extraordinaryrendition.org/ (accessed 4.2.2013). Normal rendition involves the relatively common transfer of persons from one jurisdiction to another.

prisoner into the custody of societies in which torture is known to be practised.

Many human rights groups and lawyers charge that extraordinary rendition violates Article 3 of UNCAT. The US outlaws torture on its own territory, and its constitution supposedly guarantees due process before the law. Extraordinary rendition circumvents the protections captives would enjoy if they were held within the US. Rendered suspects are denied due process, since they can be arrested without charge, deprived of legal counsel, and transferred to a country for the purpose of torture and other interrogation measures that are illegal in the US.

Many documents retrieved from the Libyan Foreign Ministry offices in Tripoli following the 2011 Libyan civil war show that the CIA and Britain's MI6 rendered suspects to Libya knowing they would be tortured and their secrets revealed. This was part of the process, even before the fall of Gaddafi, by which Libya had come in from the cold and was participating in the West's offshore torture programme, realised through the 'extraordinary rendition' of suspects. The term 'suspect' here often refers to those deemed hostile but where there is little direct evidence of 'wrongdoing', as was the case with many of those offshored to Guantánamo Bay detention camp in Cuba. Non-persons were also subject to extraordinary rendition to Egypt, Jordan, Morocco, Saudi Arabia and Uzbekistan.[32] It was recently reported that fifty-four governments were involved in the CIA's extraordinary rendition operations following 11 September.[33]

Those persons subject to extraordinary rendition are often classified as 'unlawful combatants', which means that they are not protected by relevant Geneva conventions. Supporters of torture declare that the protection of Article 3 in fact applies only to uniformed soldiers and guerrillas who wear distinctive insignia, openly bear arms and abide by the rules of war. Those who do not have such markers have 'chosen', it is said, to be outside these rules and conventions, while critics of torture note how the Taliban captured in Afghanistan neither enjoy the status of prisoner of

---

[32] Derek Gregory, 'Vanishing points', in Derek Gregory and Allan Pred (eds), *Violent Geographies* (London: Routledge, 2007), pp. 215–25.
[33] www.opensocietyfoundations.org/reports/globalizing-torture-cia-secret-detention-and-extraordinary-rendition (accessed 9.2.2013).

war, as defined by the Geneva Convention, nor have the status of persons charged with a crime, who possess some rights in most societies. It should also be noted how much of the security strategy in Iraq was outsourced to 20,000 private contractors – the 'coalition of the billing' – mostly opaque and unaccountable to public or military scrutiny.[34]

Many Taliban arrested in Afghanistan were taken to the notorious site of offshored torture, the Guantánamo Bay detention camp located in the US naval station at the isolated south-eastern end of Cuba. The US maintains *de facto* jurisdiction of this naval station but deems it to be 'foreign territory'. Within the camp many prisoners are non-citizens, reduced to what Agamben terms 'bare life' or life exposed to death.[35] Prisoners are subject to multiple forms of mental and bodily torture. Placed outside of the law, such prisoners are reduced to bare life in the eyes of judicial powers, or, as Gregory summarises, these are 'non-places for non-peoples'.[36] Holsinger describes how inmates in Guantánamo are treated almost as 'medieval men', barbaric, backward, stateless and needing to be imprisoned.[37]

Guantánamo Bay and similar detention camps exemplify 'the state of exception'.[38] In a state of exception, prisoners lose the ability to use their voice and to represent themselves. They are deprived of citizenship and agency, becoming non-persons. In such a context the hunger strike is a weapon of resistance to this bare life. The prisoners are threatened with and endure forced feeding so they do not actually die. Accusations and claims of forced feeding surfaced from 2005 onwards in Guantánamo – secrets in a mediatised world waiting to be discovered and sold.

In Abu Ghraib other secrets were revealed upon the world's media – the torturing and humiliation routinely practised at that

---

[34] Gregory, 'Vanishing points', pp. 224–5.
[35] Giorgio Agamben, *Homo Sacer: Sovereign Power and Bare Life* (Stanford, CA: Stanford University Press, 1998).
[36] Gregory, 'Vanishing points', p. 209; and see pp. 216–18 on the multiple forms of torture deployed in this non-place.
[37] Bruce Holsinger, *Neomedievalism, Neoconservatism and the War on Terror* (Chicago: Prickly Paradigm Press, 2007), p. iv.
[38] Giorgio Agamben, *State of Exception* (Chicago: University of Chicago Press, 2005); Gregory, 'Vanishing points'.

vanishing point. This theatre of cruelty was made possible by most prisoners being classified as 'security detainees' rather than as prisoners of war. They were thus not eligible for protection under the Geneva Convention. While the US has sought to demonstrate that this mediatised torture display was exceptional, subsequent evidence suggests that such torturing was more the rule and not so exceptional.[39]

Agamben argues that these camps demonstrate how the state of exception is now less the exception. The suspension of laws within a state of emergency or crisis can become a prolonged state of being and the rule. This book has shown how such offshored places are becoming much less the exception, a theme returned to in chapter 10.

Surveillance beyond borders

Central in many of these processes is how the state and corporatised security world are able both to create and to sustain new borders, both physical and digital. Within these borders many notions of public life, democracy and legality do not apply. For example, Paglen describes his visit to a military testing site, Groom Lake in Nevada: 'This is a place where the "normal" rules of society don't apply. It's a place where armed and camouflaged men in unmarked trucks have the right to kill you and prevent you from entering . . . "there's no one who can be held accountable, because the place doesn't officially exist. You might as well be on Mars".'[40]

This place is internal to the US but in effect located offshore, similar to the state of Delaware with regard to offshored financial flows. Groom Lake is a nowhere place which does not officially 'exist'. Inside the camp there is no legality or illegality, no legal designation, and no location upon government maps. It is a place of 'bare power' without connections to the rest of the US. It is also organised on the basis of an alternative geography, as there are different areas within it developed for testing different systems. These internal places include Terrortown, Korean airfield and US

---

[39] Gregory, 'Vanishing points', pp. 22–9.
[40] See Trevor Paglen, 'Groom Lake and the imperial production of nowhere', in Gregory and Pred (eds), *Violent Geographies*, p. 244, on this Kafkaesque situation.

border. Paglen describes this whole area as a place to test secrecy itself, to see how to operate outside the state's laws while located on US territory – to be offshore onshore.[41]

The securing of homeland security is troublesome for the US because of the vast flows of people and objects that move through American cities and regions. The science of logistics combined with containerisation is core to the just-in-time systems of the US economy. This logistic space is increasingly securitised.[42] The US tries to construct security as an 'away' game, producing its border as, in effect, offshore. This is intended to prevent security threats ever getting within US airspace, or upon American territory or close to the American shore, while still sustaining the logistics of flow. Security for the US is realised offshore. Admiral Keating summarises how the US national security state is 'working very hard ... so as to roll up the bad guys, capture or kill them and interrupt their attacks', long before they get anywhere near North America.[43]

This offshoring is made possible by powerful computer systems developed by private corporations and deployed within environments in the US and abroad. The integration of radio frequency identification (RFID) tags and/or GPS and/or biometric technologies located within mobiles, public transport smart cards, customer loyalty cards, credit cards, consumer goods and passports, internet use, mobile phone records, and so on, enables the movement of people and objects to be digitally recorded and monitored and the resulting patterns linked through computer algorithms. These are developed by companies routinely mining vast digital data streams and seeking to identify risky bodies, doubtful transactions and suspicious movements – or, indeed, non-movements. This digital surveillance can work in most places, offshore and onshore.

There is often mission creep. Systems developed for one purpose, such as the London congestion charging scheme, which uses automatic number plate recognition (ANPR), end up being used for another, such as law enforcement and broader 'security'. There seems to be a developing 'militarisation' of everyday life.

[41] Ibid., pp. 245–8.
[42] See Deborah Cowen, 'A geography of logistics: market authority and the security of supply chains', *Annals of the Association of American Geographers*, 100 (2010): 1–21.
[43] Quoted in Graham, *Cities under Siege*, p. 134.

Such technologies were rolled out in Iraq and Afghanistan, deploying what has been called the 'biometric automated toolkit'.[44] Key to digital systems are efforts to link together information from different databases, as also being developed in the vast Golden Shield programme within China.

A striking example of how US security is offshored is the Container Security Initiative (CSI) begun in 2002. This is designed to push out the US's borders, through the pre-screening of containers in special security zones in 'foreign' ports, before the containers and their contents are loaded onto ships and transported to the US. Each year about 108 million containers are moved through seaports around the world, transporting almost 90 per cent of the world's manufactured goods (see chapter 3 above). Fifty-eight foreign ports are part of the CSI, which seeks to minimise the security risk of the more than 10 million shipments before they arrive in the US.[45]

Air passengers are subjected to 'automated risk profiling'. This starts when would-be passengers initially book flights and before they are anywhere near their final destination. In the case of Britain's smart-border process, developed by American defence giant Raytheon, fifty-three pieces of information are automatically scanned in advance of any journey, so identifying what might be signs of risky or abnormal behaviour.[46] The algorithmic programme identifies hidden associations between people, groups, behaviours and transactions. Such 'algorithmic security', developed by vast private corporations, brings military force into close proximity to daily commuting or airport check-ins, and functions through an architecture based on the divide of friend and enemy. This is another form of security realised offshore, at least by the world's most powerful societies.[47]

---

[44] Ibid., pp. 125–8.
[45] Ibid., p. 135; 'CSI: Container Security Initiative', www.cbp.gov/xp/cgov/trade/cargo_security/csi/ (accessed 30.1.2013).
[46] Graham, *Cities under Siege*, p. 138.
[47] On this paragraph, see Louise Amoore, 'Algorithmic war: everyday geographies of the war on terror', *Antipode*, 41 (2009): 49–69, and 'Data derivatives: on the emergence of a security risk calculus for our times', *Theory, Culture and Society*, 28 (2011): 24–43.

Thus many subjects in powerful societies are treated as potential 'suspects' and subjected to various disciplinary technologies. Especially significant is what Amoore terms 'digitized dissection', the anatomical disaggregation of a person into various degrees of risk.[48] Much is rendered known, although those being digitally dissected normally have no idea that they are being so dissected by citizens from other countries. These citizens have the capacity to prevent travellers from getting to the place they seek to visit, even though they may possess appropriate ticketing and other documentation. Various persons are subject to individualised pre-emptive strikes, given the probabilities of their being a risk as revealed by data and software calculations.

During 2013 it was revealed that the scale, range and internationalisation of this digital dissection are in some societies far more extensive than official accounts suggested. Whistleblower Edward Snowden divulged the existence and functions of several classified US surveillance programmes and their extraordinary scope. These include the Prism surveillance programme, which draws data from Google, Facebook, Yahoo, Verizon and other major internet companies; XKeyscore, used for searching and analysing internet data about foreign nationals, run jointly with other agencies, including Australia's Defence Signals Directorate and New Zealand's Government Communications Security Bureau; and Tempora, a surveillance programme run by the NSA's British partner, GCHQ, which records all internet and Facebook traffic and telephone calls entering 'Europe' along the Atlantic fibre-optic cables.[49] The international character of this vast and secret data-gathering procedure enables the US to spy on its own citizens without doing so within its territory, which is formally illegal. The UK is especially useful here, since its rules protecting citizen rights are weaker than those in the US.

This cyber-security is justified in its capacity to anticipate and prevent terrorist attacks, although in most societies these are relatively uncommon. Such attacks cause less unwanted violence than do domestic violence, or homicide, or extreme weather, or traffic

---

[48] Amoore, 'Data derivatives', p. 35.
[49] See http://en.wikipedia.org/wiki/Edward_Snowden and further links to different secret security programmes (accessed 4.8.2013).

'accidents', which form the largest single cause of deaths and serious injuries each year (1.2 million deaths annually).

There is thus an emerging system of secrecy and surveillance, more or less unrelated to the comparative assessment of the actual risks involved. This has spun off, so forming a powerful self-reproducing ecosystem with many interacting elements: new socio-technical systems that enable rapid movement of peoples, messages and objects; increased inequalities providing many incentives to move personal and corporate wealth out of sight; specialist secret places for securely parking such resources; the growth of the internet, which means that nothing much is secret forever; life-threatening risks and hazards moving across borders that fuel the imagination of further dangerous risks; real and imagined risks engendering and legitimating new surveillance systems; specialist surveillance corporations, often spun out of state security, drawing upon military, internet and mobile communications software and hardware; little scientific basis for assessing just how serious risks actually are; many difficulties in limiting the scale of security being implemented because no one in a mediatised world can afford to be 'under-secured'; a mission creep whereby data gained for one purpose (such as road pricing) is then used for the surveillance of all drivers; techniques practised offshore boomeranging back and securitising populations at home; greater security and surveillance leading to more secrecy for those able to assemble their secure worlds; and so on. Thus this secrecy-surveillance ecosystem develops and spreads, becoming core to many societies. But this is not a fully stable ecosystem, and it needs continuous performance and assembling.

This book documents how offshored secrecy and surveillance are central to the functioning of contemporary societies. The security forces of a regime or a company will identify many secrets through technologies of war, torture and surveillance. But this development of secrecy and surveillance is not the straightforward consequence of a 'conspiracy', although there are some powerful conspirators here. It is more a system change. Nor should it be seen as a straightforward functional consequence of how risks move across borders or that surveillance is simply explained by the scale of such risks.

Finally, 'total security' is never fully realised. There are dreams here of a technological omniscience through employing the latest hardware and software sold to the state by powerful security corporations, promising a clear and unambiguous separation of friend and enemy. However, Graham notes: 'the new technological borders are prone to technological breakdown, ineffectiveness, errors and unintended effects.'[50] Much collateral damage often occurs as the 'wrong' people from the 'wrong' places are spied upon, imprisoned, tortured or assassinated. That in turn often engenders new enemies with a powerfully justified sense of injustice. Opponents of a regime or company will reveal secrets of illegal or unethical practices, sometimes, of course, generated through what are also covert operations. Secret worlds breed secret worlds, and there is rarely a completely assembled and secured 'security', especially as offshored relations can rarely be subject to total mastery. What is offshore can return – boomerang back to haunt the apparent masters of the universe. Security is rarely simply secure, we can observe.

---

[50] Graham, *Cities under Siege*, p. 146.

9

Out to Sea and Out of Sight

Introducing the sea

A lurking presence in most chapters of this book is the sea. The world's oceans cover nearly three-quarters of the earth's surface. Most of the surface of the planet is water, and these vast oceans contain much so far undocumented animal and plant life. There are unknown riches in the oceans as well as countless dangers. The earth is really an 'ocean world' with the 7 billion humans crowded onto just over one-quarter of its surface.[1] The sea is not the exception but the rule; it is land that is exceptional. Rachel Carson observed over fifty years ago that the sea is 'a realm so vast and so difficult of access that with all our efforts we have explored only a small fraction of its area'.[2]

For most of human history the oceans constrained human movement, providing barriers to attacking others while at the same time affording some protection from those others. This gave rise to certain 'island races'. Some sea routes did come to develop,

[1] See Philip Steinberg, *The Social Construction of the Sea* (Cambridge: Cambridge University Press, 2011); William Langewiesche, *The Outlaw Sea* (London: Granta, 2004); and Jon Anderson and Kimberley Peters (eds), *Water Worlds* (Farnham: Ashgate, 2013), for much insight here.
[2] Rachel Carson, *The Sea around Us* (New York: Oxford University Press, [1950] 1991), p. vii.

so enabling fishing, trade, piracy, exploitation and escape. Up to the twentieth century all international transport involved moving objects and people upon the surface of these dark and dangerous oceans. Those venturing to sea, the seafarers, often came to grief, as dangerous storms, mysterious currents, underwater rocks and marauding pirates drove many travellers and their goods to a 'watery grave'. For pretty well all of human history there has been an 'outlaw sea' that engendered danger, disease and death. Most coastal settlements were built with their backs to the sea and its many dangers. Only recently did a 'seaview' become desirable, as the sea was partially tamed, domesticated and subjected to the 'tourist gaze'.[3]

Oceans provided ways to assemble as secret what would otherwise be onshore and visible – hence the phrase to 'salt something away', to store it secretly. Much offshoring involves moving money, people and/or objects across the oceans, literally and virtually. To go offshore means to go out of view from land, over the horizon, beyond observation. Almost all the ocean world is literally out of sight and hence out of mind, except when viewed from the air. If one stands at the water's edge, the horizon is only 3 miles away, and almost all the surface of each ocean is over the horizon.[4] But this book documents how these watery worlds over the horizon are central for what occurs back on land. It is necessary to avoid a terrestrial-centrism.

Some 100,000 merchant ships wander this ocean world, accounting for 95 per cent of all trade.[5] Such ships demonstrate little national ownership and regulation; they are crewed by men from the world's poor countries and carry their treasure troves (containers) of goods for the world's rich. Ships regularly break up and sink. Some of the ships criss-crossing the oceans are tankers carrying enormous loads of coal and oil. Along the bottom of the oceans are communication cables. These oceans are a rubbish dump of plastics and other waste, forming vast islands of debris the size of countries. And dotted across the oceans are islands,

---

[3] John Urry and Jonas Larsen, *The Tourist Gaze 3.0* (London: Sage, 2011).
[4] Langewiesche, *The Outlaw Sea*, p. 36.
[5] Anderson and Peters (eds), *Water Worlds*.

tiny places to offload minimally taxed and documented income and wealth, as well as pleasure-seeking tourists, tortured subjects, waste and emissions, far away from prying eyes.

This massive ocean world is wild and untamed, subject, according to Carson, to exceptional 'movement and change', especially through the worldwide conveyor belts that connect the oceans to each other. Seas are dynamic, with teeming life existing at great depths, and are not at all inviolate, fixed and calm.[6] Seas are on the move, in process. But they are also unruly because of what is happening onshore, through the burning of vast amounts of fossil fuels over the past two centuries or so. This chapter considers three aspects of this 'outlaw' sea: unregulated ships, unregulated oceans and unregulated climates.

Unregulated ships

First, then, maritime shipping is a major form of offshored work, with some of the worst conditions of employment anywhere on earth. This results partly from the offshoring of ship registration, which first developed after the First World War but grew especially in the post-Second World War period. The largest of these offshore registrations, or flags of convenience or 'open' registries, are Panama, Liberia, and the Marshall Islands, which account for about two-fifths of all shipping.[7] Ships flying such flags of convenience have no real nationality and are almost literally offshore. The most striking example is the Mongolian Ship Registry; Mongolia is the largest landlocked country on earth and yet has more than 100 ships on its registry, whose main office is located in Singapore.[8] By shopping globally for registration, shipowners can choose the laws that apply to them. As the various flags competed

---

[6] Carson, *The Sea around Us*, pp. ix–x.

[7] UNCTAD, *Review of Maritime Transport 2010*, http://unctad.org/en/docs/rmt2010ch2_en.pdf (accessed 8.11.2012).

[8] See Paul French and Sam Chambers, *Oil on Water* (London: Zed, 2010), pp. 127–9; Mongolia Ship Registry, www.mngship.org/ (accessed 27.6.2012). There are also ships registered in landlocked Bolivia, while the Liberian flag of convenience is run from an office in Virginia in the US.

for business, so shipowners went 'registry-shopping' and found that 'the deals kept getting better and better'.[9]

Registration with 'flags of convenience' is normally cheap and quick (sometimes taking only 24 hours), with no taxation and little regulation. Registries normally make no demands on the size or qualifications of the crew of the ship, who are beyond the reach of national trade unions, health and safety standards, taxation or ship construction requirements (such as the required amount of steel). Oil tankers have been known to break into two because no proper regulation ensured that sufficient steel was used in their construction.

Especially problematic are the arcane ownership patterns at sea which make it almost impossible to pin down and ensure that ships are properly built, maintained and kept seaworthy. In 2002 the vessel *Prestige* broke up at sea partly because insufficient steel was used in its construction. Will Hutton notes that the *Prestige* had been 'chartered by the Swiss-based subsidiary of a Russian conglomerate registered in the Bahamas, owned by a Greek through Liberia and given a certificate of seaworthiness by the Americans. When it refuelled, it stood off the port of Gibraltar to avoid the chance of inspection.'[10] Recent inspections had judged the ship safe to sail, although it was over twenty-five years old. But it was not safe, and the *Prestige* disgorged its crew and cargo of oil into the Atlantic Ocean off Spain as it broke into two.

Those who work on board ship are an invisible workforce, mostly out of sight and out of mind. There are thought to be at least 2,000 deaths a year of such crew, most occurring on flags of convenience-registered ships. Many ship workers are employed by 'manning agents' and not directly by the shipowners. These manning agents are in turn paid by offshore management companies. Overall there are highly complex patterns of ship ownership which appear designed to avoid ownership obligations, regulatory scrutiny, decent conditions of work and the payment

---

[9]Langewiesche, *The Outlaw Sea*, p. 6.
[10]Will Hutton, 'Capitalism must put its house in order', www.guardian .co.uk/politics/2002/nov/24/politicalcolumnists.guardiancolumnists (accessed 8.11.2012). See Langewiesche, *The Outlaw Sea*, on various ships dying out at sea.

of appropriate taxation.[11] Many maritime accidents occur through the poor standards of expertise and training of the 1.2 million predominantly male seafarers who take their life into their hands when setting off for lengthy tours of duty on merchant ships. A quarter of such workers worldwide are from the Philippines.

A large oil tanker sails with twenty to twenty-five men, and most merchant shipping apart from cruise ships also employs a very small crew. There is no uniform protection of the rights of merchant seamen, partly because of offshoring through flag of convenience registration. There are poor working conditions on board, no legal rights, little chance of gaining compensation if injured, and the crew is often scapegoated by local people if there is damage or an oil spill. There is an escalating rate of maritime accidents partly because of these poor conditions. This figure is expected to increase significantly over the next few years as the number of ships doubles.[12]

Also much repair work occurs while ships are actually at sea, so minimising costly time laid up in port. Paradoxically, the one thing that might improve these conditions of work is the current world shortage of seafaring workers. At a time of high levels of global unemployment, many men are deterred from signing on as seafarers because of piracy, accidents, mistreatment and the availability of slightly better alternatives at home.[13]

Unregulated sea

I turn now to some wider aspects of this lawless world. Langewiesche writes: 'our world is an ocean world, and it is wild.'[14] The world's seas are a vast wild west, but with no sheriff riding into view. In previous times people were clear about the savagery of the sea. But it is striking how lawless the seas now are, maybe even more so than in past centuries.

---

[11] French and Chambers, *Oil on Water*, pp. 137–8; Langewiesche, *The Outlaw Sea*, pp. 1–3.
[12] Matt McGrath, 'Study finds shipwrecks threaten precious seas', www .bbc.co.uk/news/science-environment-22806362 (accessed 26.6.2013).
[13] See French and Chambers, *Oil on Water*, pp. 118–25.
[14] Langewiesche, *The Outlaw Sea*, p. 8.

While 'modernity' involved systems of normalisation and the disciplining of relations upon land, and especially in the sky, the sea remained remarkably unregulated. We can talk of the constructing and reinforcing of a 'free-market sea',[15] realised in part through the doctrine of the 'freedom of the sea'. This doctrine involves the peacetime right of ships of all nations to be able to sail the high seas, as well as the exclusive jurisdiction each state possesses over its own ships.[16] There is also the doctrine of 'innocent passage', which means that foreign ships can freely pass through the territorial waters of any other coastal country provided they do not pose a threat to that country.[17] In wartime the freedom of the sea accords immunity to neutral ships from being attacked.

The sea is thus an unruly space, not really owned and governed by states, mostly risky, free and unregulated. As Langewiesche writes of the world's ships, they are 'possibly the most independent objects on earth, many of them without allegiances of any kind, frequently changing their identity and assuming whatever nationality – or "flag" – allows them to proceed as they please.'[18] It is a neo-liberal paradise, a vision of the world almost without government, taxes and laws, and where only the powerful ships and their companies survive, with the rest sinking, sometimes literally, to the bottom. It is a frontier land but one where the frontier covers most of the earth's surface. And the kinds of damage that can now be undertaken have escalated enormously, as human habitation onshore increasingly deposits more and more unruliness offshore. There are many processes significant here, including oil leaks, the dumping of waste products, piracy and terrorism.

First, then, oil spills occur with great frequency because large oil tankers break up, or safety procedures are not followed, or there are leaks from oil platforms. Many spills occur as exploration and drilling takes place in deep and dangerous offshore locations. Especially significant is the 'atrophy of vigilance'. The performance

---

[15] Ibid., p. 13.
[16] *Collins English Dictionary – Complete and Unabridged* (New York: HarperCollins, 1991, 1994, 1998, 2000, 2003).
[17] Langewiesche, *The Outlaw Sea*, p. 36.
[18] Ibid., p. 4.

of an organisation erodes over time through familiarity, boredom, the cutting of corners, and people mechanically going through safety routines without full care and thought. This 'atrophy of vigilance' is especially significant within the oil and gas industry, where staff work on rigs and tankers out to sea for long periods.

There are many oil leaks, some of which are never reported. In the North Sea there have been over 4,000 leaks since 2000, and yet only seven companies have been fined.[19] Because oil is extracted offshore, it means that if a spill occurs then those affected will include populations who are unlikely to be recipients of that particular oil. Overall the impact of oil spills arises in ecosystems that were in the way as the spill arrived from over the horizon. Oil spills are bad news for local tourism industries – as shown in the 2010 Deepwater Horizon oil spill in the Gulf of Mexico – although its visitors almost certainly expected to arrive and depart using oil-based transport energy.[20]

More generally, the oceans are a massive rubbish dump of detritus from land but also from ships. There is much offshore dumping of waste products, and this is especially marked where large surface currents or gyres converge within the oceans. Plastic waste can come to form entire floating islands of marine debris, mainly invisible from land. The largest of these islands is thought to be the Great Pacific Garbage Patch, which is twice the size of France. It is a kind of marine soup whose main ingredient is floating plastic. UNEP calculated that an astonishing 46,000 pieces of plastic debris float on or near the surface of every square mile of ocean across the globe. This gargantuan, out-of-sight plastic rubbish dump kills a million sea birds every year.[21]

---

[19] Leo Hickman, 'Oil companies going unpunished for thousands of North Sea spills', www.guardian.co.uk/environment/2012/oct/25/oil-companies-north-sea-spills (accessed 23.11.2012); 'Oil spills and disasters', www.infoplease.com/ipa/A0001451.html (accessed 23.11.2012), lists the main oil spills since *Torrey Canyon* ran aground in 1967, spilling 38 million gallons of crude oil off the Scilly Isles. See chapter 7 above, and Langewiesche, *The Outlaw Sea*, chap. 3.
[20] William Freudenberg and Robert Gramling, *Blowout in the Gulf* (Cambridge, MA: MIT Press, 2011).
[21] www.telegraph.co.uk/earth/environment/5208645/Drowning-in-plastic-The-Great-Pacific-Garbage-Patch-is-twice-the-size-of-France.html (accessed 16.9.2012).

Seas are also increasingly unruly because of piracy. This has become commonplace, but the self-governing region in Somalia called Puntland is currently the global piracy capital. It is next to one of the busiest shipping lanes in the world, between the Gulf of Aden and the Indian Ocean. These are the world's most 'deadly waters'.[22]

Until the 1990s Somalia had not been warlord dominated, but it was unstable because of its clan structure. As the central government collapsed from the early 1990s with the emergence of various warlord-dominated regions, so Somalia's ability to control its seas declined and piracy flourished. Bahadur describes the resulting pirate ecosystem as a 'hodgepodge of rebel groups, militias, and warlords that had inherited chunks of the Somali state (along with the remnant of its army)'.[23] Some 'pirates' or 'saviours of the sea' were originally fishermen, whose livelihood was destroyed by foreign fishing fleets. Other pirates were originally trained as coastguards. Hundreds of pirates operate as a kind of loose federation. Catching a ship normally takes about 30 minutes. The ship is then moved to a safe port and, if a ransom is paid, the money is divided up between various groups involved, including the local community.

Over time piracy has become more of a business, one powerful group, known as the Somali Marines, being characterised by a military-style hierarchy able to attack ships far away from the coast and providing an alternative structure of government. The economics of piracy do not seem to generate huge income, especially for a regular crew member. But Bahadur notes how career prospects in these areas are otherwise non-existent: 'it is hardly surprising that piracy is the profession of choice for many ambitious young men.'[24]

Also, given the vastness of the sea, smuggling and piracy over the horizon is easy; waste, spills and ships can disappear, and terrorism from ships is an enduring possibility. Sea space is different from airspace. It has been an outlaw space, but it is now often

---

[22] See Jay Bahadur, *Deadly Waters* (London: Profile, 2011), which includes interesting insights into the researching of 'piracy'.

[23] Ibid., p. 31.

[24] Ibid., p. 233; Langewiesche, *The Outlaw Sea*, chap. 2, on piracy in the Strait of Malacca.

little more than a place of outlaws. Efforts to regulate that space are difficult because of the sheer scale of ships, objects, containers and people moving towards and away from the world's coasts, appearing out of the blue from over the horizon.[25] Even the US, with the world's most powerful military, does not know which ships are arriving into and departing from its ports, what each is carrying, and which ones might be full of illegal migrants, pirates, contraband or bombs. The US is increasingly not trying to govern the seas but rather mounting ramparts against incoming risks, to create a fortress world against 'monsters' appearing out of that sea.

Unregulated climate

And there is a relatively new sea monster. Analyses of the 'global warming' of the planet tend to concentrate on such warming upon the land and those living on land. Attention is focused on likely increases in heat as reflected in the rising frequency of droughts, heatwaves, and bush or forest fires and their consequences for food supplies, lack of water, loss of human and plant life, and so on.[26] These consequences are profound, especially as more and more of the earth's cultivable land turns into arid desert, as in northern Kenya. The turn to poppy production and hence opium in Afghanistan is partly because such production requires only one-sixth of the water used for wheat cultivation.[27] Many countries in the tropics are experiencing rising temperatures, with one report suggesting that a third of the earth's land mass will be desert by 2100.[28] There is 'climate chaos' for the nearly 3 billion people living on the land located between the two tropics.

[25] Langewiesche, *The Outlaw Sea*, pp. 63–70.
[26] See George Monbiot, *Heat* (London: Allen Lane, 2006), and the brilliant account of being in the eye of a firestorm in Tasmania: www.guardian.co.uk/world/interactive/2013/may/26/firestorm-bushfire-dunalley-holmes-family (accessed 26.6.2013).
[27] Christian Parenti, *Tropic of Chaos* (New York: Nation Books, 2011), pp. 9, 107.
[28] Cited ibid., p. 47.

But this captures only one side of climate change. The other side involves examining how the world's seas are being transformed and the impact of such transformations back upon most elements of life on land. Increasingly turbulent 'water worlds' result from higher CO_2 emissions, rising water temperatures and increased water vapour in the atmosphere. The seas' temperatures are rising much faster than those on land.[29] This in turn leads to greater melting of the world's vast glaciers and ice sheets, the rising of global sea levels, a greater intensity of storms and hurricanes, the loss of human and animal habitats to the sea, and the possible transformation in ocean currents worldwide. The world's oceans are not benign and show no tendency to equilibrium, even if during the Holocene period there were about 11,000 years of relative sea level stability. Especially significant in these unruly water processes is the Pacific Ocean: the 'mother of all oceans, and the other oceans, the children, obey her signals'.[30]

As global temperatures increase, climates become more sensitive to further small temperature changes. This further increases the unruliness of the sea and its capacity to generate more intense and damaging storms, although not necessarily more storms. Although such effects occur out at sea, so making the sea turbulent, these storms increasingly arrive onshore. The oceans are exacting their revenge. At least 1 billion people live by the sea, and many of the great cities of the world lie on the coast. The effects arrive onshore as the oceans deposit more and more choppy water along the coastline and also inland, with hurricanes, tornadoes, storm surges and flash flooding. Hansen notes: 'many places around the world have experienced an unnatural increase of "hundred-year" floods, which are occurring more often than their name would imply.'[31] As environmental journalist John Vidal writes:

---

[29] See Danny Chivers, 'Switching off denial: a guide', www.newint.org/features/2011/05/01/guide-to-climate-change-denial-debunking-climate-skeptic-myths/ (accessed 10.1.2013), figure 3, and John Urry, *Climate Change and Society* (Cambridge: Polity, 2011), on climate change scepticism.

[30] Parenti, *Tropic of Chaos*, p. 57.

[31] James Hansen, *Storms of my Grandchildren* (London: Bloomsbury, 2011), p. 254.

'Warning: extreme weather ahead',[32] a 'taster' of this being Super-storm Sandy, which descended upon New York and New Jersey in November 2012.

Changing temperatures transform and destabilise the oceans. Especially significant is how ice sheets are very sensitive to even small increases in global temperatures.[33] According to Hansen, if temperatures were higher by about 2 to 3 degrees, conditions would be similar to how the earth was 3 million years ago. Sea levels were then 25 metres higher than today, and most of the world's cities would be permanently under water.[34] Davis concludes how, by 2030, 'the convergent effects of climate change, peak oil, peak water, and an additional 1.5 billion people on the planet will produce negative synergies probably beyond our imagination.'[35]

Moreover, states and corporations are normally unable to cope with fast-moving and unpredicted disasters.[36] There are many instances where 'states', relief organisations and companies are overwhelmed by their scale and complexity. They necessitate improvising new kinds of mobilities and various alternative systems. Two recent examples in rich countries show this lack of system resilience: New Orleans in September 2005 and the nuclear collapse in Fukushima in Japan caused by the massive tsunami in 2011, both of which demonstrate just how organisations are incapable of responding to failures, especially as evolving processes unpredictably impact upon each other. Sheller describes through

---

[32] John Vidal, 'Warning: extreme weather ahead', *The Guardian*, 14 June 2011; see documentation at www.heatisonline.org/weather.cfm (accessed 24.12.2011).

[33] Hansen, *Storms of my Grandchildren*, p. 76, and chap. 8.

[34] Ibid., p. 141.

[35] Mike Davis, 'Who will build the ark?' *New Left Review*, 61 (201), p. 17. See Constance Lever-Tracy (ed.), *Routledge Handbook on Climate Change and Society* (London: Routledge, 2010); and Bron Szerszynski and John Urry (eds), 'Special issue: changing climates', *Theory, Culture and Society*, 27 (2010): 1–305.

[36] Chris Abbott, *An Uncertain Future* (Oxford: Oxford Research Group, 2008); John Vidal, 'Global warming could create 150 million "climate refugees" by 2050', http://www.guardian.co.uk/environment/2009/nov/03/global-warming-climate-refugees (accessed 13.5.2013).

an analysis of the January 2010 earthquake in Haiti how the dynamic intertwining of transportation, communication, provisioning, and scheduling systems can rapidly unravel in an enduring crisis.[37]

One sector of the global economy that understands the scale of these developments is the global insurance industry. It documents the rising scale, impact and cost of such climate-related events. Insurance losses worldwide have seen a sudden increase, with much evidence that extreme weather is responsible for globally rising costs. Since the 1970s, extreme weather events have increased by around 10 per cent each year. The insurer Swiss Re estimates that losses from these weather events have risen fivefold since the 1980s. Oxfam reports that, while earthquake numbers remained relatively stable, there has been an almost threefold increase in flooding and storm events over this period. Munich Re (the world's largest reinsurance company) authoritatively concludes that

> the growing number of weather-related catastrophes can only be explained by climate change. The view that weather extremes are more frequent and intense due to global warming is in keeping with current scientific findings . . . And the risk is steadily growing, for climate change harbours the potential for torrential downpours while the risk of drought in certain regions is also on the rise.[38]

Flannery argued: 'such a rate of increase implies that by 2065 or soon thereafter, the damage bill resulting from climate change may equal the total value of everything that humanity produced in the course of a year.'[39] The insurance industry doubts they could absorb such future claims. In 2005 Hurricane Katrina caused $120 billion of damage.[40] These sums are especially large partly

---

[37] See Mimi Sheller, 'The islanding effect: post-disaster mobility systems and humanitarian logistics in Haiti', *Cultural Geographies*, 20 (2012): 185–204.

[38] 'Flooding in China', www.munichre.com/cn/group/focus/climate_change/current/flooding_in_china/default.aspx (accessed 13.9.2013).

[39] Tom Flannery, *The Weather Makers* (London: Penguin, 2007), p. 235.

[40] Julia Kollewe, 'Superstorm Sandy could cost $45bn in damage and lost production', www.guardian.co.uk/world/2012/oct/30/superstorm-sandy-cost-damage-production (accessed 21.11.2012).

because of how extreme weather events destroy much property and infrastructure even in well-organised and prosperous first world cities. It is clear that rising water temperatures and storms will have long-term impacts upon levels of income and wellbeing worldwide.

Conclusion

The sea is central to analysing contemporary offshoring and indeed more generally in deciphering the changing character of global relations. These relations are as much watery as they are located purely on land. In particular, this chapter documents how there are unregulated ships where conditions of work are driven to the bottom, unregulated oceans which are becoming a global rubbish dump, and unregulated climates as the outlaw sea subjects the 7 billion humans to its heightened unruliness, intense storms, hurricanes, storm surges, rising sea levels and flooding. The sea, we might say, bites back with interest, from local effects to those which are long term and global. As emphasised in this book, that which is offshore often returns to haunt that which is onshore but in ways which are unexpected and chaotic. The distinction between onshore and offshore is unstable and being continuously redrawn.

So far this unruliness out to sea has not brought home to onshore populations just what has been done to those oceans and what humans are doing to themselves as the boomerang returns to strike onshore. This is partly because of the power of carbon capital, that complex of coal, oil and gas exploration, producing and refining companies; vehicle, plane and ship manufacturers; media, advertising and cultural corporations; and many politicians, thinktanks and consultants. The World Development Movement terms this the 'Web of power', noting that up to one-third of ministers in the current British government (2013) previously worked either for fossil fuel energy companies or for banks with extensive links to such companies.[41] The campaigning organisation Platform has analysed the 'carbon web', bringing out the

---

[41]'Web of power', media briefing, www.wdm.org.uk/sites/default/files/Carbon%20Capital%20Media%20Briefing5.pdf (accessed 3.4.2013).

related significance of London within a network of powerful fossil fuel interests.[42]

Of particular importance are interconnected thinktanks, especially within the US, that systematically seek to combat climate change science and to promote high carbon 'business as usual'.[43] Many are 'front' organisations that are intended to 'greenwash' issues. They have been remarkably significant in maintaining the fossil fuel dependency of more or less all societies, even though mounting evidence showed this was almost certainly transforming global temperatures in an irreversible upward direction. There are many powerful interlinked thinktanks combating climate change science and promoting fossil fuel business as usual.

These often secret thinktanks cast doubt on the sciences of climate change, which pretty well agree that the burning of fossil fuels over the past few centuries is causing climate change, and exploit the nature of science, which should be full of controversy and uncertainty. They both overemphasise the scientific uncertainty found, for example, in IPCC reports and often operate secretly, implying that there is far more opposition to climate science than there really is, so 'manufacturing uncertainty'.[44]

Such carbon capital has been enormously effective in the US, the Russian Federation, parts of Africa and Latin America, and most Middle Eastern countries. Climate sceptics 'manufacture

---

[42] 'Unravelling the carbon web', www.carbonweb.org/showitem.asp ?article=67&parent=3 (accessed 3.4.2013).

[43] Such as the American Enterprise Institute, Americans for Prosperity, the Cato Institute, the Competitive Enterprise Institute, Energy for America, the Global Climate Coalition, the Heartland Institute, the Marshall Institute, the Nongovernmental International Panel on Climate Change (NIPCC), the Science and Environmental Policy Project, the Science and Public Policy Institute, the Heritage Foundation and the World Climate Council.

[44] See Sharon Beder, *Global Spin* (London: Green Books, 2002); Naomi Oreskes and Erik Conway, *Merchants of Doubt* (New York: Bloomsbury, 2010); Urry, *Climate Change and Society*, on climate change scepticism. See Suzanne Goldenberg, 'How Donors Trust distributed millions to anti-climate groups', www.guardian.co.uk/environment/2013/feb/14/ donors-trust-funding-climate-denial-networks (accessed 17.2.2013), on the massive scale of corporate funding of the many climate sceptic groups.

uncertainty' about climate science and as to the likely importance of the peaking of oil supplies. These thinktanks seek to argue that the increasingly unruly sea has absolutely nothing to do with burning all that fossil fuel upon the land.

The final chapter brings out just how problematic offshoring has been. For both democratic control and post-carbonism it will be necessary to mobilise a radical programme of on- or reshoring. But financial and carbon capital are powerful opponents and unlikely to sit idly by if work, wealth and waste were to be brought back onshore.

10

Bringing It All Back Home

The Dubai model

Dubai symbolises the wild offshore world that grew so rapidly over the past three or four decades. This Islamic society was rapidly transformed into almost the world centre for offshoring – of taxation, goods, leisure, property, energy, consumption, islands, expertise, crime. You name it and Dubai offshored it to excess.

Dubai illustrates what Roubini and Mihm maintain, that 'capitalism is not some self-regulating system . . . rather it is a system prone to "irrational exuberance" and unfounded pessimism. It is . . . extraordinarily unstable.'[1] Many offshore worlds such as Dubai were the product of such irrational exuberance and then of intense pessimism. They especially experienced the dramatic collapse of real-estate values and financial failure during the economic meltdown beginning in 2007–8. Budd generally argues: 'all financial crises are rooted in real estate market crises.'[2] The effects of financial collapse turned such real-estate assets toxic, with

---

[1]Nouriel Roubini and Stephen Mihm, *Crisis Economics* (London: Penguin, 2011), p. 43 and chap. 2; John Urry, *Societies beyond Oil* (London: Zed, 2013).
[2]Leslie Budd, 'Re-regulating the financial system: the return of state or societal corporatism', *Contemporary Social Science*, 7 (2012): 1–19.

many dire impacts. The astonishing growth of Dubai went into reverse. Expats fled, leaving their cars bought on credit at the airport, thousands of construction workers were laid off, property values fell 60 per cent, half the construction projects were put on hold or cancelled, 'The World' island development started slipping back into the sea, major companies such as Dubai World defaulted on huge debts, the population shrank, and Dubai was bailed out by Abu Dhabi.[3]

Does this rise and possible fall of Dubai index a general peaking of offshored consuming, tourism, property development and tax 'limitation'? Is offshoring on the way out? Does offshoring entail such high carbon costs that future oil shortages and more extreme weather events will bring offshoring worlds to a slowdown or even an abrupt end? Or does the exceptional scale of economic and social practices that escaped offshore, and were often made 'secret', show that we have seen nothing yet in the irrational exuberance that is contemporary offshoring? Is offshoring an irreversible system change?

The scale of offshore

I have documented the scale and reach of the economic and social practices involved in this offshored world which reaches into almost all societies. It restructures global power through moving resources, practices, peoples and monies from one territory to others, often along routes hidden from view. Such secret route-ways were intriguingly revealed in early 2013 by the exposure of a Europe-wide conspiracy whereby cheap horsemeat was sold as though it were more expensive beef. This fraud resulted from extensive international networks of slaughter houses, agents,

[3] www.cnn.com/2009/BUSINESS/12/14/dubai.10.billion.bailout/index.html (accessed 5.3.2010). It has also been noted that a US/Israeli strike on Iran's nuclear facilities would make Dubai and the rest of the Gulf region more or less uninhabitable in what would be the world's largest environmental disaster: Wade Stone, 'Good-bye Dubai?', www.globalre-search.ca/good-bye-dubai-bombing-irans-nuclear-facilities-would-leave-the-entire-gulf-states-region-virtually-uninhabitable/5334737 (accessed 18.5.2013).

transport companies and supermarkets, each apparently operating somewhat secretly and where there were few testing mechanisms for the meat that the poor consumers across Europe were eating.[4] Some companies involved in this conspiracy were registered off-shore and linked in to other criminal activities.

Contemporary offshoring involves the most sustained of attacks upon governance orchestrated through national states and especially upon efforts to regulate and legislate on the basis of democratic control. Offshoring involves getting around rules in ways that are illegal, or go against the spirit of the law, or use laws in one jurisdiction to undermine laws in another.[5] Most offshoring practices are not incidental features of the contemporary world but are systemically engineered and legally reinforced to avoid regulations, to be kept secret and to 'escape' offshore, helping to form and sustain an offshore world at the expense of open borderlessness.

I noted above how Bauman emphasises the power of the 'rich class' to be able to 'exit' and thus to act irresponsibly.[6] Elites can escape many kinds of formal and informal sanction and set up the conditions for further extending their income and wealth. This inaccessibility makes elites less responsible for their actions, especially in the very societies in which their actions would appear to be occurring.

Moreover, we have seen how these elites increasingly meet as secret societies, such as the offshored annual meetings of the Bilderberg Group.[7] As elites circulated spatially, with meetings often in places of offshore leisure and pleasure, so they developed connections and capacity to extend further offshored worlds and discourses that promote offshoring. Private meetings and more

---

[4] Jamie Doward, 'Horsemeat scandal linked to secret network of firms', www.guardian.co.uk/uk/2013/feb/16/horsemeat-scandal-victor-bout-firms (accessed 17.2.2013).
[5] Giorgio Agamben, *State of Exception* (Chicago: University of Chicago Press, 2005).
[6] Zygmunt Bauman, *Liquid Modernity* (Cambridge: Polity, 2000).
[7] Ian Richardson, Andrew Kakabadse and Nada Kakabadse, *Bilderberg People: Elite Power and Consensus in World Affairs* (London: Routledge, 2011); Charlie Skelton, 'Bilderberg 2012: bigger and badder and better than ever', www.guardian.co.uk/world/us-news-blog/2012/jun/01/bilderberg-2012-chantilly-occupy (accessed 15.5.2013).

public thinktanks helped to orchestrate this offshore world and its corporate, individual and policy world beneficiaries.

It is common to criticise 'conspiracy theories' for their simplistic analysis of social and political processes. But there does seem here to have been a series of overlapping semi-secret conspiracies against the power of states, their realisation of collective interests and rationally planned onshore worlds. During much of the post-war period there was a struggle to 'liberate' large corporations and rich individuals from what was seen as the yoke of an over-bearing state. As noted in chapter 1, the 'rich class' is waging class war and winning it, although this 'class' is constituted of very many different and competing elite groups and is not unified simply in its interests or conspiratorial form. Especially significant is how this class struggle was partly orchestrated by powerful thinktanks ('organic intellectuals' of the rich class) that counter-posed the many freedoms of the market to what was deemed to be the repressive serfdom of the state.[8]

Among offshoring processes by which this rich class has so far got much richer and is winning this war are fragmenting and offshoring production to cheaper sites; systematically reducing tax liabilities and hence heightening inequalities; creating many secret offshore companies; engendering new forms of financialisation; developing expertise in novel ways of marginalising workforces; extracting infrastructural investment from states; externalising the costs of waste and emissions; using moments of crisis to force through neo-liberal restructuring; mobilising various discourses promoting marketisation; and creating astonishing new products based upon new 'needs', including for security. These all derive from the global freedom to move monies, income, wealth, people, waste and loyalties from pillar to post. This dizzying 'mobile' world, bright and dark, open and secret, free and destructive, is difficult to regulate, especially as anti-Keynesian discourse became a flood from around 1980, with progressivism and statism being systematically rolled back.

In particular, the dizzying 'mobile' world systematically impedes necessary forms of global cooperation across most domains of desirable governance. This generates the problem of 'global

---

[8] See as an example, Madsen Pirie, *Think Tank: The Story of the Adam Smith Institute* (London: Biteback, 2012).

gridlock'.[9] Particularly significant in such 'gridlocking' has been the fragmentation of the large industrial corporation. Ownership was increasingly located with financial institutions concerned with short-term 'shareholder value'.[10] Simultaneously the industrial working class was subjected to 'disorganising', even though global inequalities were mushrooming. The growth of inequality has engendered powerful interests to protect and further extend the bases of such unequally distributed global income and wealth.

Offshoring is part and parcel of the realising of such unequal interests. And such inequalities matter a great deal, since access to 'services' will come to depend upon each person's income and wealth; the more unequal these are, the less chance there is that people will be regarded as in any way equal. The rampant marketisation of almost everything crowds out many other reasons why people may act towards each other, such as fairness, service, duty and sociability.

The term 'big bang' captures this break from Keynesianism, as capitalism was 'disorganised' from top to bottom. Banks grew into behemoths too big to fail. The power of finance spun off from forms of national regulation and from rules separating investment from high-street banking. Derivative contracts grew tenfold in value in the decade up to 2007–8, reaching a colossal US\$500 trillion, many times greater than global GDP.[11] Vast offshore flows grew through the growth of new markets and 'products', while manufacturing industry and many consumer services remained much more onshored. This was how a global rich class came to make and extend itself over the past third of a century.

Disorganised or neo-liberal capitalism saw the ending of many barriers to the flows of money, with extensive offshored financial markets and accelerated algorithmic trading.[12] This dictatorship

---

[9]Thomas Hale, David Held and Kevin Young, *Gridlock* (Cambridge: Polity, 2013).

[10]See Scott Lash and John Urry, 'Disorganizing capitalism and its futures', *Work, Employment and Society*, 27 (2013): 542–6.

[11]Andrew Haldane and Robert May, 'Systemic risk in banking ecosystems', *Nature*, 469 (2011): 351–5.

[12]See UK government report *Economic Impact Assessments on MiFID II Policy Measures related to Computer Trading in Financial Markets*, www.bis.gov.uk/assets/foresight/docs/computer-trading/12-1088 -economic-impact-mifid-2-measures-computer-trading (accessed 9.2.2013).

of accelerated financial trading redistributed income and rights
away from the 'real economy' to a less taxed and governed 'casino
capitalism'. Crucial was the growing structural significance of
flows of finance and what has been termed the 'survival of the
fattest', not the fittest.[13]

Haldane and May argue that many very large financial institutions have grown 'too big, connected or important to fail'.[14] This
magnifies the probability of system failure because 'excessive homo-
geneity within a financial system – all the banks doing the same
thing – can minimise risk for each individual bank, but maximise
the probability of the entire system collapsing.'[15] From a complex
systems perspective, the danger is herding as each bank engages in
similar behaviour, so heightening the likelihood of system failure.

Such a neo-liberal gridlocked capitalism was 'assembled' in the
1970s and 1980s and resulted in offshore worlds which no one
conspired to produce in detail, but which have many dysfunctional
system consequences, for economic stability, security, climate,
incomes and democracy. In the rest of this chapter I elaborate
some features of the contemporary world which could and should
be onshored. I begin with the small problem of democracy and its
possible reshoring, which would begin at least to help to deal with
the problem of gridlock.

Finance and democracy

Keynes outlined two problems about finance. First, when two
parties trade with each other, buying and selling goods and services, there is rough equality between them, since each wants what
the other has. But with finance there is no equality, since finance
is always in command. Keynes critiqued how industry is subservi-
ent to finance and often to geographically distant forms of finance.[16]
Offshore accounts make these relationships especially unequal.

---

[13] Haldane and May, 'Systemic risk in banking ecosystems', p. 351.
[14] Ibid., p. 354; and see the surprising 'Inequality and the crisis: still
pre-Occupied', www.guardian.co.uk/commentisfree/2012/oct/30/andy
-haldane-occupy-bank-of-england (accessed 6.11.2012).
[15] Haldane and May, 'Systemic risk in banking ecosystems', p. 353.
[16] John Maynard Keynes, *The General Theory of Employment, Interest
and Money* (London: Macmillan, [1936] 1961), p. 376.

Second, most investment by financial institutions is speculation in secondary markets. Keynes considered this problematic, since 'the remoteness between ownership and operation is an evil in the relations among men'.[17] These secondary markets and the development of offshore escalate the chasm or remoteness between the ownership of companies and their actual operation through 'skilful evasions'.[18] This is gambling against the future market position of companies, currencies and countries. Trading is for the sake of trading. And, through automatically trading algorithms so as to hedge one's bets, money can often be made whether the market is falling or rising.[19]

Because of the dangers of excessive 'capital flight', Keynes strongly argued for nationally organised exchange controls to be exerted over financial flows. But exchange controls were relaxed from 1979 onwards, partly because Hayek, Friedman and free-market disciples criticised and campaigned against the 'siren song of exchange controls'.[20] This removal of exchange controls helped to generate a change in financial relationships, from freedom to dictatorship. Because Keynes thought that there should be transparency in financial flows, he would have regarded secrecy jurisdictions as counterproductive to effective economic management. The requirement for good governance is transparency. Keynes was in favour of the free trade of goods and non-financial services but regarded finance as too important to be left to unregulated offshore flows.

Secrecy jurisdictions are centrally implicated in the growth of the shadow, unregulated financial system where trading is often out of sight, and which brought the world economy to its knees a few years ago. Capital in its various forms moves from nation-state to nation-state, choosing the regime most conducive to its changing

---

[17]John Maynard Keynes, 'National self-sufficiency', *Yale Review*, 22 (1933): 755–69, at p. 756.
[18]Keynes, *The General Theory of Employment, Interest and Money*, p. 372.
[19]Although they can fail, as with the Delaware-incorporated Long-Term Capital Management that involved Nobel Prize-winners, which collapsed in 1998.
[20]Steve H. Hanke, 'The siren song of exchange controls', www.cato.org/publications/commentary/siren-song-exchange-controls (accessed 1.8.2012).

interests. There is 'regime-shopping'. The growth in hedge funds from the 1970s onwards occurred especially as exchange controls were being disbanded. Such funds are not regulated by central banks and do not have to be transparent in their dealings, with most being owned offshore. Entry to them is confined to the rich because of initial capital requirements and strict vetting procedures. Currently there are said to be 10,000 or so hedge funds.

The offshore world is based upon secrecy and concealment, including providing advantages to 'foreigners' not available to a society's own citizens. Offshoring and democracy are in direct conflict. The scale and significance of offshoring makes it impossible for new kinds of post-national democracy to gain traction. Neo-liberal capitalism has brought about a systemic disorganisation of potential democratic structures. The flows of money, finance, manufacturing, services, security, waste and emissions which are in various ways offshored are catastrophic for transparent governance. Such transparency necessitates debate and dialogue being able to determine and implement policies through citizens being aware of, and having control over, a clear set of onshored resources. The absolute requirement for good governance is transparency, and that is what secrecy jurisdictions preclude. There is here an offshoring of democracy, since money and resources are rendered invisible and unaccountable.

Democracy requires money and resources that are subject to clear, transparent and accountable contestation between the members of a given society. It needs activities to be brought back 'home' and the interests of *its* citizens to be regarded as primary. Much should be reshored so as to re-establish potential democratic control by the members of a given society over the activities and resources that are specific to them.

The only entities that might begin to bring about anything like an effective reshoring are nation-states. This poses democracy as located within a 'nation-state-society'. It might be said that framing the issue in this way ignores the development of new notions of global and cosmopolitan democracy developed by various theorists.[21] The problem is that so many resources have been moved

---

[21] See, for example, David Held, *Global Covenant: The Social Democratic Alternative to the Washington Consensus* (Cambridge: Polity, 2004); John Urry, *Sociology Beyond Societies* (London: Routledge, 2000).

offshore and hidden from view, legally protected and not subject to potential democratic oversight, control and regulation. Only reshoring to each nation-state can ensure that there is, as Palan well expresses it, a 'national life predicated on mutual responsibility, which is at the heart of the modern system of popular sovereignty'.[22] This national life based on mutual responsibility is in direct opposition to the power and influence of the dozens of financial centres that emphasise the special interests of rich and powerful 'virtual citizens', the 'rich class' that, we have seen, straddles the globe.

Moreover, Haldane and May maintain that the 'structure of many non-financial networks is explicitly and intentionally modular. This includes the design of personal computers and the world wide web and the management of forests and utility grids.'[23] This modularity found in realms outside finance prevents contagion infecting the whole network if failure happens within one node. It ensures system resilience. If there are more gaps, firewalls, local and national specificities or borders, then contagion and catastrophic herding will be much less likely. Modularity may reduce the profitability of individual companies, but it also lessens the likelihood of system failure. How to engender modularity?

The onshoring of much economic and social life behind barriers would re-establish democratic control by the members of a given society over the activities and resources that are in some sense specific to that society. What is required is an agreed international discourse and a robust system of procedures to ensure that resources generated within a society are subject to transparency and taxation within that society and that the interests of foreign money are not treated better than those owned by a society's citizens. This should not, however, be couched in terms of an anti-foreigner discourse.

But this requirement is formidably difficult to achieve because of what this book has documented, namely, widespread internationalisation, outsourcing and offshoring over the past decades. Very few products, services and practices are the 'nationally'

---

[22]Ronen Palan, *The Offshore World* (Ithaca, NY: Cornell University Press, 2006), p. 159; Mathias Risse, *On Global Justice* (Princeton, NJ: Princeton University Press, 2012).
[23]Haldane and May, 'Systemic risk in banking ecosystems', p. 355.

specific outcome of activities locatable within a given society. Even the contents of a modest beefburger, we now know, travel between various societies before ending up to be eaten in a specific fast-food restaurant. The poor consumers can have no idea whether they are indeed eating British beef, for example, and not Irish horse. A 'nationalisation' of production is even more difficult to achieve within smaller and poorer societies around the world. Achieving modularity is a demanding requirement.

A recent report from the Tax Justice Network does begin to outline some steps towards a more modular framework for national taxation at least.[24] This report proposes a transformation of the legal basis for taxing multinational corporations. At present companies are taxed on the basis of the legal forms that they take, with corporations being thought of as a loose collection of separate legal/economic entities, a notion dating from the early part of the last century when transnational businesses were less developed and complex.

This loose form taken by corporations results in the system problem that transfer pricing of flows of goods, services and income internal to the corporation enables companies to declare varied profit earnings within countries with very different tax rates and arrangements. Almost all transnational companies operate complex transfer pricing. Most have many accounts in tax havens often structured in a complex layering (as with Goldman Sachs). Many large transnational companies pay little 'corporation-type' taxation anywhere they operate. For example, the UK branch of Starbucks pays a very large 'royalty' to its headquarters in the Netherlands, so minimising its potential tax payments within Britain, even though much coffee is sold there and the company boasts to shareholders of the high earnings generated within its British cafés. Overall it is often impossible for tax authorities to determine if the royalties or transfer prices are justified.

Instead of this, the Tax Justice Network proposes that the taxation of corporations should be based upon treating a corporation as a single entity around the world. Companies would have to

---

[24] See Sol Picciotto, *Towards Unitary Taxation of Transnational Corporations* (London: Tax Justice Network, 2012), for the following paragraphs.

submit one set of consolidated accounts for that entity and appor-
tion activities to countries according to their actual 'economic'
presence within each country. This presence would be formula-
based, relating to the number of staff employed, the geographical
location of the company's fixed assets and the value of its sales.
Of course these are all immensely difficult to determine, especially
because many services are outsourced by large corporations.

Corporations will no doubt mount a robust defence of the
status quo and find many reasons why such a 'unitary' taxation
would not work. However, it was recognised as early as the 1930s
that national authorities should examine a firm's overall accounts
so as to ensure a fair split of total profits between different areas.
The state of California used such a notion to prevent Hollywood
film companies from siphoning profits through affiliates in neighbouring low-tax Nevada.

Today there are steps being made by some US states and by the
EU to develop the basis of such a unitary taxation methodology.
The EU established the Common Consolidated Corporate Tax
Base to apply to all companies operating within the Union. This
measure was passed by the European Parliament in 2012, but it
is unclear how effective it will actually be.[25] This depends partly
upon whether the shaming of companies for tax evasion or aggressive tax avoidance will gain further traction and whether there
will be concerted NGO and social media/movement organisation
around issues of tax justice. Will companies continue to suffer
major reputational damage for their apparent failure to pay taxes
roughly in proportion to where their activities are located and
profits are generated?

By early 2013 it was reported that the Tax Justice Network,
Global Witness, Cafod, ActionAid and Save the Children are all
now campaigning for 'country-by-country' reporting for taxation.
This has already been imposed on mining and oil extraction
groups by the US, and something similar is being developed by
the EU for banks operating in Europe.[26] Developing such a reporting system is a precondition for transparency and democracy.

---

[25] Picciotto, *Towards Unitary Taxation of Transnational Corporations*,
pp. 10–16.
[26] Reported in *The Guardian*, 8 May 2013, p. 23.

It should also be noted that companies are not in fact independent entities. Most have a legal form in which the owners or shareholders possess limited liability if that particular business collapses. This is a huge privilege which is granted by nation-states to the economic enterprises operating within its borders. If the company goes bankrupt, the shareholders lose only their shareholding and are not themselves made bankrupt. It is thus reasonable for the state to expect in return for this limited liability some responsibilities, among which we can include the requirement that companies pay taxes roughly proportionate to the scale of business in which they are involved within each society.

Interestingly, the countries that maintained exchange controls have grown faster than those that reduced controls and participated most in the bonanza of offshoring and tax limitation. The only alternative is to bring it all back home, and that must mean that home is the complex of nation-state-society. Because of the scale and power of offshoring, only the nation-state-society could be the form to which reshoring should take place.[27]

Reshoring the material

But it is not only taxation and finance that must be onshored along the lines just described; so too must the material elements of everyday life. A system of national accounts should be developed that enables tracking of the material flows of waste products and goods manufactured within each society.

With regard to waste, the UNEP's Basel Convention developed the important proximity principle.[28] This principle states that waste should be disposed of as close as possible to its source. There are two problems. Not all countries have signed up to this – in particular the US – and there is inadequate monitoring of the removal chain to ensure enforcement. Such removal chains can involve many different companies, but little information is passed

---

[27] Although see Anthony Giddens, *Turbulent and Mighty Continent: What Future for Europe?* (Cambridge: Polity, 2013), on the possibilities of 'bringing it home to Europe'.
[28] www.basel.int/ (accessed 3.1.2013).

between them. There is currently no standardised information model for how and where waste moves, although it is clear that 'proximity' should be the default position here.

A prototype system for tracking the movement of waste was the Trash Track project from MIT.[29] This documented not the supply chain but the 'removal train' after products had been used. Small, smart location-aware tags were attached to items of rubbish, and these enabled the tracking of the lengthy and complex removal process. The rubbish travelled very long distances, a process otherwise impossible to document using non-digital means of tracking.[30]

Scaling up this monitoring globally is a major challenge, but one interesting finding of the Trash Track project was the high concern that volunteers showed in just where their rubbish actually ends up. This concern is reflected in the reasonably high levels of recycling of domestic waste in certain societies, which necessitates a quite significant expenditure of time and effort to sort through and distribute. We might say that there is an emerging politics of waste, and that this is now something many citizens do care about and will organise to rectify if they believe that there are robust systems in place to move on their waste once it goes out of sight.

But overall the scale of global rubbish production makes it impossible for all items to be tagged and tracked.[31] This is also partly because much waste consists of food, a significant proportion of which is edible. We noted in chapter 7 that food is the largest component of solid waste in landfill sites; wasted food could not be tracked. So while some tracking and tracing is desirable there also needs to be a clear international legal framework

---

[29] http://senseable.mit.edu/trashtrack (accessed 28.12.2012).

[30] See 'Urban digestive systems', http://senseable.mit.edu/papers/pdf/2011_Offenhuber_et_al_Urban_digestive_Sentient_City.pdf) (accessed 10.10.2012), on the complex methodological issues involved in attaching tags to rubbish and then in tracking where the objects moved to, as well as the subsequent disposal of the tags and their minute batteries.

[31] See www.dosomething.org/actnow/tipsandtools/11-facts-about-recycling (accessed 28.12.2012) on the extraordinary scale of US rubbish production.

to ensure that societies deal comprehensively with their own rubbish, especially food.

In chapter 3 we saw a rather different way that material onshoring might develop – through 3D printing. This could transform the very notion of 'manufacturing', which normally takes place in large factories often thousands of miles distant from consumers. A new system may evolve whereby 'manufacturing' gets relocalised and undertaken on a smaller scale and closer to consumers. This 'system innovation' would eliminate some elements of manufacturing as a separate and spatially distant activity. This would parallel the internet, whereby music or films or books are accessed and downloaded and not actually owned and sold. Downloading designs and then printing would be part of an 'access' economy which has so mushroomed in other spheres of the digital economy.[32]

There are various possible futures of 3D printing.[33] First, it could develop as the basis of a major new system of localised manufacturing. There would be many 'factories' throughout the world 'printing' objects which would then be delivered locally using new distributed consumer-based logistics. Additive manufacturing undertaken locally would eliminate the long-distance transport of many manufactured objects, and this would be a game-changing innovation likely to reduce offshoring very significantly.[34]

A second possibility is the more rapid development of community printing centres or 'makerspaces'. This is a future of commons-based peer production drawing partly on the internet model

---

[32] Jeremy Rifkin, *The Age of Access* (London: Penguin, 2000). Much downloading is illegal, and this will be a major issue in 3D printing/manufacturing.

[33] See Thomas Birtchnell, John Urry, Chloe Cook and Andrew Curry, *Freight Miles: The Impact of 3D Printing on Transport and Society*, ESRC Project ES/J007455/1, Lancaster University/Futures Company, 2012; Thomas Birtchnell and John Urry, 'Fabricating futures and the movement of objects', *Mobilities*, 8/3 (2013): 388–405, http://dx.doi.org/10.1080/17450101.2012.745697. See Giddens, *Turbulent and Mighty Continent*, for one of the few social scientific analyses of 3D.

[34] See http://dsi.dhl-innovation.com/en/node/256 (accessed 16.08.2011) on how logistics giant DHL is concerned about the implications of this possible future.

of 'democratised innovation'. Consumers and producers would be oriented towards 'not-for-profit' through the widespread availability of open-source designs, modifications and individualised production.[35] This set of developments would constitute a major change in manufacturing but does not eliminate all offshore manufacturing.

Third, 'desktop factories' in the home could become widespread. Here 3D printing is ubiquitous, rather like the way in which 2D printers are widespread in many homes. In 2013 the first high-street 3D printer was advertised in Britain.[36] At first jewellery, kitchen utensils, toys, models, homework projects and replacement parts of consumer objects would be designed and printed at home, often by children, so not needing to be mass produced on the other side of the world and then shipped in containers to customers.

Thus additive manufacturing could be a world-changing innovation generating a new long wave of socio-technical change and reversing the offshoring of much manufacturing. Analysts of long waves of economic development note that the structure of goods and services, of dominant technologies, firms and social activities, does dramatically change over decades. Much of what now exists will not necessarily be directly replaced, but growing up alongside it will be a cluster of new technologies, firms and social activities now mostly unknown except within laboratories. Some of these new 'systems' will become core to life in the mid-twenty-first century, though we do not know what they will be. 3D printing/manufacturing could be one of those systems and the basis for reshoring manufacturing.[37] It would involve a fundamental worldwide restructuring of the geography of manufacturing, employment, income and investment.

---

[35] This vision is set out in Chris Anderson, *Makers* (New York: Random House, 2012), especially the Appendix, as well as p. 46, where Fab Labs are described.

[36] See http://www.dailymail.co.uk/sciencetech/article-2358357/Velleman -K8200-First-3D-printer-available-high-street-goes-sale-700.html (accessed 9.7.2013).

[37] See Ken Green, Simon Shackley, Paul Dewick and Marcela Miozzo, 'Long-wave theories of technological change and the global environment', *Global Environment Change*, 12 (2002): 79–81.

There are at least two dangers, however. One is that the technological promise of 3D turns out to be limited, and it remains only a specialist niche for manufacturing prototypes rather than a game-changer. If so, manufacturing would probably become even more offshored over the next few decades, with container ships getting even bigger. Alternatively, manufacturing through 3D becomes so fashionable and available that greater quantities of material stuff are produced and there is even more exploitation of the world's finite resources. Anderson argues for this in his techno-enthusiastic analysis: 'what we will see is simply more' being produced rather than less.[38]

But what is globally needed is the exact opposite of this – to improve the 'material efficiency' of manufacturing, to make more but with less, or even much less, as Buckminster Fuller famously argued.[39] This making more with less entails developing longer-lasting products, modularisation and remanufacturing and component reuse, as well as designing products with less material in the first place. There needs to be a thoroughgoing dematerialisation as part of a broader low carbon future, as analysts in many domains are now demonstrating.[40] There has to be the widespread reversal of offshoring, so developing a 'human economy' rather than one that is finance-dominated.[41]

Various commentators report that leading companies such as General Electric and Apple are now restarting production in the US while the Raspberry Pi is beginning to be made in the UK.[42] These are early signs of a change in the organisation of manufacturing, away from global value chains and towards more localised, smaller-scale distributed manufacturing. Many American firms now consider that the offshoring of work went too far, especially since wages in offshore locations are no longer dramatically lower,

---

[38] Anderson, *Makers*, p. 229.

[39] http://peakenergy.blogspot.co.uk/2009/02/buckminster-fullers-critical-path.html (accessed 28.7.2013).

[40] See Julian Allwood, Michael Ashby, Timothy Gutowski and Ernst Worrell, 'Material efficiency: a white paper', *Resources, Conservation and Recycling*, 55 (2011): 362–81.

[41] Keith Hart, Jean-Louis Laville and Antonio David Cattani (eds), *The Human Economy* (Cambridge: Polity, 2010).

[42] www.raspberrypi.org/archives/tag/made-in-the-uk (accessed 29.7.2013).

while shipping costs have risen greatly as oil shortages increasingly impact.

Some analysts argue that global production will no longer be the default approach for large-scale production and that regionalisation and potentially localisation will occur in various sectors, such as transport, computers and electronics, fabricated metal products, machinery, plastics and rubber, electrical appliances and equipment, and furniture.[43] A related American development is the 'Reshoring Initiative: Bringing Manufacturing Back Home', whose website offers a method for calculating the full costs of offshoring through the Total Cost of Ownership Estimator.[44] According to Giddens, the trend will be not only for American manufacturers to relocate, but for foreign companies to move to the US.[45]

Finally, there is the strange story of the offshoring of libel.[46] Many wealthy foreign celebrities and businessmen have taken advantage of Britain's draconian libel laws and have gone offshore to Britain in order to sue for libel, even when there was no connection among those involved with Britain. But this offshoring is now viewed as a major problem. Some US states passed specific laws to prevent unreasonable libel rulings made in British courts from infringing their own freedom of speech. The chair of the Culture, Media and Sport Select Committee at Westminster stated that it was time the courts ended this 'libel offshoring' by refusing to hear cases where Britain was not the appropriate jurisdiction. It was maintained that such cases should be heard in the country which is the main home of the claimant or defendant or the place where most examples of the libel allegedly occurred. Thus this Select Committee maintains that libel should be 'returned home' and not offshored to where it seems the highest awards for damages might be made. Is this the start of a major reversal?

---

[43] See Finbarr Livesey and Julian Thompson, *Making at Home, Owning Abroad: A Strategic Outlook for the UK's Mid-Sized Manufacturers* (London: Royal Society of Arts, 2013).
[44] www.reshorenow.org/ (accessed 10.1.2013).
[45] Giddens, *Turbulent and Mighty Continent*, chap. 2. He also notes that some call centres are being reshored.
[46] See www.telegraph.co.uk/news/7301403/How-libel-tourism-became-an-embarrassment-to-Britains-reputation.html (accessed 25.8.2012).

Offshoring up or powering down

Offshoring is very problematic not only for democracy but also for developing effective policies to deal with rising CO_2 emissions. Powering down to a low carbon future requires a strong mutual indebtedness of people around the globe and especially of current generations towards future generations, including those not yet born. The need for this public or social indebtedness is powerfully expressed in many global documents, such as the UNESCO Declaration on the Responsibilities of the Present Generations Towards Future Generations (12 November 1997). However, realising this is a massive challenge which offshoring has made much more intractable.

Such social indebtedness between people has been overwhelmed in much of the world through what can be called financial indebtedness, which ties people, states and corporations into obligations. This financial indebtedness and the large-scale offshoring of potential taxation revenue make it very hard for social indebtedness to develop and gain traction. Without sufficient tax revenues post-carbon futures are unlikely, since both public money and a strong notion of public interest are necessary to plan and orchestrate low carbonism. Offshoring and the effective powering down of economies and societies are in direct contradiction with each other.

Tax havens favour large corporations rather than small and medium-sized companies. The offshore world makes it hard for 'innovative minnows' to compete, and if they prosper they are likely to become parts of large multinational corporations with income flows substantially offshored.[47] Such companies can face unfair competition, since markets favour large companies that may avoid taxation and hence undercut small and medium-sized enterprises. It was noted in chapter 1 that ninety-eight of the FTSE 100 companies in the UK possess offshore accounts. This financialisation runs counter to a productive low carbon economy and society made up mainly of relatively small companies innovating

---

[47]Nicholas Shaxson, *Treasure Islands* (London: Bodley Head, 2011), pp. 190–1; see research in 'Tax havens cause poverty', www.taxjustice.net/cms/front_content.php?idcat=2 (accessed 26.11.2011).

low carbon products and related services, but which could potentially move to a much larger scale.

With regard to money, Mellor argues that a 'steady state economy would be possible if the money system was not driven by the demands of debt-based money, financial accumulation and profit-driven growth.'[48] She maintains that money should be reclaimed and democratised for the benefit of each society and for the state of the physical world. Money and taxation should be controlled by the localities and nations where incomes are generated.[49] Recent developments in peer-to-peer currency and lending are the first steps in pushing back finance and re-establishing to a modest degree the public role of money. There are now several thousand examples of alternative money schemes; current examples include LETS, Time Dollars, Bitcoin (a P2P digital currency) and Zopa (a P2P lender). The website of Zopa interestingly states how 'Zopa is a marketplace for money. Lenders get lovely returns, borrowers get low-cost loans and money becomes human again.'[50]

More generally, many developments worldwide are emerging of 'alternative' economic practices, and especially low carbon practices, that are based upon a strong sense of local or regional indebtedness between people. Conill, Castells and others document the extensive alternative economic practices emerging in Catalonia, including agro-ecological production and consumer cooperatives, exchange networks, hacklabs, social currency networks, urban orchards, shared parenting networks, ethical banks, and so on.[51] One-third of a million people are involved in these networks of alternative economic practice. Also Castells documents the emerging power of many different social networks in

---

[48] Mary Mellor, *The Future of Money* (London: Pluto Press, 2010), p. 175.

[49] Shaxson, *Treasure Islands*, pp. 26–7.

[50] http://uk.zopa.com/ (accessed 3.1.2013). On connections with Simmel, see Nigel Dodd, 'Simmel's perfect money: fiction, socialism and utopia in *The Philosophy of Money*', *Theory, Culture and Society*, 29 (2012): 146–76.

[51] Joana Conill, Manuel Castells, Amalia Cardenas and Lisa Servon, 'Beyond the crisis: the emergence of alternative economic practices', in Manuel Castells, João Caraça and Gustavo Cardoso (eds), *Aftermath* (Oxford: Oxford University Press, 2012), pp. 214–15.

the internet age, most of which undermine or reverse the power of finance within public life.[52] They are typically organised horizontally, emphasising solidarity and cooperation, and are often strongly organised by and through various digital worlds.

We can indeed talk more generally about the putative development of a 'low carbon civil society' constituted of tens of thousands of experiments, groups, networks, prototypes, laboratories, scientists, universities, designers and activists looking to innovate and develop various reshored low carbon practices. This low carbon civil society, especially using the resources of the internet and of social media, seeks to develop, promote, demonstrate and scale up many kinds of low carbon practices.[53] These often involve making connections between post-carbon practices around the globe partly through developing new digital worlds, including the App economy. There is here an emerging social force oriented mainly to relocalising the 'economy-and-society', even as it deploys the mobile techniques of digital worlds.

These many practices and movements are seeking to transform society such that, as Mellor expresses it, money becomes 'human' again.[54] But in terms of normal economic measures most people would be apparently 'poorer' in a lower carbon society.[55] GDP indicates the sum of measurable market transactions within a country, and this can apparently increase, even though much of what is measured adds nothing to wellbeing. Indeed, increases in GDP through finance can go along with reduced levels of wellbeing. There have been efforts to develop better wellbeing measures, such as the 'Happy Planet Index' devised by the New Economics Foundation.[56] Many argue that societies should be measured in

---

[52] Manuel Castells, *Networks of Outrage and Hope* (Cambridge: Polity, 2012). And see the inspirational Rob Hopkins, *The Transition Companion* (Totnes: Green Books, 2011).

[53] See Elizabeth Shove, Mika Pantzar and Matt Watson, *The Dynamics of Social Practice* (London: Sage, 2012), chap. 8, on promoting transitions in social practice. And see Urry, *Climate Change and Society*, chap. 8.

[54] Mellor, *The Future of Money*.

[55] David Halpern, *The Hidden Wealth of Nations* (Cambridge: Polity, 2010).

[56] www.happyplanetindex.org/ (accessed 3.11.2011). Costa Rica was rated at number one on the index in 2009.

terms of the quality of life or wellbeing and not measurable GDP or GDP per person. Societies should be assessed in terms of the quality of life, of 'prosperity', but not of measurable offshore-generated growth.[57]

Significantly, societies with high levels of economic and social wellbeing are those which are relatively equal and with much social connectivity (such as Norway). Wilkinson and Pickett document how life expectancy, the wellbeing of children, rates of literacy, social mobility, and levels of trust tend to be higher in more equal societies.[58] Society is weakened through greater social inequality. Moreover, after a level of income is achieved, increasing personal incomes may not generate more wellbeing. Extra goods and services are in effect 'wasted', with money being spent on replacement TV sets, extra unworn clothing, more trips to exotic islands, many unused toys, or the temperature of buildings being set too high.[59] Thus low carbon societies should enhance the 'capabilities for flourishing' rather than just increasing 'income' and consuming what may be very many 'wasted' commodities, including many of those designed for children. Jackson trenchantly argues for broadly enhancing the 'capabilities for flourishing'.[60]

It further follows that high status in a low carbon society should not be based on possessing extensive offshored connections involving travelling and communicating around the world. 'Success' should emphasise the achievements of those living 'localised' and not 'mobile' lives. Status should be relocalised and based upon people's contributions being made and recognised locally.

Many studies following on Jacobs's *The Death and Life of Great American Cities* show how human wellbeing is enhanced by proximity and developing mutual responsibilities between people. She showed the attractions of neighbours living close

[57]Tim Jackson, *Prosperity without Growth* (London: Earthscan, 2009).
[58]Richard Wilkinson and Kate Pickett, *The Spirit Level: Why More Equal Societies Almost Always Do Better* (London: Allen Lane, 2009).
[59]See, on heating comfort, Elizabeth Shove, Heather Chappells and Loren Lutzenhiser (eds), *Comfort in a Lower Carbon Society* (London: Routledge, 2009); on the wellbeing of children, see Sharon Beder, *This Little Kiddy Went to Market* (London: Pluto Press, 2009).
[60]Jackson, *Prosperity without Growth*.

together, that residences should mix with businesses through a lack of zoning, that slow modes of travel are preferable, and that there are many gains from the absence of extreme differences in income and wealth between those living near together.[61] Overall her argument shows that the de-zoning of activities within built environments would significantly contribute to onshoring.

Research on the social response to a major heatwave that occurred in Chicago in 1995 brought out the importance of such neighbourliness.[62] In the areas in Chicago that afforded opportunities for people to get out and about and to visit shops and local services, deaths from the intense heatwave were significantly lower. The connectedness of houses with habitable streets, accessible parks, shops, cafés, neighbours, and so on, provided opportunities for walking, meeting and especially talking with others. Where opportunities were rich and diverse, people would go out but were less likely to die from heat. In neighbourhoods where residents rarely socialised and the elderly were isolated, death rates were correspondingly higher. Ironically, wealthier neighbourhoods with more people living offshored lives were less likely to develop a strong localism, and death rates were greater than in some poorer neighbourhoods.

Thus a low carbon society would need to make a virtue out of neighbourly social practices – 'making your community more resilient in uncertain times', according to the transition movement,[63] notions that are developed in various visions for 'transition towns/cities'. This movement promotes local solutions to the global issues of the peaking of oil supplies and of climate change, in part through developing local Energy Descent Action Plans (EDAPs).[64] The transition movement is a widespread phenomenon, with over 3,000 transition towns, projects and initiatives

---

[61] Jane Jacobs, *The Death and Life of Great American Cities* (New York: Vintage, [1961] 1992).

[62] See Eric Klinenberg, *Heatwave* (Chicago: University of Chicago Press, 2002); Jane Jacobs, *Dark Age Ahead* (New York: Random House, 2004).

[63] See many inspiring examples of community resilience in Hopkins, *The Transition Companion*.

[64] www.transitiontowns.org/ (accessed 8.1.2010); see Shaun Chamberlin, *The Transition Timeline* (Totnes: Green Books, 2009).

around the world, and advocates innovation that is viral, open source, self-organising, iterative and enjoyable.[65]

Developing transition towns/cities would involve very significant changes. In such a relocalised world, friends would have to be chosen from neighbouring streets, families would not be able to move away at times of new household composition, distant family members would not be regularly visited, and households would mostly not live apart. Movement and education would be relocalised. Owen argues that the greenest city in the US is New York, since it provides many local connections while making it almost impossible to own and use private cars.[66] In general he advocates a threefold policy for promoting low carbonism: to live smaller, live closer and drive less. Interestingly, various commentators now report that, in the rich north of the world, there may be a modest plateauing of car-based travel, with the next generation less likely to be licence-holders, car owners and drivers.[67]

But this is a formidable challenge. Moving to a low carbon economy-and-society necessitates 'reversing' most of the systems set in motion during the twentieth century which generated such extensive offshoring. Crouch argues that this is made so difficult because of the 'strange non-death of neoliberalism', even after its clear responsibility for almost ending the world economy in 2007–8.[68] Overall the long-term path-dependent patterns of existing systems, including offshoring routines and habits, engender a forward momentum that makes it difficult to find and engage reverse gear.

There is also the power of 'high carbon' advertising and marketing. The world's media circulate countless images of the good offshore life and the importance of global brands, products and services. 'Celebrity-isation' through the world's media is inconsistent with developing and sustaining the mutual responsibilities

---

[65] http://frontlinecopy.com/wp-content/uploads/2012/07/Transition-Initiatives-Around-the-World.png (accessed 13.9.2013); Hopkins, *The Transition Companion*.

[66] See David Owen, *Green Metropolis* (London: Penguin, 2011).

[67] See *Transport Reviews* special issue on 'Peak Car', 33/3 (2013); http://tinyurl.com/o4mxuk4 (accessed 12.9.2013).

[68] Colin Crouch, *The Strange Non-Death of Neo-Liberalism* (Cambridge: Polity, 2011).

necessary within societies organised around low carbon systems and practices. So reducing the power and reach of the media, of old media but especially of new media, is crucial to ensuring that people offshore very much less.

There are many difficulties in developing a global polity to reset global agendas away from the interests of large-scale and often virtual companies and individuals. Slowing down the interconnectedness of global systems is crucial especially through implementing taxation on financial transactions, a policy currently being developed by the EU. It is astonishing that there is no equivalent to VAT levied on such transactions. Even a very modest tax would potentially raise very large sums of money and reduce the rate at which finance system dysfunctions would move around the world. Offshoring would be significantly reduced, but that is the very reason why most financial institutions campaign so vigorously against such a financial transactions tax.[69] Latouche proposes that the World Trade Organisation should be replaced by its opposite, a World Localisation Organisation.[70]

Thus finding reverse gear is extremely challenging, and that is why the futurist Buckminster Fuller once maintained: 'You never change things by fighting the existing reality. To change something, build a new model that makes the existing model obsolete.'[71] Societies should therefore seek to develop a cluster of 'new models' that would make the existing offshoring model obsolescent. Developing a cluster of onshored low carbon systems and related social practices is *the* challenge for the next few decades. But it will encounter much organised hostility and opposition from many elites making up the offshore rich class.

Offshoring or onshoring?

This book thus documents how the world's oceans provide both routes and metaphors to assemble as secret what should be onshored and visible. People, objects, money and waste are moved

---

[69] See Robert Holton, *Global Finance* (London: Routledge, 2012), chap. 5.
[70] Serge Latouche, *Farewell to Growth* (Cambridge: Polity, 2009).
[71] 'The Buckminster Fuller challenge', http://challenge.bfi.org/movie (accessed 4.11.2011).

across oceans and out of view from land, over the horizon, beyond observation. Especially significant are islands and small states, places to offload far from prying eyes minimally taxed and documented income and wealth, as well as waste, pleasure-seeking tourists and tortured subjects.

There is also much that is offshore but not literally out to sea. There is a vast secret world which washes around the globe, both at home and away, and is central to the neo-liberal order assembled and systematised over the past few decades. The secret realm has become the essence of the global economy, as well as of global crime, social life, pleasure, finance, waste and damaged environments.[72]

The social sciences have been mostly indifferent to this vast powerful offshored world. Part of the argument here is to show how the social sciences must energetically develop analyses of the changing ecosystem of the mobile offshore world and of its corrupting interests. Without examining these offshore worlds, which stem from a particular kind of international class struggle, analyses of globalisation remain superficial.

Efforts to deepen democracy and to power down societies will lack traction without confronting the ecosystem of these multiple, overlapping offshored processes. Researching offshore worlds is central to deciphering future global trajectories. Offshoring *or* reshoring is the global issue core to how economies, politics and societies will unfold over the next decades.

Were Dubai and other offshore centres the forerunner of an even more offshored twenty-first century? Will a new burst of extreme offshoring emerge the like of which has not yet even been imagined? Are there waiting in the wings new offshored centres that will make contemporary Dubai seem small scale by comparison? Is the strategy of the rich class more extreme offshoring? Or are the many forms of offshoring just one step too far and many societies will in fact move back to a more reshored future, especially if resource shortages begin to impact with interest and

---

[72] William Brittain-Catlin, *Offshore: The Dark Side of the Global Economy* (New York: Picador, 2005), p. 199; Sven Opitz and Ute Tellmann, 'Global territories: zones of economic and legal dis/connectivity', *Distinktion*, 13(2012): 261–82, on 'non-resident' money and subjects.

threaten societal 'collapse'? Will potential forms of reshoring develop momentum within many nation-states, this being good for democracy and essential for reducing the probability of runaway climate change?

It has been argued here that offshoring has reorganised many societies over the past few decades. It is hard to imagine how societies can simply reverse such a powerful set of processes that have been unleashed worldwide, with enormous momentum and tied into the unambiguous interests of various elites making up the rich class. Any challenge to this will involve campaigning for, orchestrating and seeking to realise a wide range of on- or reshoring processes. This is tremendously hard to achieve, and so far the only entity to which such reshoring might occur would have to be each nation-state-society, as we have seen in various proposals outlined in this chapter.

But such reshoring will not result simply from nationally specific programmes and policies. Rather it will stem from the forcefulness of a 'low carbon civil society' made up, as noted above, of tens of thousands of experiments, networks, prototypes, laboratories, cities, universities, designers and activists around the world. These are looking to innovate various reshored practices especially through deploying resources of the internet as well as of horizontal meetings. Also many international organisations may enhance the conditions for engendering such reshored social practices, including the EU across much of Europe.[73]

Such a civil society is key to developing, promoting, demonstrating and scaling up many kinds of low carbon reshored practices. There is here a potential social force oriented to relocalising each economy-and-society, even as it partly deploys the mobile techniques of digital worlds. Combating offshoring requires a powerful social force. A global low carbon civil society needs to be developed so as to bring about reshoring in and across many different societies. The aim of this civil society must be to ensure that much that has been offshored should 'go back onshore, reattached to the body of society, in league with nature, where freedom must move people together, not push them apart'.[74]

---

[73] Giddens, *Turbulent and Mighty Continent*.
[74] Brittain-Catlin, *Offshore*, p. 239.

Index